# Ward
## of the
# Court

## The Lost Children of Ireland

## My Story
# Noreen Anne Roche

Copyright © 2023 by Noreen Anne Roche

For information regarding permission, please write to:
info@barringerpublishing.com
Barringer Publishing, Naples, Florida
www.barringerpublishing.com

Cover, graphics, and layout by Linda S. Duider
Cape Coral, Florida

ISBN: 978-1-954396-24-1
Library of Congress Cataloging-in-Publication Data
*Ward of the Court: The Lost Children of Ireland* / Noreen Anne Roche

Printed in the United States of America

*This book is dedicated to all the children who passed through the cloisters and hallways of St. Dominick's School at the Good Shepherd Convent, Co. Waterford.*

*A special thanks to my husband, Ross, who has encouraged me to write this book. Also, thanks to my three children, my Irish and English families and the dear friends who have enriched my life.*

# Contents

# Prologue

It was the late evening knock on Nanny's front door that instantly changed my life.

My mother died unexpectedly, aged thirty, when I was four years old. Prior to her passing, I lived with my parents, an older sister, and two younger brothers in a modest cottage at the foothills of the lush Comeragh Mountains in County Waterford, Ireland. Although we shared a simple existence, love reigned in the arms of our mother's warm and comforting embrace until it was cruelly snatched away by the agonizing jaws of death.

Without the nurturing and emotional support of both parents, my life took on a new meaning. In the confines of my mind, I existed in an isolated and lonesome place that only I alone would understand.

It was the 1950s. Catholic Ireland was suffering from great poverty, sparse opportunity, and mass emigration. For those left behind, the church and local governments took harsh and unusual measures regarding the lives of children from broken families by making irrational and emboldened decisions. Children born out of wedlock or left without a parent were most at risk. Fathers who lost their spouses following childbirth were often considered unfit to raise children single-handedly without the finances or domestic support of a spouse in the house.

1

Weeks after my mother's death, my life was tossed into a disturbing turmoil. My father, left with no other choice, split up my three siblings and me and sent us to live with other relatives. My eight-year-old sister, Margaret (Peg), went to live with our grandmother and six-month-old brother, Johnjoe, was adopted by my father's brother and his wife. This arrangement left my three-year-old brother, Thomas, and me without any clear plan. We were the middle siblings, and most affected by the split in our family. In a two-and-a-half-year span, we were shipped off to live with two different sets of aunts and uncles who were negligent and cruel. After two unsettling incidents, we were removed from their care and returned to live temporarily with our grandmother.

Soon, the social services stepped in and took control of our situation. Against my father's pleas, Thomas and I were made wards of the court and sent to live in Church-run orphanages. Thomas was assigned first to St. Michael's School in Cappoquin, in Co. Waterford, and then to St. Joseph's Christian Brothers School for boys, in Ferryhouse, Clonmel, Co. Tipperary. I was sent to live at The Good Shepherd Convent, an institution for girls, in Waterford.

My life at The Good Shepherd Convent profoundly affected my well-being as a child and endured well into my adult years. As a result, I became painfully shy, nervous, withdrawn, and insecure. I craved the love and affection I had once known before my mother's passing. Traveling through life, I yearned to repair the fractured family picture that once was whole and coveted what was left.

As my character evolved, I became more perceptive, secretive, sensitive, sympathetic, and tactful, ensuring to always avoid conflict. Being Irish, I was wary of my own people and was especially cautious around my peers. The first and most apparent questions asked of me were, where did I come from, and what school did I attend? It was only natural of them to ask. But how was I supposed to explain to them about something they would never truly understand unless they walked in my shoes? Because they had never been one of us, they could never comprehend our circumstances. I was too beaten down and embarrassed to tell folk; I hailed from a poor family, was just four years old when my mother died, and I was raised in an orphanage.

Early in my life, I quite cleverly developed a knack of being evasive amongst strangers, and covered up my pain by shifting conversations that might focus on me and my youth. I knew if I were to freely divulge my secret, I would be labeled and slotted into a category that would cripple my very existence and block my ability to grow and fulfill my future. To protect myself from curious invaders, I built an invisible wall around me, allowing only a trustworthy few to breach it. Because people can be unwittingly cruel, I found it hard to trust them. This was especially true when I heard derogatory words spoken about people in similar situations to mine. To many people, I was an enigma they could never quite fathom.

Since I had no close family to celebrate annual holidays and milestones, I became popular when working as a nurse in the UK. My co-workers liked it when I offered to cover their holiday work duties, because it enabled them to spend quality time with their families. When asked why it never bothered me to work on Christmas Day, I would laugh and brush it off, telling them it was because all my family were in Ireland, and too far away for me to travel.

I was still the little girl trapped in my childhood. For my very survival, I choose to hide in the shadows of life, while keeping my childhood wrapped tightly intact until it was safe enough to unravel and look back inside.

Once I discovered my strengths and weaknesses, I became more secure about myself. I especially enjoyed the company of gentle, genuine, and witty folk, who were fun to be around. My curious nature and voracious appetite for learning gave me the stamina and willpower to strive and survive.

With the presence of a handful of good relatives, friends, and my faith, I forged ahead alone. My life spread before me in twists and turns and weaved a path of adventure and uncertainty. I would have been blind not to sense the presence of divine intervention throughout my journey. As my independence grew, I knew any mistake I made was mine alone to fix. No matter where life was taking me, I tread carefully and played it safe.

Those who know me well often remark on my memory for details, an ability I subconsciously developed in early childhood. Although my good memory has served me well, it has also been a disturbing curse in keeping the details of my childhood ever present on my mind.

In the last fifty years, science and psychology have uncovered a greater understanding of childhood trauma, and how it shapes and changes who we become. Research has shown that without solid nurturing and guidance in early childhood, one is often left directionless.

However, the reward has been the mental acuity with which I was blessed. This has helped me to compartmentalize and resolve the conflicts of my youth.

On reflection, I often wonder how my life would have progressed if my mother had lived and it was my father that passed? Would she have been allowed to raise her own children alone or would we have been removed from her care as had been the case for my father?

There's no greater imprint left on the mind of a human being than that of their early childhood. No matter where life takes one, childhood memories, good and bad, remain on the human mind throughout life.

By a chance encounter in 1984, at age thirty, I found my soulmate and husband. Feeling safe with someone I could finally trust, I gradually dropped my guard and shared with him the secrets I had so long been burdened with. My life soon became stable and durable. While sharing my life with him, he gave me the confidence to express who I was and loved me for the person I had become.

# Chapter One

# MAM

In the stillness of my mind, I am transported back to a Sunday morning when I was barely four years old. It was the late 1950s, and I am with my family in the countryside of Rathgormack, County Waterford, Ireland, when an image of my mother emerges.

I am seated at the kitchen table beside my two-year-old brother, Thomas, watching my Mam. She is standing in front of a small wall mirror pinching her cheeks with her long fingers, and then pushing her dark eyebrows into perfect arches. She is wearing a buttoned-down, Kelly-green frock, with a matching waistband. On her head is a pink and yellow floral scarf where a neat bow is tucked beneath her chin. After applying ruby red lipstick to her lips, she rolls and smacks them together before dropping the tube into her navy clasp handbag. Giving her appearance a final check, she then turns around and walks over to Thomas and me. Looking down at us from her slim frame, she is smiling.

"We are off to mass now. I want you to be good children. When I come home, I will have a big bar of chocolate for the two *a ye*," she said.

Then she bent over my brother and me and gave each of us a kiss on our foreheads. As she makes her exit, a sweet aroma from her lipstick wafts around me.

That special scent of my mother's lipstick has remained with me ever since. Although I recall many fond memories of her, the kiss she gave me on my forehead and the scent of her lipstick is one of the most vivid and lasting images I have of her.

Mam was in the prime of her life when she died, aged thirty, on January 8, 1958. I was at my grandmother's cottage when the news of her death was delivered by telegram.

Earlier in the day, my four-year-old mind sensed something was amiss. Family members had gathered in Nanny's kitchen and spoke in unusually hushed tones with each other. While in their presence, some gave me odd and sympathetic looks, others fussed and offered me sweets and biscuits to eat. Soon the day turned dark, and Nanny's kitchen swelled with an increasing number of unfamiliar faces. Cigarette smoke swirled overhead and hung in the dank air.

At some point that evening, my eight-year-old sister, Peg, feeling bored and bold, hatched a plan. She took my arm and had me crawl under the kitchen table with her. She figured it would be genuine fun to hide beneath the vinyl tablecloth and tickle the ankles of unwary guests that stood close to the table. My feet were bare and felt cold on the stone floor. At first, I was apprehensive and shy about touching people's ankles, and waited until Peg did it first. When a stiletto-heeled woman stood close to the table, Peg stuck out her hand and bravely tickled her ankles. The woman jumped back in fright. When we saw the woman's reaction, it made us both squeal with delight. Most people gathered around the table were fully aware it was only Peg and me and played along with our antics. Other strangers were genuinely taken by surprise, believing a field mouse had found its way under the table. Once they discovered we were under the vinyl cloth, they were relieved. "Oh, my God, you gave me a wicked fright. I thought a mouse or spider was crawling up my leg," one woman said.

"For a minute, I thought the same thing," a male relative joked.

Hearing their cries of shock only encouraged Peg and me to keep up our mischievous adventure. Life was all that life should be in those childhood moments, and we were both happy children.

Suddenly, there was a loud rapping sound on the front door, and the crowded room fell eerily silent. Sensing the change in the atmosphere, Peg and I gave pause from our play and listened while the front door opened. I heard a man talking in a quiet voice. Then the front door was latched again. Within seconds, a gut-wrenching wail echoed in the room. Although I couldn't see her, I recognized my grandmother's voice.

A gasping ripple of shock and loud sobbing ripped through the crowd. Feeling panicked, Peg and I swiftly crawled out from under the table. Looking up, I eyed the people around me. Many were crying and mopping their tears with hankies. I wasn't sure why they were crying but felt it must be something incredibly sad and bad. A woman I had never seen before, stood in front of me. She attempted to hold my hand and talk to me, while tears rolled down her face. In my disturbed confusion, I pulled my hand away from her. Then I heard my mother's name mentioned. "Poor Mary. I hope the poor thing didn't have to suffer much. May God rest her blessed soul. And, poor Stevie. I wonder what will happen *ta* him now with the *young wans*."

The sound of my mother's name magnified in my mind. I began to shake and let out a deafening scream. "It's my mammy. She's dead. My mammy is dead," I hollered.

Uncle Johnny, hearing my screams, came to my rescue and quickly scooped me into his arms. Holding me tight, he tried to console me while mopping tears from his own eyes with the loss of his sister. "*Whished* now. Your mammy has gone and left us. She's up there in heaven now with Holy God, and looking down at you," he said, pointing his finger to the ceiling. While he held me, neighbors, friends, and relatives came and offered their condolences and kissed my cheeks and hands. One relative gave me buttered Marietta biscuits. She knew I liked them because my mother often gave them to me as a treat. When I finally calmed down, Uncle Johnny attempted to put me down, but I clawed onto him and would not let go. My feet were bare and cold. For the first time, I sensed abandonment and began to understand my mother would never again be around to hold me.

Two days after her passing, her remains were brought to the Old Church graveyard in Rathgormack, Co. Waterford. A neighbor took care of my siblings and me, because we were not allowed to attend our mother's funeral.

That fateful evening, a telegram was delivered to my grandmother by a local postman. My father had sent the telegram upon my mother's passing. He had been called to Ardkeen Hospital in Waterford earlier that day. He only became aware of his wife's tragic passing when he got there. Nanny was heartbroken to lose her daughter so suddenly and took it upon herself to blame my father for her untimely death.

*1940—Mother's Confirmation Day.*

*1945—Mom with two of her friends.*

*1947—Mother center, with her brother, Michael (L), and sister, Alice (R).*

Chapter Two

# LIVING WITH MOREY AND PEG

## February 1958

Two months after my mother's passing, my father shipped my brother, Thomas, and me off to live with Uncle Morey, his youngest brother, and his wife, Aunt Peg.

My aunt and uncle were both in their early twenties. They lived in a three-bedroom cottage with their six-year-old daughter, Aine, and six-month-old son, Timmy. Their home was without plumbing and electricity and was located three miles outside the village of Clonea Power, in Co. Waterford.

I shared a single bed with Thomas in a small box room. This room was off a narrow hallway and directly across from my aunt and uncle's bedroom. Cousin Aine had her own bedroom off the main living quarters. The living quarters were inside the front door. This also served as a kitchen and dining area. A large open-hearth fireplace with a black sooty hob dominated the room. Two long wooden benches straddled both sides of the fireplace. On frigid days, I enjoyed huddling on one of the benches to soak up the warmth of the fire.

When I wasn't at school, or on rainy, cold days, I spent much of my time playing with Thomas and Aine in her bedroom. On one such day, I figured out how to tie a bow under my chin. My aunt had given me a multi-colored woolen hat that Aine no longer wore. It was pretty with a peaky red pom-pom ball on top and had two long knitted strings that hung down either side. Looking in a small wall mirror, I kept admiring the hat. I tied the strings repeatedly, until I was finally able to create a bow. I felt utterly proud of my accomplishment and beamed with satisfaction.

At four and a half years, I entered the National Primary School in the village of Clonea Power. Each morning before 9:00, I set off with Aine on a three-mile walk down a steep hill to the village school. Both of us had brown leather satchels on our backs, and in our coat pockets, we carried small 'Paddy' whiskey bottles filled with hot cocoa. Once we arrived at the school, a teacher took our bottles of cocoa and placed them in front of a blazing fire to keep them warm. When it was time to drink my cocoa at 11:00 a.m., (*elevenses*) a thick skin already had formed in the neck of the bottle. I enjoyed poking my finger inside the hole and lifting out the slimy rubbery skin to eat it.

There were about fifteen other four-year-old girls in my class. We were known as 'The High Babies' and our teacher was Miss Donaghue. She taught us the alphabet by lining up large wooden block letters to form words and had us sing counting songs to learn our numbers. Before chanting our numbers in song, she tapped a tuning fork on her desk to ensure we were all on the right key. I liked her class because I loved to sing and was eager to master any new song. My favorite song was:

One, Two, Three, Four, Five.
Once I caught a fish alive.
Six, Seven, Eight, Nine, Ten,
Then I let him go again.
Why did you let him go?
Because he bit my finger so,
Which finger did he bite?
The little finger on the right.

Aine was in a class higher than me. When my classes ended, I had to wait for her at the front door of the school and then we left together and climbed a high hill back to her parents' home. The walk home from school took a lot longer because of the steep hill we had to climb.

One evening before supper, Aunt Peg sent Aine and me to the local water pump to fill a bucket of water. When we got there, we saw two local women at the pump. After acknowledging our presence, they continued their conversation. They were talking about strange sightings that had been observed at a cottage close to where we lived.

The house they spoke of had once belonged to an elderly lady and was left abandoned when she died. "Sure, that place must be haunted. I'd be frightened of my life to go near it with the way *dem* curtains do be *bouncin'* around the windowsill," one woman said.

After hearing what the women said about the house, Aine and I were genuinely spooked. This was a house we passed going to and from school. I already had a fear of ghosts because of the Banshee stories my grandmother spoke about when I stayed with her.

The following morning, heading to school, we averted our eyes and sprinted past the house on the opposite side of the road. Aine never told her parents how scared we were of passing the house, or what we heard the two women say about it. However, the more we talked about the house, the more heightened Aine's curiosity became. She wanted to sneak inside to see what the fuss was all about.

Returning from school one sunny Friday, she decided we should venture inside and have a look. Feeling nervous about what we might find, I clung to the back of her frock while stepping inside the partially opened rusty gate. A short weedy path led us to the front door of the house. Aine stopped at the window on the left of the front door first, and I followed her. The window was higher close-up than we expected it to be. To clearly look inside, we had to grab the grimy windowsill, and stand on our tippy toes. The sun was shining on the windowpane, showing a thin crack on the lower right side. Holding onto the windowsill with one hand, we cupped the other around our eyes to block the sunlight. All we saw was a faded, shaggy lace curtain, with canopies of long grey cobwebs. Some were attached to the side of the window, and others hung freely in grey clumps. With nothing unusual inside this window, Aine nudged me to move to the window on the right side of the door. We were back on our toes again, craning our necks and straining our eyes to spot any movement. The curtain on this window was torn and dangled sideways on a broken cord.

Suddenly out of nowhere, there was a rapid bouncing of the lace curtain. Feeling anxious, I grabbed hold of Aine, and began pulling at her to leave. We were about to take off, when we saw two black Jackdaws suspended from the curtain which made it sway from side to side. Their black claws dug into the curtain and their bright eyes looked angry and appeared to be staring at us. One of them then flew onto the window latch and pecked at the windowpane. Fearing the birds were going to break free and attack us, Aine quickly grabbed my arm, and I ran with her until we were well outside the gate. Both of us huffed and puffed trying to catch our breath, as we recovered from our wild adventure. Before heading home, Aine made me promise not to tell her parents or anyone else about our daring exploits.

Aunt Peg was waiting for us when we got home. Although we were sweaty and flushed and later than normal, she never questioned us. Both of us felt relieved knowing our secret was safe.

Days later, when Uncle Morey came in from work, he announced alarming news of the two Jackdaws discovery. While telling the story, Aine and I sat quietly and listened. He said that one of the Jackdaws flew into the face of a local man who went inside the house to investigate the cause of the moving curtains. Despite this revelation, Aine and I still believed the house was haunted, because it was so foreboding looking. Thereafter, walking to and from school, we continued to run past the house with our eyes covered, and never daring to enter there again.

Sundays were different than the weekdays at my aunt and uncle's house. After attending mass in Clonea Power Church, all of us except Uncle Morey came back to the house to have lunch. He only returned home when the local pub closed for the afternoon. After supper on Sundays, he headed back to the pub again. Sometimes Aunt Peg joined him, and left Aine in charge of minding her six-month-old brother, as well as Thomas, and me. By the time they got home, we were already in bed. Uncle Morey frequently returned home drunk and his loud singing and bumping into furniture would always wake Thomas and me up. The songs he sang were slow and slurred like he was mournful and crying. Aunt Peg quarreled with him to keep his voice down and reminded him he wasn't the only person living in the house.

"Will *ya whished* up for Jaysus sake, and *gesh yerself inta da* bed. You're *goin'* to wake up the young *wans* if *ya* don't be quiet."

After a time, he settled down and the house went quiet again.

The next morning, Aine and I were awakened by Aunt Peg to get ready for school. Once we were dressed, we sat at the breakfast table for a slice of bread, and a cup of tea. It was usual for Uncle Morey to emerge from his bedroom at this point. Taking a seat on the wooden stool by the fireplace, he sat there without acknowledging us. Aunt Peg quickly boiled water in the kettle to prepare him a mug of hot tea when she saw he was up. Before handing it to him, she cooled it down by pouring the hot tea onto a saucer. Uncle Morey, feeling the need to quench his thirst, lifted the saucer to his lips with a shaky hand, and taking a deep breath, he sapped the tea into his mouth in noisy slurps. Once he swallowed it, he let out a satisfying burp. His rude burping permeated the air with a stench of stale beer that emanated from his breath. The corners of his mouth showed brown, cracked remnants from the Guinness he imbibed the previous night. His strange habits always frightened me, and I hated having to look at him. Aine, on the other hand, was used to seeing her father's Monday morning behavior. While eating her breakfast, she quietly watched every move he made without uttering a word to him.

As the weeks turned into months, I increasingly disliked living with my aunt and uncle. I found them both to be harsh and unkind, and I missed my mother terribly. I had only seen my father once since he sent us to live with them, and I yearned to be back in Rathgormack with my family.

My only real link to my family was Thomas. Returning from school each day, I always looked forward to seeing him. At three and a half, he was still too young to start school and spent his days with my aunt and his baby cousin, Timmy. Sometimes, when I came in from school, he was standing naked from the waist down and I could see he had been crying. He still had accidents and wet his pants. This angered Aunt Peg, and she walloped him on the behind for "being very bold," she said.

She figured spanking him would make him break the habit. Even though my dad had given my aunt a supply of nappies for Thomas to wear, she never put them on him. Somehow, Thomas never wet the bed I shared with him. The accidents he was having only occurred during the day. When my aunt spanked him in front of me, he cried. As young as I was, I knew my brother was doing something he had no control over. To protect myself from her spanking me, I tried to do everything right to please her.

One winter's evening, shortly after moving to their home, Aunt Peg told Thomas and me to get ready for bed. We promptly obeyed her and dressed in our night clothes while she stood at the bedroom door watching us. Thomas climbed into bed first because he slept against the wall, and I got in beside him. We both snuggled down under the blankets but jumped up again and screamed when we felt something stinging our feet. Sitting at the top of our bed, we cried while rubbing the bottom of our feet because they itched and stung. Aunt Peg watched us and roared out laughing when she saw our reaction. Feeling panicked, I immediately pushed the bed covers back to see what had stung us. Halfway down the bed, I saw a bunch of wilted nettles hidden between the bedsheets. Realizing what it was, I looked at Aunt Peg, terror-stricken. Then she walked over to our bed holding a scrap of newspaper she had in her hand and picked up the nettles. To scare us even more, she dangled them in front of us as we cowered in the corner. She was still chuckling when she told us to get back under the covers before latching the bedroom door behind her.

When it was safe, my brother and I sat up again. The room was pitch black, and we continued to scratch our itchy and stinging feet and toes. I discovered that by rubbing my saliva around the blistered bumps, it helped ease the irritation. Sitting beside my brother, I took his hand in the blinding darkness, and showed him how to do the same. At some point, we lay down under the covers again, and finally fell asleep in a world of confusion.

This would not be the last time my aunt and uncle showed their evil ways.

One rainy Sunday afternoon, I was in Aine's bedroom playing with her and Thomas when Uncle Morey arrived home for his lunch. After he had eaten, he retired to his bedroom, something he generally did on a Sunday afternoon.

Not long after, Aunt Peg called for me to go back to their bedroom. When I entered, I found her sitting at the end of her bed, and Uncle Morey lying stretched out on top of the bedcovers. Curious to learn why I had been called there, I stood looking at both of them.

"Your uncle wants to play the game 'Horsey' with *ya*," my aunt told me, while getting up to shut the bedroom door.

I looked at Uncle Morey when she said this. He was gaping at me, wearing a beaming wide grin. "Ah, *gwon*. Sure, *ya* love playing that game with me, don't *ya*?" he said.

I didn't react but continued to stare at both of them. I knew the game 'Horsey' he talked about. He sometimes played it with Aine and me on the kitchen floor. First, he would lay on his back, and then Aine and I took turns climbing up on his knees. Once balanced on top of his knees, he hoisted us into the air while we made clicking sounds with our tongues, pretending to be riding on galloping horses.

"If *ya* want to play, you'll have *ta gesh* up on *da* bed with me," he said.

I looked at Aunt Peg for approval. Not wanting to disobey either of them, I was wary of climbing up on the bed because Aine was always with me when I played the game with him. Instinctively, I sensed it was strange playing the game 'Horsey' without having Aine present. But knowing my aunt was also there, I obeyed and climbed up on the bed beside my uncle.

He immediately took hold of me and lifted me up onto his knees. Then he raised his legs and hoisted me into the air. I felt awkward and was not at all interested in playing with him or making the usual clicking sounds. Aunt Peg sat watching and thought the whole spectacle was hilarious. She laughed heartily every time she saw my uncle lift me high into the air. After hoisting me up several times, he finally stopped and dropped me down beside him. Believing the game was over, I sat up. I was about to climb off the bed to go back to play with Aine when Uncle Morey put his hand out and stopped me.

"Do you want *ta* play *anoder wan* with me?" I did not know what the other game was because he only ever played the 'Horsey' game with me.

"Why don't *ya gesh* under da blankets *wit* me and I'll show *ya*," he said, climbing under the bedcovers. He raised the covers higher for me to join him, displaying the same silly grin.

Not knowing what to do, I looked at Aunt Peg again to see if it was okay. She didn't say anything except look at me and smile. My mind was muddled. I didn't want them to get angry with me, so I lay down under the blankets with my uncle. I was barely down when he grabbed me and lifted me up on top of his chest. My face was close to his mouth, and I got a strong whiff of beer from his toothy grin. He pulled me tighter to his chest and then began moving me back and forth on his body. I wasn't sure what game he was playing with me or what he was doing. Soon, I felt something hard beneath me. I could no longer see my aunt, but I could hear her laughing. Suddenly, my uncle rolled me over, and looking down at me, he lifted my dress and slid his hand inside my underwear. Feeling trapped I began to panic when he roughly fondled my private parts. I attempted to bring my legs together and to push his hand away, but he held me back. Feeling helpless, I screamed when I heard him make strange grunting noises and attempted to pull away from him again. When he didn't let go of me, I let out another scream.

Only then did he remove his hand from my underwear and fell back on his bed. I laid under the bedcovers, shaking and gripped with fear. Knowing my aunt was still at the end of her bed, I pushed back the bed covers and sat up. When she saw the look on my face, she laughed aloud. Feeling helpless, I jumped down off the bed and ran to the door wanting to flee from my ordeal. I stood at the door, clawing it, and waiting for her to unlatch it to let me out. When it wasn't happening, I let out another piercing shriek. Uncle Morey was annoyed and yelled for me to shut up.

"*Will ya gesh* her *ousha* here," he shouted to Aunt Peg, sitting up on his pillow.

My aunt stood up and before opening the door, she slapped me across the face. "Now, *dat'll give ya something ta cry aboush*," she said.

Trying to stifle my crying, I touched my stinging face and wept from the force of her hand.

"*Gesh ousha here,*" she said, unlatching the bedroom door.

With the door open, I quickly ran across the hall to my room and threw myself on my bed. Cradling my knees to my chest, I sobbed into my pillow. I was in utter turmoil and my face throbbed and private parts hurt. I knew what my uncle did was wrong. Yet, the image of Aunt Peg remained on my mind. She sat on her bed laughing while her husband tried to hurt me.

The following morning when I woke up, the left side of my face was swollen, and my eye was partially closed. When Aunt Peg came to my room to wake me up, she saw my swollen face and told me she was keeping me out of school that day. Then, for some reason, she moved me to Aine's bedroom and told me to climb into her bed while Aine dressed for school. Why she did this was a mystery to me. She told Aine she would have to share a bed with Thomas until I got better. I believe she wanted to keep an eye on me while she worked in the kitchen and was guilty for what she did to me. For the rest of the week, each morning, she came to Aine's bedroom and inspected the swelling on my face. I only returned to school when the swelling and bruising subsided.

Not long after that incident, Uncle Morey announced one evening at supper he was taking Thomas and me on a visit to see our grandmother. Nanny lived in Rathgormack, five miles from Clonea Power and he was taking us there with his donkey and cart.

I was excited knowing I would be seeing my family in Rathgormack again. It had been months since I had seen them, and I especially missed my sister.

The next morning, we rose early. While Thomas and I ate breakfast, Uncle Morey prepared his donkey and cart for the journey. The cart was wooden with two long slats on the sides, and a short one that opened at the rear. Before Thomas and I climbed in, Uncle Morey loaded two grey, speckled, woolen blankets and a pillow for us to sit on.

As soon as the cart was ready, we set off. The sun was shining that morning, and the air was crisp. Puffs of white clouds were scattered across the blue sky and a sheen of morning dew glistened on the grassy dykes. The cart swayed from side to side when the large wheels struggled over rocks that were strewn about on the unpaved road. Occasionally, the squeaking of the noisy wheels was broken by the sounds of swallows chasing each other across the morning sky.

Suddenly, a herd of cows blocked the road as they came ploughing out of a field ahead of us. My uncle got angry when they surrounded us. He tried to push the cart through the herd, but they wouldn't move. I leaned over the edge of the cart and touched the head of a cow closest to me. It was brown with large brown eyes and long eyelashes. Cows didn't scare me because I was used to seeing them in the field across the road from dad's house. Some of them moo'ed loudly and flapped their tails to swat away the flies that landed on them. Thomas and I moo'ed back at them and laughed at the way they licked their noses with their long, wet tongues.

"*Gesh oush of ish, ya ejits. Gwon, Gwon,*" Losing his patience with them, Uncle Morey hollered and tried again to push the bony, dirty rear ends of the cows out of his way. But the cows barely budged.

Minutes later, a sheepdog sprang out of nowhere behind us. He was barking wildly running around the cows. The cows moo'ing grew stronger and they set off into a clumsy gallop to a nearby field. After they were gone, I looked over the sides of the cart and saw the huge wheels roll over the cow pads and squish and flatten them. The cows had left a steaming stench and big mess on the road. I held my nose to avoid having to smell it.

We were a few miles into our journey when Uncle Morey told Thomas and me to lie down under the blankets. "*T'won't* be long now until we get to Nora's (Nanny). *Ye* don't want to be tired when *ye* get there, so *ye* better get some sleep."

Thomas lay down to the left of me and I was on the right, close to where our uncle sat guiding the donkey. Although I wasn't cold or sleepy, I snuggled under the blanket next to my brother. Any passerby would never have noticed we were both hidden beneath the blanket. I was restless thinking of my anticipated visit and found it hard to relax. I rolled onto my back and pulled the blanket under my chin. Looking up at the morning sky, I watched the puffy clouds move aimlessly. Some were big and looked like cotton wool balls. I began to daydream about my mother. Uncle Johnny said she would always be watching over me. In my reverie, I imagined her gazing down at Thomas and me while floating on one of the big fluffy clouds. I turned to look at Thomas to share my thoughts with him, but his eyes were closed.

Staring up at the moving puffs of clouds, I was lost in my own world until I felt the blanket slowly lifting. Coming out of my trance, I looked up and saw Uncle Morey leaning back on the cart. He had his hand under the blanket and quickly slipped it inside my underwear. I tensed, knowing what was happening, and raised my head. He wasn't looking at me but looking straight ahead guiding his donkey. I began to whimper, and furiously pushed his hand away. This time, he stopped what he was doing, and didn't try to fight me. Then he turned around briefly and stared at me. "You'd better not go *tellin'* Nora (my grandmother) or *yer fadder* about *dis*, or I'll give *ya* a good *hidin'* when *ya* come back home," he said.

I understood what he meant about giving me a *hidin'*; he meant he would beat me if I told anybody what he had done. I didn't say anything, but quietly put my head under the blanket and didn't dare move for fear he might try to hurt me again.

"Wo back, wo back," I heard Uncle Morey making a command to his donkey.

The cart had come to a halt, and I guessed we had arrived at Nanny's cottage. I slowly lifted my head from under the blankets and through squinted eyes, I sat up and looked around me. Thomas was already sitting up with a big smile on his face. Coming out to greet us, were Nanny, Dad, sister Peg, and Uncle Johnny. My father, happy to see us, lifted Thomas and me out of the cart one by one. The minute he sat me down, I ran over to my sister, and stood beside her. The excitement I previously had about seeing her, and my family was now overshadowed by perplexity. Uncle Johnny noticed how withdrawn I was. He began teasing me a little and gave me a lucky bag filled with sweets to try and cheer me up.

Once inside, Nanny served lunch around the kitchen table. I was seated next to Peg, and Uncle Morey sat opposite me beside my father. He kept eying me while I ate, and I attempted to keep my head down to avoid his stares. Even though I was in the trusted security of my family, I felt uncomfortable knowing I would be going back to Uncle Morey's house again.

When we finished eating lunch, dad gathered Peg, Thomas, and me and took us to the village store in Rathgormack to buy us ice cream. The walk to the village was over a mile from Nanny's cottage. When we got there, the grocery store owner, Mrs. Kennedy, greeted us warmly. She was especially glad to see Thomas and me because she had not seen us since our mother's passing. While we waited for her to prepare us ice-cream wafers, she gave each of us free orange barley sticks to suck on.

Heading back to Nanny's again, we carefully held our ice cream wafers and licked and savored the sides to catch the melting ice-cream drips. About half-way up the hill on our trek, dad decided to stop and take a rest. He found a grassy clearance on the dyke. Removing his jacket, he threw it down on the ground for us to sit on. Thomas was full of excitable energy after his long nap and ice cream and wouldn't sit still. Dad took him and held him on his lap to calm him. Then he asked Peg to mind him. She found some plants with round fluffy dandelion heads and blew them into the air for Thomas to catch.

As she blew away the seeds, she counted how many hours it took to blow all the heads off. "one o'clock, two o'clock, three o'clock, four o'clock," she said, until all pollen seeds were blown into the air.

Thomas enjoyed the game and put his hand out to try and catch them. But most escaped through his fingers before he could snatch a few.

Sitting next to my father, I quietly watched Thomas. I wanted to join in and play with him but felt reluctant to. My mind was preoccupied with having to return to Clonea with Uncle Morey. I could not understand why I had to live with Aunt Peg and Uncle Morey. I wanted to stay at Nanny's house with my sister. The more I thought about leaving, the more morose I became. What my uncle had done to me played around in my head, and I feared he might do the same if I returned to his home. Dad, sensing how quiet I had become, asked me if I wanted to play with Peg and Thomas. I didn't answer him but rested my head against his shoulder. "Are *ya feelin' alrish*?" he said.

"Daddy. Can I stay at Nanny's house because I do not want to go back to Uncle Morey's house," I begged tearfully.

My father looked at me wearing a deep frown. "And, what's wrong *wit ya* going back *dere*?"

Wiping my tears on his shoulder, I tried to pull myself together. Then I suddenly blurted out what had been bothering me.

"Uncle Morey hurt me and made me sore when he touched me here," I said, pointing to my private parts.

Hearing what I said must have shocked my father. He dropped his head between his hands and fell silent. Seconds later, he lifted it again and looked at me. "What are *ya tryin' ta* tell me? When did *dat* happen?"

"Today, he did it coming here in the cart. And another time after mass," I said.

His brows scrunched tightly while he absorbed what I was telling him. Then, a strange look appeared on his face. "Now don't *ya* be *goin' sayin'* wicked *tings* like *dat*," he said.

"But he did. Aunt Peg saw him do it, and she slapped me across the face and made my face swell-up because I was crying."

"What did she have *ta* go *hittin' ya* like *dat* for?"

He sat for a few moments and pondered. Then, taking a deep breath, he abruptly stood up, and told us it was time to be makin' our way back to Nanny's. Holding my brother's hand and mine, he walked us down the hill, barely saying a word.

The disturbing information I had given him was slowly sinking in. But all was not in vain. In a matter of days, my childhood was about to take another strange twist.

Chapter Three

# IN THE STILL OF THE NIGHT

After eating supper on Sunday evening, July 14, 1957, I went outside with Thomas to play in the backyard of my aunt and uncle's cottage. It was a sunny summer's evening and we chased each other around the back field. Noting Uncle Morey's donkey grazing in the field, we stopped to pet and feed him some grass. Suddenly, a whooshing sound swept around the back of my head. Unsure of what it was, I covered the back of my head with my arm and crouched down for protection. After the sound passed, I looked up and saw two swallows swooping down toward the branches of a low-hanging Hawthorne tree. Then they swiftly soared back into the sky before disappearing over nearby trees.

Since living at my aunt and uncle's, I had never been down to that corner of the field before. Being curious, I took my brother's hand, and we ran down to have a look.

As we drew closer, I spotted an elongated shaft of evening sunlight penetrating the chinks of the dense tree branches. When I crawled under one of the branches with my brother, I discovered a gully of shimmering water with thousands of tadpoles squirming around in a narrow stream. On instinct, I knelt and put my hand in the water to try and catch some. But they wriggled through my fingers and plopped back into the water like jelly blobs. Playful moments passed as my brother, and I tinkered with the tadpoles. With the sheer excitement of my discovery, I wanted to run back to the house and get Aine to show her what I found. Then I remembered her mother had asked her to feed her baby brother a bottle of milk.

Pretty soon, the hollering voice of Aunt Peg calling for Thomas and me echoed under the branches of the tree. I told my brother we had to go and jumped to my feet. We quickly scrambled out from under the branches, covered in mud. When I looked up, I saw my aunt standing at the top of the field with her hands on her hips. Obeying her calls, I took my brother's hand and ran towards her. But then I noticed she was heading down in our direction in long, determined strides. From the angry look on her face, I knew we were in trouble. When she reached us, she took each of us by an ear and began marching us back inside her house. "Who told *da two a ye* to go off down there? Look at *da* state of *da* two a *ye. Ye* are rotten with *da* dirt. Now *ye'll* have *ta* have a *bash ta* scrub *da* dirt off *ye*," she said.

My feet barely touched the ground trying to keep up with her as she dragged us along the tufted grass. She was holding our ears so tight that we both squealed from the pinching pain. Once inside the kitchen, she told us to strip naked. Cousin Aine was sitting on a bench by the fireplace, and quietly eyed us while holding her baby brother on her lap. Her mother went outside and returned, dragging in a large tin tub, and set it down in the middle of the kitchen floor. Carrying a large milk jug, she went back outside to fill it with rainwater from the barrel at the side of the house. She poured it into the metal tub and didn't stop until she was satisfied with the water level. Then she ordered Thomas and me to climb in.

I stepped into the tub first, but quickly scampered out when I felt the icy stab of the cold-water swirling around my legs. She commanded me to get back in, but because the water was so cold, I ignored her order and stood on the stone floor. It annoyed her that I was refusing to get back into the tub, so she angrily reached over it and forcefully dragged me forward until I fell into the tub of frigid water. Sensing the numbing shock of the freezing water on my body, I screamed with fright. Next, she took a hold of Thomas, and lifting him up, she dunked him down into the water. Like me, he stood up, and immediately tried to climb out. Aunt Peg turned him around and spanked him on his bare buttocks before sitting him down again in the tub of icy water. Both of us sat opposite each other, bawling and shivering. Through my tears, I watched drools of slick saliva dropping like icicles from Thomas's nose and mouth. Aunt Peg, ignoring our cries, picked up the milk jug, and after she filled it with some tub water, she poured it over my head first. In sheer fright, I caught my breath. As the water washed over my eyes, it momentarily blinded me, before it came cascading down my face and back. I began to panic and felt around for the rim of the tub, to climb out. My aunt, watching this, clamped down on my arm to keep me where I was. When she was done, I sat in the water shaking while she performed the same act on my little brother. Both of us didn't stop crying.

Uncle Morey appeared from his bedroom when he heard all the commotion. Believing he might save my brother and me, I looked up at him through blurry tears.

"What's up with *da* two *a ye*? he said.

Aunt Peg told him we went down in the gully and got filthy dirty.

"It serves *ye* right *so*. If ye hadn't gone off getting' *yerselves durty*, *ye* wouldn't be *needin'* a *bash* now, would *ye*?" he said with a cunning smirk.

Once we were finished bathing, Aunt Peg got us out of the tub and handed both of us a towel. "Sit on *da* bench *dere* and *ta* dry *yerselves* off," she said.

Thomas and I sat huddled together with the towels wrapped around us in front of the waning fire. The water from my drenched hair trickled down my face and onto the towel, but I was too stunned and cold to even care.

Aunt Peg and Uncle Morey left the house a short time later. Before going, my aunt instructed six-year-old Aine to mind her baby brother, Thomas, and me. The baby had already fallen asleep on Aine's lap, and she laid him down in her parents' bedroom.

After they were gone, the house became eerily quiet. The only sound heard was from the slow rhythmic tick-tock of a small, round-faced clock that sat atop a nearby cabinet shelf. Its calming sound comforted me, while I rocked back and forth on the wooden bench.

Around 7:00 p.m., there was loud rapping at the front door. Wondering who it could be, I looked at Aine. Then the door latch lifted, and my dad walked inside. The instant relief in seeing him, caused Thomas and me to cry. Standing at the open door, he observed our condition.

"Aine, where's your mammy and daddy?" he asked, looking around him, expecting one of them to appear any second.

Aine told him her parents had gone off to the 'Pattern of Mothel,' and that she was minding us. Dad walked over to Thomas and me and told us we had to get dressed. "I'm *takin' da* two *a ye* away with me," he said.

Following us back to our bedroom, he helped us get our clothes on. When we were ready, he told Aine he was going to Mothel to look for her mother and father and bid her farewell. Outside, he had left his bicycle leaning against the wall at the front of the house. First, he picked Thomas up and secured him on a small seat at the rear of his bike, then he lifted me up and sat me on top of the handlebars. Moving his bike away from the wall, he hopped up on it, and cycled off, leaving Aine behind with her baby brother.

After a short, hilly ride, we arrived in Mothel. Dad got off his bike and set Thomas and me down. He rested his bike against a whitewashed wall and holding our hands, he walked us in the direction of a busy pub. As we drew closer, the road was crowded with countryfolk, and a celebration was in full swing. They were singing and dancing to honor two sixth-century patron saints, Quan and Brogan, who hailed from Mothel and Clonea Power. Some people we passed recognized my father. They shook his hand, while others simply waved at him.

"Have you seen any sign of Morey or Peg?" dad called out to a small group of men.

One man told him he had seen Uncle Morey sitting in a ditch and pointed in a direction ahead of us. Dad thanked the man and headed off in search for his brother and wife.

After a short walk, he found Uncle Morey leaning against a grassy ditch talking to a woman. At first, he didn't see us because his head was turned. When the woman spotted us, she nudged him. He turned around to face us, with a cigarette in one hand and a bottle of Guinness in the other. He was speechless when he saw us and raised his eyebrows in surprise. "Well, hello, *dere* Stevie. What's up with *ya*? Did *ya decide ta* come out and bring the young *wans ta* The Pattern?" he said, wearing a wet grin.

Dad stood glaring at him for a few moments, and then leaned forward and whispered something into my uncle's ear. Whatever dad said, it quickly wiped the smirk off Uncle Morey's face. He was furious and pulled himself away from the ditch. Resting his drink in the dyke, he then stubbed his cigarette out in the grass. In a flurry of seconds, he stepped forward in front of my father and punched him squarely in the face. Dad, shocked by the surprise attack, stumbled backwards, knocking his peaked cap clear off his head. A small crowd of onlookers gathered around to watch the brothers' spat. Feeling overcome and embarrassed, Dad steadied himself and brushed his mop of thick hair off his face. Thomas ran to where his dad's cap fell, and picking it up, he proudly placed it on his little head.

Word of the brothers' fight spread. The earlier celebrations were almost at a standstill as the number of onlookers grew. Uncle Morey, feeling elated by all the attention he was getting, snickered when he saw Dad pull an old grey handkerchief from his trouser pocket. Dad's nose was bleeding, and he used the handkerchief to mop it up. Giving his nose and mouth a final swipe with the handkerchief, he slipped it back in his pocket. Straightening himself up, he rushed over to his brother and decked him in the face. The force of the punch caught my uncle off guard and sent him toppling backwards into the dip of the grassy dyke. Thomas felt great excitement to witness his uncle's fall. He had a big smile on his face and began singing his father's praises.

"Hit him, Daddy. Hit him, Daddy," he repeated, punching the air with his tiny fists. Uncle Morey, unable to retaliate, remained in the dyke, nursing his injured face.

My father, feeling satisfied with the outcome, asked Thomas to give him back his cap. Gathering up his mop of wavy black hair, he placed his cap back on his head. Ignoring the mob, he took my brother's hand and mine, and slowly led us away from the scene. As we walked past the people, some men clapped my father on the back. Others gave him approving nods, waves, and words of triumph.

After picking up his bike, we continued on foot in the direction of Clonea Power village. As we drew close to the village, a woman my father recognized was walking toward us. She greeted us and told my father she heard about the brawl. Looking at my father's face, and my brother and me, she invited us to her home, so dad could clean up.

When we got to the house, her husband guided us into the sitting room. The house was bright and pretty. The walls of the sitting room were decorated with floral wallpaper with matching heavy floral curtains that adorned a large window. Two cushiony armchairs were on either side of the fireplace which the man beckoned Thomas and me to sit on.

His wife gave us tumblers of orangeade and biscuits and provided dad with a basin of water and a face towel to bathe his face. Once dad had freshened up, he sat with the couple at the kitchen table, and spoke to them in low whispers. While munching on my biscuits, I felt so contented and comfortable sitting in the big easy armchair. It was a happy home, and a place where I wished I could stay forever.

It was getting dark outside. Dad told the nice people he needed to head for home. He said he was taking a shortcut through the fields and asked them to hold his bike until he came to pick it up. He thanked them and we departed.

Dad walked us along a quiet country road until we came to a high ditch made of big rocks and dirt. The ditch was full of nettles and long thorny briars. Dad found a big stick and cleared them away before stamping down on them with his shoed feet. Once cleared, he lifted me up on the top of the rocky ditch. I waited there until he picked up Thomas and put him up beside me. Then he climbed up to join us, before lowering himself down the other side into a large field. He then reached up and lifted Thomas and me down beside him. Holding both our hands, we trudged through the field in the dark, until we came to another ditch. Following the same routine, we climbed over it. Some of the fields had sheep, and others, cows. They were barely visible apart from their bulky silhouettes. Close to the end of our journey, my foot sank into a soft pad of cow dung. I sensed it when I heard the squelching sound it made and couldn't walk because my foot got stuck in it. The cold sensation of the cow pad freaked me out. Dad had to stop and help me remove my shoe and he blindly scraped off the dung in a patch of grass. With my shoe back on my foot again, he had me roll it side to side to remove any excess dung.

Thomas was getting tired and fussy, and dad carried him on his shoulders. He cried every time dad put him down on the grass or he had to lift him on top of another ditch. He didn't stop crying until he picked him up to carry him again.

Daylight was breaking when we finally reached Graigavalla, my father's home. I was desperate to sleep and could barely keep my eyes open. My father laid Thomas down in his bed, and after removing my dirty sandals, he tucked me in beside him.

We slept for several hours. After we woke up, Dad took Thomas and me back to live with our Nanny.

Less than a week after our return to our grandmother's, a large brown bulky parcel arrived in the post. It was from Aunt Peg and Uncle Morey. It was tied with twine and wrapped in brown paper. The outside of the paper was stained and damp. When Nanny opened it, she found a wet nappy covered in oatmeal kernels. The nappy belonged to Thomas. Nanny was shocked as well as puzzled at how spiteful our aunt was to mail a dirty nappy to her house. My father knew it was in retaliation for the punch he gave Morey.

Although my father had given Aunt Peg nappies for Thomas to use, never once had I seen Thomas wearing one. For weeks after that incident, Nanny repeatedly told her neighbors and friends about the parcel she received. She and my father knew how despicable Aunt Peg and Uncle Morey were. My father admitted to my grandmother how sorry he was that he ever sent my brother and me to live with them.

Once again, another chapter was closing in on our young lives. In a matter of weeks, Thomas and I were on the move again.

# Chapter Four

# DAISY

After Dad's fist fight with Morey, Thomas and I lived temporarily with our grandmother. Less than a month later, we moved to what my father believed would be our permanent home.

We arrived at the home of my father's sister, Aunt Cora, and her husband, Uncle Mack. They lived in Fews, a village in Co. Waterford.

Walking up the narrow path to their front door with my dad and brother, I sensed an inviting warmth from the array of colorful pansies that spilled over the sides of the narrow footpath. Their friendly faces smiled as if to welcome us to our new home.

Aunt Cora and Uncle Mack were in their mid-forties. They lived in a modest house with their eight-year-old son, Mick, and fourteen-year-old daughter, Meg. Thomas shared a bedroom with cousin, Mick, and I shared a bedroom with Meg. Both of us slept in brown wooden cots we had outgrown. My aunt and uncle had some older children who had already left home by the time we came to live with them.

Aunt Cora was tall and buxom, with an intimidating presence. She had a ruddy complexion, against her black and wavy hair. She wore it short and kept in place at the side of her head with a large metal hairgrip. In contrast, Uncle Mack was short and wiry with a balding head and some missing teeth. They eked out a living running a small sheep and goat farm.

Soft sheepskin rugs decorated the floors in the living areas. All the sheepskins were white except for the few black ones that were proudly draped on the backs of the armchairs. I enjoyed touching their plush softness but avoided getting too close to them, because of the gamey odor the wool gave off. That smell, and the stench of the boiled cabbage my aunt cooked daily, appeared to linger, and wafted throughout the house constantly.

School was on summer break when I first arrived. This allowed Thomas and me time to play with our cousin, Mick. He was older than me, and both Thomas and I looked up to Mick as a big brother.

Cousin Meg was my aunt and uncle's only daughter. Although she kept to herself, I discovered early on that she could be a menacing tattletale. Quite often, she accused me of saying or doing something I never did, and then took pleasure in watching her mother spank me for it. I was defenseless against her lies, and too young to understand that Meg was envious of me because I invaded her bedroom space.

At five and a half, I attended Fews National Primary School. Thomas had also started school and was in the high baby's class. The school was only a short distance from the house, and we set out with Mick each day.

Uncle Mack had an appetite for rabbit meat. He kept a constant supply of dead brown rabbits hanging upside down on metal hooks. He tied their hind legs together with twine and hung them on the back of his shed door. Mick knew his dad liked trapping rabbits and searched for them in the dense undergrowth of the ditches on our way to school. Occasionally, we spotted one, but then it hopped away.

One morning we found a large one in the thicket of weedy grass. The rabbit stared at us with a sad-looking, bulging eye. Mick asked me to keep an eye on it while he ran back to the house to fetch his father. I felt sorry for the rabbit, knowing what my uncle was going to do to it, so I shooed it away. This angered Uncle Mack. He felt he had gone out of his way to catch it, and I let it get away. Later, I understood the bulging eye the rabbit had was caused by a virus called myxomatosis.

Across the road from the house was a field where Uncle Mack kept his flock of sheep. The field was hidden behind a high ditch of grass and rocks. After breakfast when the weather was fine, Mick, Thomas, and I excitedly climbed over the ditch to play with the sheep and lambs. The first time I saw the ewes they scared me because they looked so much bigger up close. Over time, I learned how docile and harmless they were when I fed them bunches of fresh grass. Most of the ewes kept their offspring standing close to them and allowed us to stroke them. The lambs were cuddly and playful, and I liked patting their curly fur. When they spotted us on top of the ditch, they announced our arrival with a cacophony of bleats and baa's.

There was one lamb I had grown particularly fond of. Whenever it saw us on the top of the ditch, it frolicked about in the grass with excitement while staying close by its mother. It reminded me of the type of dog I dreamt of owning one day, because of its white, soft fluffy coat.

I named the lamb, Daisy, because of all the daisies I saw scattered throughout the field. Daisy loved getting attention, and when I stopped giving it, she came to me and nudged and nuzzled her warm head against my legs for more. She was cuddly and cute, and I wanted to keep her as my pet friend forever.

One chilly Saturday morning in October, Uncle Mack saw Mick, Thomas and I head over to the field to play with Daisy. Mick had been telling his father for weeks about Daisy and how she bounced around when she saw us. Up to now, his father hadn't paid much attention to the fascination we had with Daisy, except for that Saturday morning.

"Mick, why don't *ya* go over *dere* and bring Daisy back over *ta* me. I want *ta* have a look at her," he said.

Excited to show our pet to Uncle Mack, all three of us happily climbed the ditch. We were thrilled when we saw Daisy standing on the other side, waiting for us beside her mom. We played with her until Mick picked her up and carried her to the top of the ditch. While he held her, I rubbed her furry belly. She baa-ed with contentment, for she had my complete trust.

Uncle Mack was outside his workshed when we returned with Daisy. Mick proudly set her down on the ground for his dad to see. After assessing her for a few moments, I watched my uncle take a thick rope and bind Daisy's hind legs together. Daisy became distressed and attempted to walk but tripped over, falling onto her nose. My uncle gave the rope a tug and hoisted Daisy upside down on a large rusty hook that was attached to the wall outside his shed. Mick, Thomas, and I looked on, confused by his strange actions. Daisy wriggled around upside down trying to break free while Mack went inside his shed. When he came back out, he had a long, skinny knife in his hand. He walked over to where Daisy hung, and effectively slit open her abdomen from tail to throat in a split-second motion. I was momentarily numbed by what I had witnessed, then I screamed. Daisy's eyes looked directly at me like I had betrayed her. Blood splattered to the ground, and her innards spilled out in glistening globs before us. Feeling helpless for Daisy, I let out another scream.

"*Gesh ousha a* here. The lot *a ye,*" Uncle Mack yelled angrily.

In our frightened state, Mick, Thomas, and I ran shrieking and sobbing until we reached the far end of the house. Aunt Cora heard us and came to the front door. "What's up *wit da lot a ye?*"

Through choking sobs, Mick tried to tell her what his father did to Daisy. "Sure, there's no need for *ye* to be *whinging* like that? It'll be a fine feed tomorrow for the Sunday dinner," she said.

Hearing what she said made the unbearable pain of losing Daisy more paralyzing for me.

Later that afternoon, still reeling from what we had seen, Thomas, Mick and I sat on the front doorstep. Uncle Mack approached us, holding Daisy's bloodstained fur. "Here, why don't *ye* make *yerselves* useful and wash *dis, den* put it on the hedge over *dere ta* dry," he said, throwing the fur on the ground at our feet.

Mick was aware his father had a short fuse. He obediently stood up and went inside the house to find a bucket. He came out of the house and filled the bucket with rainwater from the barrel at the side of the house. As soon as he dropped Daisy's fur into the cold water, it turned bright red. Although I felt squeamish, I put my hand in the bucket of cold water and carefully touched the softness of the fur. I winced when I felt the sticky, slimy underside, and tears rolled down my face. It was hard to conceive that Daisy was no more. Even though I played with her only hours before, I felt guilty for helping bring Daisy back to my uncle.

The following morning, I woke up feeling nauseous and shaky. I left the bread and honey Aunt Cora had put in front of me for breakfast. I feared she would get angry with me, but she didn't seem concerned because she was in a hurry to rush us out to Sunday mass.

After mass, she prepared lunch. An aroma of cooked meat wafted from the kitchen to the front yard where I sat on a grassy area with Mick and Thomas. When she was ready, she called us inside for lunch. I took a seat beside Meg at the kitchen table. Aunt Cora walked over to the table and placed a platter of neatly piled portions of meat in the middle. The smell of the meat whirled around me. I was mindful it was Daisy and didn't want to look at it or touch it.

My aunt forked some of the meat onto my plate with mashed potatoes and cabbage. The stench of both the meat and the cabbage caused me to silently retch. I sneakily held my nose, repulsed by what was in front of me. I glanced at Mick and Thomas, and saw they were both enjoying their meal. I wasn't sure if they knew the meat they were eating was Daisy? Everyone was eating their meals, but my plate was still untouched. Meg observed this and informed her mother. "Mammy, she won't eat her food," she said.

"What's up with *ya*? *Sish* up and *aish* that grand food I made *ya*. If *ya* don't, I'll have *ta* come over *ta ya* and make *ya aish* it."

Uncle Mack was seated on the other side of the table. He leaned over and looked at my plate. "Listen *ta* her; You'd better *aish* up."

He was wearing a mean look on his face. I knew if I didn't obey, he would whip me with his belt. I gingerly picked up my fork and sunk it into the mashed potatoes and ate some. As soon as they took their eyes off me, I discreetly buried the lumpy meat beneath the mashed potatoes.

Aunt Cora, noting my plate of food was still basically untouched, rose from her chair, and stood over me with a cross looking glare. "Why aren't *ya aishing*? I'm going *ta* make *ya aish dat* food if *yer nosh goin' ta*," she said.

Then she picked up my fork and scooped up some potatoes. I saw some meat stuck to the fork. "Open up *yer moush* wide," she said.

I closed my eyes and pursed my lips tightly. When I didn't do as she asked, she grabbed both sides of my jaw and forced my mouth open. Then she pushed the food onto my tongue. Dropping the fork on the table, she clamped my mouth shut.

"Now, chew *itsh* and *swally* it," she said, letting go of my mouth to chew the food.

I let the meat roll around on my tongue, and unable to tolerate it any further, I gagged and spat it back onto my plate. Aunt Cora lost her patience and slapped the backs of my hands hard. I sobbed when she asked me to open my mouth again. I just couldn't do it. In anger, she pulled me off the chair, and walloped the backs of my bare legs. My legs hurt and I hollered louder from the stinging pain.

"Right. *Yer goin'* back to *yer* bed where you can stay for *da* rest *of da* day," she said. Then she dragged me into the bedroom, unlatched the cot, and dumped me like a rag doll onto the mattress. Before leaving, she scolded me some more and told me my father would be hearing about my refusal to eat my food.

The next day, I remained in my cot. I could no longer eat and only wanted water to drink. The backs of my hands were puffy and swollen and I felt hot. Although Aunt Cora came to the bedroom to give me toast and tea, I didn't touch it. She also got me out of the cot to use the *Po* (chamber pot) and frequently reminded me how my father was going to hear all about how bold I was.

45

By mid-afternoon on the third day, I was laying in my cot in a sleep-like state. I was disturbed when I heard some movement around my cot and opened my eyes. I saw Meg standing by the side of my cot. I thought she was there to get me out of the cot to use the *Po*. Her mother sometimes asked her to go to the bedroom and perform that task too.

She was holding a beige painted metal mug with green trim in her hand. In my groggy state, I watched her poke the mug through the wide rungs of the cot. Without making eye contact, she carefully lifted my bed covers and I watched her pour a liquid onto the middle of the mattress close to my bottom. Then she carefully brought the mug from between the wooden slats again and left the room. The cold liquid seeped into my nightdress and cooled my warm body. I lay in my cot perfectly still.

Minutes later, Aunt Cora came barging into the bedroom. When I saw her red face, I pulled the bed covers up under my chin.

"Did *ya wesh* the bed?" she yelled, looming over me. I was too scared to tell her I saw Meg put water in my bed. She hastily unlatched the cot and ripped the bedcovers out of my hands. Pushing me to one side, she found my nightdress and cot sheet saturated. Without saying another word, she hauled me out of the cot. Standing on the floor wet and scared, I began to tremble. Uncle Mack stood inside the bedroom door, affirming the lie his daughter told them. After yanking the sheet off the mattress, my aunt turned me around and maniacally whacked me on the buttocks through the wet nightdress. "You're *nottin' bush* a big troublemaker, *wettin'* the bed and *nosh aitin'* yer food. I'll have a lot *ta* tell *ye'r fadder* when he comes here," she said.

Feeling helpless, I stood bawling from my sore bottom, and from Meg's deceitfulness.

Uncle Mack chimed in. *"Tis dis ya'll be* gett'ng' the next time if *ya wesh da* bed," he said, pointing to his waist-belt.

That same weekend, Dad came to visit Thomas and me. Several weeks had passed since we had last seen him. He told me he was attacked by a ram while fetching a bucket of water from the well across the street from his house, causing him to sustain some broken ribs.

As I lay in my cot, he showed me the large strips of white plaster across the left side of his chest where the ram had gored him. Even though he was nursing his own injury, I believe he was shocked when he saw how frail, sick, and thin I had become.

The following morning after his visit, my aunt wheeled me in my cot to the entrance of her open front door. Although it was mid-October, a cool breeze cooled me down, while the soft rays of sunshine played upon my face.

At some point, two tall men stood over me. They lifted me out of the cot and onto a stretcher. When I opened my eyes, I saw Thomas. He was beside me, standing on his tippy toes wanting to get a glimpse of me as I was being wheeled to a waiting ambulance. I heard him say, "Bye, bye, sissy," before the men lifted me into the back of an ambulance.

I was taken to Ardkeen Hospital in Waterford City and admitted to St. Brigid's Children's Ward. After a physical assessment, I was diagnosed with severe malnutrition, scurvy, and physical abuse. As well as having a high fever, the backs of my hands were swollen, and I had black and blue bruising on the backs of my legs.

The doctor in charge of my care came often to check on my progress. Sometimes when I woke up, I discovered him listening to my chest with a stethoscope or looking inside my mouth with a small mirror. He prescribed me liquid vitamins and a sweet iron tonic to take daily. At breakfast, I was served a hard-boiled egg in a pretty egg cup with white toast.

The nurses working on St. Brigid's ward were nurturing and kind. Each morning before the day shift began, I looked out the ward window from my cot to see which nurse was walking along the path to the ward. It made me happy when I saw my favorite nurse walking down the path. She always stopped outside the window to wave before coming to the ward to care for me.

It was getting close to Christmas, when I had a surprise visit from my English Aunt Pat and Uncle Sean. Uncle Sean was one of my father's six half-brothers and he was home from England visiting his family. I barely remembered meeting him before then, but knew it was my first-time meeting Aunt Pat. The moment she stood over my cot to greet me, I felt a radiance of loving warmth emanate from her. I embraced the gentle way she spoke to me and hugged me. She was the mother I was missing, and I didn't want her to leave me.

I shared a room with a boy who was a few years older than me. He was recovering from the mumps. Each evening his parents came to visit him. On their visits, they also remembered to bring me sweets and biscuits. Their son kept telling his mom and dad he wanted me to go home with him when he left the hospital. When he said this, his parents would just look at me and smile.

We were both discharged from the Ardkeen Hospital on the same day. Shortly after breakfast that morning, the nurses got us up and ready to leave. Assuming I was being dropped off at the boy's house, I felt content and secure. On our journey, the ambulance came to a complete stop. I guessed the driver had pulled up outside the boy's house.

The attendant opened the back door of the ambulance, and I got up to leave with the boy. When the driver saw me standing beside him, he instructed me to sit down. "No love, this it isn't your house. I will be dropping you at your house next."

Crestfallen, I wondered which house he was taking me to. Once the boy left the ambulance, I didn't see him or his parents anymore as we rode away. The ambulance didn't have any back windows, so I never got a chance to wave goodbye.

After a short drive, the ambulance came to a halt. I didn't know where I was but knew it must be where I was being dropped off. I tensed when the driver opened the back door, and I realized I was at Uncle Mack and Aunt Cora's house. Feeling fretful, I pulled back from the attendant and told him I didn't want to go to that house. The attendant, not understanding my fears, picked up my belongings, and lifted me out of the ambulance. He took my hand and after much persuasion, he encouraged me to go with him. When he knocked on the front door, Aunt Cora opened it. Because of her large frame, she almost filled the doorway. Standing behind her was my little brother, Thomas. He was poking his head around Aunt Cora's skirt, wearing a beaming smile when he saw me. We had been apart for so long that I had almost forgotten about him. I let go of the attendant's hand and I walked inside my aunt and uncle's house to join my brother.

The following day, my father arrived at his sister's house. He packed up my brother's clothes and mine in a small suitcase and took us back to our grandmother's house once more.

At six and a half years old, another new chapter of my childhood was about to unfold.

## Chapter Five

# A NEW JOURNEY

## June 1960—Six Years and Seven Months

I felt something was amiss that sunny day at Nanny's house. I had been living with her since leaving Uncle Mack and Aunt Cora's home. After eating lunch that day, Nanny called Thomas and me back to her bedroom. On her bed, she had clothes laid out for both of us to change into.

"Aren't *dey* lovely. Chrissy Whelan gave me *dem* for *da* two *a ye* to wear. The two *a ye* are *goin' ta* look grand altogether in *dem* fine clothes," she said.

Nanny's neighbor, Chrissy, often gave her hand-me-down clothes and shoes for my siblings and me to wear. She had a multitude of children, and when they grew out of their clothes or shoes, she passed them on to other neighborhood children as well as to us. Without her generous support, Nanny would never have had the funds to clothe us. Yet, that day, I wondered why I had to change out of the dress I was wearing because it was pretty and clean. I didn't ask Nanny why I had to change because that would have been bold.

The frock she laid out for me was also pretty. It had a mint green background and was decorated with tiny yellow daisies with speckled white centers. While I changed, Nanny helped Thomas dress in a pair of short brown pants and a white shirt. Once I was ready, I stood in front of her to seek her approval. "Well, will *ya* look at *yererself*. *Dat* frock fits *ya* grand. Don't be *goin'* off *an'getting yerself* all *durty*. *Twon't* be long now til *ye'r fadder* is here," she said.

I was puzzled as to why my dad was visiting. He mainly came at weekends, or when it suited him.

Nanny gave me a white, button-down cardigan to wear over my dress. Before leaving her bedroom, she told me not to go far, that I had to wait until Thomas was ready. While waiting for Thomas, I slipped out of her room and into Uncle Johnny's bedroom. He had a large wooden wardrobe with a long mirror attached and I wanted to see how I looked in my fresh, new clothes. Admiring myself in front of the mirror, I smiled at my reflection and twirled around to see the back of my frock. I couldn't wait to show it off to Peg. She was outside in the half-acre waiting for Thomas and me to go out and play with her.

When Thomas was ready, I ran outside with him to the half-acre to display my new frock to Peg. She gave it a quick look and wasn't at all bothered about it. She was only interested in playing on the haystack our uncle had assembled for us the day before. Uncle Johnny had several other haystacks scattered about the half-acre, but only allowed us to play on this one. To prevent it from tipping over, he told us we had to climb up on it, one at a time.

Lining up, Peg climbed up first. When she got to the top, she slid back down the other side. I went next and Thomas followed me. We enjoyed taking turns climbing up and down the haycock and were careful not to knock it over. Because of what Nanny had said earlier about keeping my clothes clean, I was mindful not to soil my new frock, and reminded Thomas to do the same with his new clothes.

When it was my turn to climb up again, I scampered to the top and sat there for a few moments. Feeling on top of the world, I looked down at my sister and brother, smiling and waving down at them.

As I was preparing to slide down the other side of the haycock, I spotted a shiny black car pulling up outside my grandmother's front gate. Motor cars were rare in Rathgormack, and this was the second time I had seen the same car. The last time was when dad took Thomas and me to live with Aunt Cora and Uncle Mack.

I sat on the haycock for a few moments fixating my gaze across the yard. A rush of confusing thoughts raced through my mind. I wondered if I was going back to live with them again. Was that why Nanny gave Thomas and me fresh clothes to wear? Then I watched her walking across the front yard, to meet the driver. I froze when I saw the same driver stepping out of the car to talk with Nanny.

Peg was getting impatient with me. When I wasn't coming down off the haystack, she began to climb up. I was aware it might topple over if both of us sat on it. Feeling overwrought, I nervously slid down, and dashed across the yard, through the front door of Nanny's cottage.

In my panic, I fled inside Uncle Johnny's open bedroom door and forcibly slammed it, so the latch clicked shut. At first,

I was going to jump into the wardrobe, but changed my mind when I figured I might easily be discovered.

Uncle Johnny's double bed was pushed tightly against the wall-papered wall. Laying on my belly, I squeezed myself underneath the bed. His empty chamber pot (*Po*) was in my way, and I pushed it aside to create more room. Scooting on my elbows inch by inch, I kept my head lowered because of the sagging mattress and broken coiled springs. My new clothes were no longer clean. They were getting blacker from the years of settled dust and dirt I was crawling over. Once I reached the upper far corner of the wall, I laid on my side and brought my knees up to my chest. My heart was pounding in my chest, but I felt safe, and lay there as still as a mouse.

Before long, I heard my grandmother and father in the kitchen calling out my name. One of them was in the bedroom I shared with Peg, opening and slamming the doors of the heavy mahogany dresser. Then someone lifted the latch on Uncle Johnny's bedroom door and walked inside. I held my breath when the wardrobe doors squeaked on their hinges. Then, the bedroom door closed again. I guessed it was Nanny. She was outside the door telling my father I wasn't in my uncle's bedroom.

All went quiet again, and I didn't move an inch from my spot. I knew I was being bold and would surely be scolded once I was discovered. The image of the shiny black car was fresh in my mind, and I was determined to remain where I was. I simply didn't want to go back to live with Uncle Mack and Aunt Cora.

Moments passed before a cacophony of frantic voices echoed through my uncle's bedroom from the kitchen. "Noreen. Noreen. Where are *ya*? Come out of wherever you're at."

My uncle's bedroom door was opened again. The sound of the wardrobe doors being opened aggressively and slammed shut again caused me to shudder. Floorboards creaked when footsteps drew closer to the bed, and then paused. I hid my face when I noticed someone's head resting on the linoleum floor. Peeking out from under my elbow, I discovered it was my dad. He had his eyes shielded to take a better look under the bed. After staring intently at my curled-up shape in the corner, he discovered my hideout.

"There *ya* are. Sure, we're all worried about *ya*. "*Whash* are *ya doin'* hidin' under *dere*? Come *outsha' dere* like a good little girl."

I burst out crying, with relief, hearing his voice.

Nanny rushed into the room and saw dad kneeling on all fours. He told her I was under the bed. When she heard this, she prayed to Jesus and His Blessed mother that I had been found. She stepped outside the bedroom and yelled for Uncle Johnny's attention. He entered his room with Peg and Thomas. Dad was still crouched on the floor pleading with me to come out, but I wouldn't stir. Thinking of a way of pulling me out, he stretched his long arm under the bed, but I was tucked too far away in the corner for him to reach me. I was being disobedient and stubborn but was also paralyzed with fear.

"Come *oush fer yer* daddy. *Tis* wicked *bould* of *ya ta* be hidin' under *da* bed like *dash*?"

When my father's hopes of coaxing me out were lost, my grandmother and Uncle Johnny took turns in trying to lure me out. After their repeated efforts, I sensed they were growing impatient when I wasn't accepting their bribes.

Nanny got down on the floor a second time and cracked a safety match to see me more clearly. The light of the match was bright, so I turned my head into my folded arm.

"Look *ash whash* I have here *fer ya*, some Bullseyes *swates an'* a half-crown. I'll give *dem ta ya* if *ya* come *oush* a *dere*," Nanny begged persuasively.

She knew I loved sucking on Bullseyes, but not even they were going to win me over, and I chose to ignore her bribery.

The cajoling continued and time was passing. My dad was down on the floor again.

"*Meself* and Johnny will have *ta* pull *da* bed away from *da* wall and get *ya* if you won't come *outsh*," he said.

I had never been as naughty as I was now and knew I was losing the battle. I started to whimper with this stern warning.

"I won't come out because the man in the car is going to take me back to Aunt Cora and Uncle Mack again," I told him through sniffling sobs.

"Who told *ya* such a *ting*. *Ye're* not *goin'* back *to dem* again. He's only here *to* take me down to *Washurford* City with *yerself* and Thomas. The poor man has been *waitin'* outside for *ya* all *dis* time. I can bring him in if you don't believe me, and he'll tell *ya* himself," my father said.

This was the first time I heard about going to Waterford with my father and Thomas. I had never been there before, and only heard about how big and crowded it was.

Someone went outside and brought the driver in to talk to me.

"Sure, *yer fadder* is tellin' *ya* the *trush alrighsh*. I am only here *ta* take *ya* down *ta Wasuerford*," he said.

"Don't be *keepin'* the poor man *waitin.'* He came here especially for us today," my dad said.

My six-year-old mind told me my father meant what he said. I had already defied him and didn't wish to further disobey. My eyes were filled with tears, and I wiped them with the sleeve of my cardigan. Overcome by what I had done, I decided to crawl out. I stretched my body out from its curled up position and pressing down on my elbows, I slowly dragged myself away from the corner until I was fully out. When I stood up Nanny gasped when she saw how dirty and disheveled I looked.

"Will *ya* look at the state of *ya*. *Ye'r* a holy fright. *Dem* clothes are no good *fer ya* now anymore," she said.

Feeling shaky and disoriented, I put the back of my hand to my eyes to shield the bright light streaming through the bedroom window.

"First, you'll have *ta* have a *scrubbin'* before *ya* head down *ta Wasuerford. Den ya* can have *dem swates* and the half-crown, I promised ya," she said, fussing and brushing the dust off my dress.

I looked down at my clothes and saw that my cardigan and frock were full of dust balls, and my hands and legs were covered in streaky smudges. Feeling sorry for what I had done, I stood beside my father and grabbed his trouser leg for protection. He allowed me to cling to him for a few minutes before Nanny pried me away to get cleaned up. Walking away from my father, I caught a glimpse of myself in the wardrobe mirror. My face was covered in rivulets of grey grime, and my clothes and shoulder-length hair were matted in dust.

Nanny removed my dirty clothes, and then washed my face, legs, arms, and my hair with a bar of carbolic soap. When she was done, she picked through the donated clothing and chose a pink, seer-sucker frock, and another white cardigan for me to wear. Although I was still in a sulky mood, I liked the pretty frock. It had little pink heart-shaped buttons decorating the front, with a matching pink sash.

My face lit up when she handed me a bright red coat to wear. Red was my favorite color, and it fitted me perfectly. It had a furry brown collar with a double row of dark brown buttons lined up in the front of the coat. Nanny helped me button them up, and taking my hand, she walked me outside to the waiting car.

Thomas was already in the back seat. He was happy because the driver had allowed him to play with the steering wheel, while waiting for me to get ready. Climbing in beside him I got a strong gamey whiff from the maroon leather seats. The driver closed the car door and slowly drove away from the gate and onto the road. Uncle Johnny, Peg, and Nanny were standing by the gate waving goodbye as we drove off. I smiled and waved back, believing I was going to see them when I returned from my day trip to Waterford City. I continued to gaze out the back window at them, until they disappeared on the other side of the hill.

My father, feeling satisfied that his plan had worked, turned around in the passenger seat and said, "Well, we're off at last. *T'will* be a grand *oul'* spin going down to *Washerford* City."

# Chapter Six

# SEPARATION ANXIETY

I began to create a fuss on my journey to Waterford City. Looking out the car window at the landscape, I felt certain the driver was on the same road that led to Aunt Cora's and Uncle Mack's home.

"Daddy, is the man taking us back to Aunt Cora's house again?" I anxiously asked.

"No," he said, with a touch of irritability in his voice. "I told *ya* already. We're *goin'* down to *Washerford*. *Tis* a big city and a grand place altogether," he said.

My earlier shenanigans hiding under Uncle Johnny's bed hadn't helped. He told me before leaving Nanny's house that he might be late getting down to Waterford because I held the driver up.

My sense of insecurity eased when I saw the small villages and roads looked different than the road to Fews. I moved in closer to Thomas. He was transfixed on the driver and all the shiny fixtures in the car. When the driver made a right turn, he saw the triangular orange indicator pop out on the outside of the car and squealed with excitement.

The driver, trying to meet his deadline, speedily weaved around curvy mountain bends to make up for lost time. Sometimes, when he made a turn, I slid across the backseat and bumped into Thomas.

A light, misty rain was falling when we pulled into the Waterford Quay. Dad walked us across the street to the shops and tall buildings. The sidewalk was bustling with men, women, and children going back and forth carrying bags of shopping. I became giddy gazing in at the large windows showcasing toys and games. One toy shop had a huge, brown teddy bear on display inside a tall shiny glass window. Dad wasn't happy with us dawdling too long because he was in a hurry. Feeling proud in my new red coat, I held his hand and skipped beside him as he hurried us along the crowded street. We soon turned up a side street and approached a large grey building with two wooden doors. Walking inside, a lady greeted us warmly and guided us down a hallway to a large room. Inside, I got a distinctive smell of wax polish. It was the same scent from the polish I smelled on Aunt Cora's furniture. The walls of the room had dark wood paneling from floor to ceiling. I walked with dad and my brother to the front of the room and sat on a long wooden bench. Other people were already seated. Some smiled endearingly at Thomas and me.

The room fell silent when a tall man in a black gown stepped out from behind a side door. He walked to a high chair behind a big wooden desk and sat down. His stature and black robes intimidated me, causing me to cling to my dad's coat.

Then he looked up from his desk, and in a deep, crisp voice, he called out my name first, and then my brother's. "Will Noreen Roche and Thomas Roche, please rise," he said.

Hearing this stranger stating our names, made me bury my face in my father's coat sleeve. Dad stood up, and taking my brother's hand and mine, he escorted both of us to the man seated at the large wooden desk. Feeling shy of the man, I hid my face in my dad's coat and peeked out at him with one eye. He leaned over his big desk and flashed a warm smile at my brother and me. When he sat back in his seat, his attention shifted. He quietly spoke with my father and then gave him a paper to sign. When my father handed the signed paper back to the man, I heard the man in the black gown utter words that have echoed in my head ever since.

"They are now Wards of the Court."

I didn't understand what 'wards of the court' meant, but I looked up at my father and watched him nod his head. Taking our hands again, we returned to the same bench and sat down. Soon, a man and woman with friendly faces stepped forward and introduced themselves to dad. The lady, wearing a big smile, held out her hand to me, and I took it, and the man took Thomas's hand. They both ushered us back through the same door we had entered. I turned around to see if dad was following us. He was standing alone, with a forlorn stare on his face. When we walked outside, I looked for my dad, but he wasn't behind me. Feeling confused, and unaware of what was happening, I tried to pull away from the lady to run back inside to get my dad.

But she had a tight grip on my hand and wouldn't let go. I let out a deafening scream and started to sob inconsolably.

My brother was walking ahead of me with the man. When he heard me, he too began to cry. The man walked Thomas in a different direction from where the lady was taking me. I began to throw a temper tantrum and refused to walk with her. Then she tugged my hand and quickened her pace. I kept pulling away from her, and she kept pulling me back.

She stopped outside a parked black car. The driver got out, and quickly opened the back door. The lady let go of my hand and nudged me inside to the back seat, and promptly climbed in beside me. When the driver closed the door, I continued to cry. Feeling trapped, I grabbed the door handle and attempted to jump out. The lady pulled my hand away and clasped both my hands firmly on my lap. I tried to push her hands away, and when she wouldn't let go of me, I kicked her leg. She didn't get angry with me, but calmly moved her legs to the side. I was shocked by my own audacity because I had never been so brazen to act this way before.

As the car pulled away from the curb, I was teary-eyed, and upset. I looked out the window searching for my father and brother, but they were nowhere to be seen. The lady released her grip on my hands when she saw I was calming down. Then she patted my head, but I moved her hand away. I was sad, lost and confused and I didn't know where she was taking me. I turned my head away from her and blankly stared out the car window.

After a short drive, the car turned off the main road and swung in between two enormous arched wooden gates. The driver continued up a wide driveway and didn't stop until he arrived in front to a sprawling, grey, stone building.

I turned and looked at the lady. Smiling, she announced, "This is the Good Shepherd Convent, and it will be your new home now."

Feeling bewildered by what she said, I turned away from her, trying to make sense of why I was at this place.

*Good Shepherd Convent (main entrance).*

*St. Dominick's School.*

## Chapter Seven

# THE GOOD SHEPHERD CONVENT

I stood with the lady outside a big, wooden door while she knocked on a curved, brass door knocker. I was vexed and sullen about being at this place and kept my head down.

When the door opened, I saw a strange person standing in the doorway. Only half the face and hands were visible, and a black veil flowed over a long, beige dress.

"Say hello to Mother Teresa. She's one of the nuns who will be taking care of you now," my escort said, moving me towards her.

Although only half of her face was shown, her striking, pale blue eyes stood out against her other features. Around her neck she had a huge silver heart, and her hands poked out from below the buttoned sleeves of her long dress. A string of heavy, wooden, rosary beads hung from her thick leather waist belt and draped down the right side of her beige dress. On the left side of her belt was a medium-sized pair of silver scissors that hung from a white string.

Wearing a gentle smile, she looked down at me and put her hand out to greet me. Unsure of whether to take her hand or not, I shyly recoiled and hid behind my escort. Her odd clothing and the leather belt she wore made me wary of her.

"Come, let me see you, dear. I've been waiting for you. There's no need to be shy. We have many girls your age here that you can be friends with," she said.

She leaned forward and gently took my hand in hers. I wanted to take it back, but when I felt how warm and soft it was, I continued to hold it.

She thanked my escort, and then walked me inside and closed the door behind her. "You must be awfully hungry, dear. But don't worry. It will be suppertime soon. First, you will need to have a bath and change out of the clothes you're wearing. So, we need to head over to see Mother Cyra. She will take good care of you," she said.

She opened a door that led to a long, shiny, tiled cloister. It was patterned in different sizes and colors of red, beige, and grey. The corner walls displayed two enormous, alabaster angels, with pointed, white wings. They loomed high above in sweeping sculpted clothing and were painted in white and blue colors. Their beady black eyes seemed to watch us as we passed. Walking beside the nun, my black-laced ankle boots squeaked with every step I took, and the shiny cloister emitted a waxy scent.

When we reached the mid-section of the cloister, Mother Teresa opened a side door. This led to a small gravel yard and to a small building with a low grey door. Above the door hung a hand carved sign that read, 'Laundry Room.' Mother Teresa opened the door, and I walked inside with her.

As we entered, a draft of humid air and the scent of carbolic soap enveloped us. Against the far wall, I spotted a row of wooden sinks.

The floor beneath the sinks showed small pools of soapy, grey water.

Seconds later, a heavyset nun wearing thick black spectacles emerged from a room at the back. She was wearing a habit identical to Mother Teresa's, except hers hung sloppily around her waist, and displayed an uneven hemline. As she approached us, I noticed she walked with a limp and her forehead glistened in sweat. Mother Teresa introduced me to Mother Cyra. Without acknowledging me, Mother Cyra eyed me up and down, then turned to Mother Teresa.

"Is she in from the country?"

"She comes from Rathgormack, in Carrick-on-Suir," Mother Teresa told her.

"Sure, that's the country alright. They're always filthy when they come here from the country. No doubt about it, she'll definitely be *needin'* a bath," she said.

As she callously derided me, her top and bottom teeth wobbled in her mouth, and swam in a pool of her saliva. Mother Teresa informed her that she would be back to pick me up in time for supper, and then left.

Limping over to the sinks, Mother Cyra instructed me to follow her. She handed me a dark grey pinafore and told me to remove my clothes and shoes. The pinafore was long and heavy. When I slipped it on over my head, it hung off my shoulders and trailed onto the stone floor. Standing beside the nun, I hoped she would see how big it was on me, but her back was turned. She was busy rolling up her habit sleeves which revealed her white, puffy forearms. To protect her habit, she tied a white apron around her waist. Then she pulled two shiny black beaded pins from her black veil and used them to secure the top of the apron to her shoulders. Reaching over a sink, she rotated two t-shaped bronze knobs. Water immediately spluttered and splattered from both. I stood in awe, watching a whorl of steam, rising to the low ceiling. This was my first time seeing running water.

When the sink was half-filled, she moved a small wooden stool in front of it and told me to step in. I hoisted the oversized pinafore above my knees and stood on the stool. After I managed to lift one of my legs over the lip of the tub, I climbed in. The sink was small and narrow and at six and a half years, my legs were growing, and I had to bend my knees. I felt awkward soaking in the sink, but I took comfort from the embracing warmth of the water seeping through the thick serge fabric of the pinafore.

Mother Cyra picked up a bar of red carbolic soap. She rubbed it into a facecloth, and gruffly swiped it across my face. The soap had a stinky odor, and I held my breath, so I didn't have to inhale it. A grimace appeared on the nun's face when she picked up one of my hands to wash it.

"Just look at the dirt of *them* nails. Sure, they're long enough to grow spuds under," she said, pushing her black veil over her shoulders like it was her long hair.

Her chubby red face was soaked in sweat, and her thick, jam-jar type eyeglasses were fogged up from the steam. I wondered how it was possible for her to see my fingernails through the glasses she wore. Lifting a pair of scissors from her leather waist belt, she began clipping them. The tips flew off my nails, into the sink and onto the floor with each snip.

My legs were entirely hidden by the heavy fabric. She had to push the pinafore aside and straightened one leg at a time to wash them. She left the covered part of my torso untouched. Creating a lather in both hands from the carbolic soap, she rigorously washed my hair and then rinsed it off with the sink water. When she was done, she pulled the copper chain and stopper. While the water drained out of the sink, she told me to stand up. I found it difficult to pull myself up because my pinafore was saturated, and its weight kept dragging me down. Seeing I had difficulty, she helped me climb out and onto the stone floor. I stood in a pool of water as it ran off the pinafore. She instructed me to lift the pinafore off my shoulders, and let it drop on the floor while handing me a grey towel to wrap around my naked body.

"Now, go over here and sit on that chair," she said, pointing to a small wooden chair by the window.

"I will need to check your hair for *boodies* and nits."

I didn't know what she meant. Standing behind me, she lifted parts of my hair. When she was done, she picked up a pair of large scissors from the windowsill and proceeded to chop off my hair, piece by piece. The snipping and cutting continued until my hair was high above my ears. To finish off, she cut a straight fringe to the top of my forehead. My neck felt bare without my shoulder-length hair. She then placed a basin on my lap and asked me to lower my head towards it. I shuddered when I felt her douse my head with a cold solution that ran down my neck and the sides of my face.

With my head still lowered over the basin, she towel-dried my hair thoroughly. Then, lifting my hair, section by section, she shook some strange smelling powder on it. "That's to kill the boodies and nits," she said, massaging the stinging powder into what was left of my hair.

When she was done, she told me to remain seated while she went to the back room. On the windowsill, I noticed a tubular canister with the letters DDT 'powder for lice' printed on the front. I hadn't seen it there before she gave me the haircut, and guessed it was the powder she used on my hair. Touching the front and back of my shorn hair, I felt how short it was. It made me want to cry because I never had such short hair before. Everything and everyone I loved was being taken away from me by strangers today.

Mother Cyra returned carrying a pile of fresh clothes and shoes. She gave me a pair of white plastic sandals and another pair of brown lace-up shoes, to try on. When she saw they fit, she handed me a pair of underwear, a gymslip and cardigan to wear. I really wanted to have my pink dress back, but I couldn't see any sign of it. That had disappeared along with my boots, and my new red coat. Mother Cyra never mentioned anything about them, and I was too disoriented and timid to ask her about them. Once I was dressed, she told me to sit on the chair to wait for Mother Teresa. While she was cleaning up after my bath, I jumped when I heard a loud clanging noise of bells.

**Dong. Dong. Dong. Dong.** The bells pealed in slow, solemn tones. Mother Cyra paused from her work and told me to go down on my knees and follow her in prayer. Clasping her hands together, she closed her eyes and recited a prayer:

*"The Angel of the Lord declared unto Mary,*
*And she was conceived by the Holy Ghost.*
*Hail Mary full of grace . . ."*

When the ringing stopped, she permitted me to stand up. "That was the six o'clock Angelus call to prayer. Those bells ring every day, at noon and again at six in the evening. No matter what you're doing, you will have to stop and pray the Angelus," she said.

A few minutes passed and Mother Teresa returned to pick me up. "Don't you look lovely with your new haircut and clothes? Did you thank Mother Cyra for the splendid job she did on you?" she asked me smiling.

I looked at Mother Cyra shyly and thanked her.

"No, dear," Mother Teresa intoned. "That is not how you address Mother Cyra. The proper and respectful way to thank her, is to say, thank you, Mother."

I repeated what she told me to say, and Mother Teresa rewarded me with a wide smile of approval. Taking my hand, she led me out of the laundry room and walked me down the long cloister. At the end of the cloister, she opened a door that led onto a hallway. In front of me was a massive wooden door. Over the top, the word 'Refectory' was spelled out with large wooden letters.

# Chapter Eight

# OBEDIENCE

When Mother Teresa opened the large door to the Refectory, I anxiously squeezed her hand. Inside was a huge room with high windows, and facing me, stood a short nun and numerous girls of all ages. They obediently stood in groups of four around pink and turquoise four-top laminate tables. As soon as they saw me, they gawked with curiosity. Feeling overwhelmed, I lowered my head and peeked out from under my eyelashes. Mother Teresa introduced me to the nun. Although I had my head down, I saw her acknowledge my presence with only a nod.

Her name was Mother Concillio. She had a round face with rosy-red cheeks, beady brown eyes, and thin, pursed lips. Over her habit, she wore a white, starched apron that was pinned at the shoulders. Dangling from her habit, I spotted a long skinny black whip. The sight of her whip immediately made me tense. She informed Mother Teresa she had a place ready for me at one of the tables. Mother Teresa gently let go of my hand and told me I needed to sit down and eat my supper; moments later, she left.

An awkward void crept in after Mother Teresa was gone. Standing at the front of the refectory, I heard a fluctuating wave of whispers resonate from the girls. Mother Concillio, aware of their murmurings, clapped her hands to get their attention, and I looked up.

"Listen up. We have a new girl here at St. Dominick's. Her name is Noreen Roche."

The mention of my name caused me to blush with unease and I dropped my head again. Because of my awkwardness around them, I didn't hear Mother Concillio calling for me to follow her. I jumped and looked up when she raised her voice. "Are you deaf? I said for you to follow me," she said sternly.

At first, I wasn't sure she was talking to me, until I saw her angry red face. Feeling nervous, I had an unexpected urge to urinate. When I attempted to walk over to her, I found myself glued to the floor. I knew all eyes were on me and the nun was getting agitated. Then, she marched over to me, and grabbing my arm, she hurried me to a table two rows back from the front. Running alongside her, I felt a stream of warm urine trickling down my legs. When I got to my table, she pressed my arm in a downward motion to ensure I didn't move from where she left me, before letting go of me. Then she swiftly swept back between the tables to the front of the room again.

Three other girls stood behind their chairs at the same table where she left me. They quietly sized me up without uttering a word. Feeling out of place and ashamed, I feared they might have noticed my unplanned accident. I stopped myself from urinating any further because I knew my underwear was soaked.

From where I stood, I had a clear view of Mother Concillio. She had her head bowed and didn't appear to notice I had wet clothing. Her hands were joined together at her chest, and she began saying a prayer, with the girls following her in unison:

*'Blessed O Lord*
*For These Thy Gifts*
*Which of Thy Bounty*
*We Are About to Receive*
*Through Christ Our Lord*
*Amen.*

When the prayer ended, there was a scraping sound of chairs being dragged across the red-tiled floor as the girls took their seats. I was the last person standing. I pulled my chair out from under the table and sat down. The girls at my table continued to eye me. I tried to avoid their stares by looking at the place setting in front of me.

It had a starched, dark green serviette rolled up into a point that sat vertically in a green ring holder. To the right and left side of the setting, was a knife, fork, and spoon. A white cup and saucer were placed on the upper right side. Out of the corner of my eye, I watched the girls lift the cloth serviettes from their holders and place them on their laps. I wanted to copy them but felt uneasy because I had never used a serviette before.

The girls at my table still hadn't spoken to me, but I overheard girls at the table on the right of me whispering my name behind their shielded hands. I shifted slightly to the right, and keenly listened to what they were saying. Were they talking about my dreaded secret?

*Girl 1, "What do ya think of that new girl?*

*Girl 2, "I don't know. She's real gawky looking."*

*Girl 1, "How old would you say she is?"*

*Girl 2, "I'd say she's around my age, and will be sleeping in my dormitory."*

It was a relief to hear they weren't talking about my shameful situation. But everything was bothering me. Nothing had gone right for me since the black car arrived outside my grandmother's house today. At that moment, I was desperate to jump out of my chair and flee, to where I did not know. My head was crowded with confusing and disturbing thoughts.

*Why was I brought to this place with all these girls?*

*Where was my father? He never said anything about me coming here. He didn't even say goodbye to me or Thomas.*

*Where was my brother?*

*How come my sister, Peg, didn't have to come here? Would my father be coming back to get me?*

It all seemed like a very bad dream.

I snapped back to reality, and my dark emotions halted when the older girl at my table spoke. "You're not the only one here called Noreen, just so you know. There's another girl called Noreen sitting over there," she said, pointing to the far corner of the room.

Although I didn't respond, I followed her finger to the table where the other girl with the same name sat. A silence passed between us before she spoke again.

"I'm Josephine, and that's Nellie and Tess," she said.

Nellie and Tess looked at me and smiled when she shared their names with me, and I timidly smiled back. It was easy to see Tess was the youngest girl at the table. She was pretty with wavy blonde hair and had two missing front teeth. Nellie looked a little older than me. She had mousey brown hair with freckles covering her entire face. Josephine was the eldest. She was well-developed, and had light brown hair, slanted blue eyes, and a long face. At first, I didn't know what to make of her, but the more she talked to me, the less fear I had of her. She gave me a brief rundown of the nuns and the supper service. "See that fat little nun? That's Mother Colette. She works in the kitchen."

"The short skinny one is Mother Concillio. None of us like her because she's always lashing out at us with her whip. She makes the older girls go into the kitchen to help Mother Colette. Soon, they'll be coming around with our supper. After that, Mother Colette will bring out a big tray of bread. She leaves it up there," she told me, pointing to a large cupboard at the front of the room.

"The bread goes quickly, so you better grab some fast, if you like it," she said, smiling with a row of crooked top yellow teeth.

Although l liked eating bread, there was no way I was going to stand up and get some with my wet underwear. Besides, the girls might pick-up on the smell of urine from me.

No sooner had Josephine told me about the service, than Mother Colette came to our table and served me a plate of green peas, brown meat, and mashed potatoes. I was very hungry but didn't like the look or smell of the meat. It had a ring of yellow fat around it and since what happened to Daisy, I hadn't touched any brown meat. I watched the girls eat their food and picked up my knife and fork. I ate all the mashed potatoes and peas but left the meat on my plate. I already understood that if

Mother Concillio ordered me to eat my meat; I would have to promptly obey her.

An older girl came to the table and poured tea in my cup. I could tell by the white appearance of the tea, that milk had already been added. I loved drinking tea and wondered if sugar had also been added. At Nanny's house, I often heaped teaspoons of sugar in my tea and enjoyed drinking it that way. I was tempted to try some, but feared if I did, it might make me want to urinate again. Since arriving at this place, I hadn't been to the toilet and was too scared to ask where I should go.

"Hey, look. The bread is out," Josephine announced, leaping out of her seat.

Tess and Nellie got up and followed her. Within seconds, the majority of the girls were out of their chairs and rushing between the tables, eager to be the first to get some bread. They slowed down when they saw Mother Concillio standing guard at the front with her whip in her hand.

"Stay in your line. You're acting like a bunch of hooligans. You're only allowed to take one slice of bread," she bellowed.

The girls heeded her command and waited in line for their turn. When Mother Concillio wasn't looking, one girl grabbed more than her share of bread. As she was about to walk back to her table with it, Mother Concillio turned around. "I saw what you did. Put that bread back, you greedy brat."

After the girl dropped the bread back in the large wooden tray, Mother Concillio picked up her whip and lashed her across the back of her legs with it. The girl screeched and lowered herself to the ground to ease the pain. Mother Concillio, standing over her, ordered her to get up and go back to her table. She stood up and limped back to her table. She was crying and kept her head down, in shame and in pain. Her table was close to where I sat. Feeling sore and embarrassed, she tearfully buried her head in her arms.

The girls at my table returned, each carrying a slice of bread. When they sat down, they took turns passing a plate of butter around the table. Each of them slathered their bread with it, before devouring every crumb.

Nellie finished her supper first. Gathering her cutlery together, she stood up and dipped them in a ceramic bowl of warm water that sat in the middle of the table. After rinsing them, she used her serviette to dry them. I watched her neatly fold her serviette and place it back in its ring. Josephine helped Tess clean her cutlery and told me I had to do the same. I took my unused serviette out of its holder and attempted to reach for the water bowl from my seated position, but it was impossible. Mindful of the girls behind me, I carefully stood up hoping they wouldn't notice the back of my damp frock. But I didn't hear them say anything. After I rinsed my utensils, Josephine showed me how to fold my serviette. Using her own serviette, she gave me a demonstration. "First, you must make a half triangle, and then roll the narrow ends into the center before putting it back in the ring holder," she said.

Mother Concillio walked around the tables supervising the routine. Feeling satisfied, she went back up to the front. Then picking up a large hand bell with both hands, she rang it until everyone stood up behind their chairs. I was conscious of my frock, and quickly glanced around me. The girls were not looking at me but straight ahead at the nun. Then the room went strangely quiet when Mother Concilliio joined her hands together, and the girls followed her in prayer again.

*We Give Thee Thanks*
*O Almighty God*
*For All Thy Bounty*
*Who Lives and Reigns*
*World Without End*
*Amen.*

With the prayer over, the girls instinctively formed lines between the rows of tables. I got in line with the girls at my table and slowly followed them as they made their way to the front. Moving along with my group, some girls checked me up and down. I was glad none of them had noticed my damp dress or detected an odor from me.

Mother Concillio was standing at the front door of the refectory, holding her whip in her hand. I filed past her, quietly and orderly, until I was outside the refectory door with the other girls. I looked down the long cloister outside the refectory, hoping to see the nice nun, Mother Teresa, but there was no sign of her.

The line continued into a hallway until we came to a door leading to a playground. Once we were outside, the line dispersed. I stood alone on the playground, unsure of what to do. Feeling lost and lonesome, I put my hands to my face and began to sob.

One girl came over to me when she saw me. "Why are you crying?" she asked.

I was too choked up to tell her why. She stood by me and patiently waited while I pulled myself together. I told her I felt sad and missed my sister Peg.

"Have you a mammy and daddy?" she asked.

When I told her my mother was dead, she told me her mother had also died and her father lived in England.

Her name was Marian. She was pretty with short blonde hair and hazel eyes. She made me feel more relaxed, so I told her I needed to use the toilet. She showed me where the toilets were at the far end of the playground. When I came back outside, she was waiting for me. I sat with her on a grassy area at the bottom of the playground close to three swing-sets.

We soon discovered we were the same age, slept in the same dormitory, and I would be in the same class as her at school.

A short time later, the sound of the handbell rung at the front of the playground. This was a signal to line up to go to our dormitories. Marian stayed close to me as I entered a strange world of uncertainty and fear.

Marian remained my best friend for a few years. Then, one day, she and her sister left for England to live with their father. It was a secret departure. On the Saturday morning before she left, she sat on my bed and told me not to tell anyone she was leaving the convent. She gave me a gift of an orange and told me she would always be my friend. After she left, I felt a huge void in my childhood.

## Chapter Nine

# THE NUNS

Situated on the outskirts of Waterford City, the Good Shepherd Convent was a massive, sprawling, grey stone building. It was divided into three separate sections and surrounded by a twelve-foot-high stone wall.

Each section was independent of the other. All three areas served different purposes and had separate kitchens, dining rooms, recreational areas, praying areas, and sleeping quarters. The nuns' convent was in the middle of the building, attached to a large church. This building housed about fifty nuns of all ages. The majority of the nuns who worked and lived in the convent were rarely seen.

St. Mary's building was situated on the left side, hidden behind the convent. That building was on three levels and was better known as the Magdalene Laundries. At least forty or more young girls and women lived and toiled there. Most were forced to labor long hours as punishment for becoming pregnant out of wedlock, while others were there for disciplinary reasons. Some had been transferred from other institutions around Ireland.

Getting 'in trouble,' pregnant out of wedlock, in Ireland before the 1950s and decades later, brought a shameful stigma not only to the fallen girl, but also to her family. This unnecessarily fiendish dogma caused great humiliation to entire families. It ran so deep that often parents were not only forced to shun their daughters but banish them from ever returning home.

Facing the Cork Road and College Streets was St. Dominick's School. This was on the far right side of the building where I lived. It also had three levels and was identical in look and size to St. Mary's. Fifty girls, aged two to sixteen plus years, were housed here. Most had lost one or both parents and were sent to live there when they were made wards of the court.

In the mid-1800s, The Good Shepherd order came to Waterford from France. They erected the first section of the Good Shepherd Convent building in 1858. This part had a church and convent where the nuns lived and prayed. Years later, St. Mary's building was added. This was used to house unwed mothers and other women, and where the Magdalene Laundries were set up. The Magdalene Laundries were situated throughout Ireland and were profit-making operations for the church. The girls toiled to launder soiled linens and clothing for the business community, upper class families, as well as for the needs of all who lived inside the grey walls of The Good Shepherd Convent. The women were used as slave labor to atone for their sins. The construction of St. Dominick's building soon followed.

As a young girl, I looked at the Good Shepherd Nuns with both awe and fear. The strange clothing they wore was imposing and intimidating. At times, I thought they were immortal beings.

Some Good Shepherd Nuns kept their hands under their scapulars in church. I used to think they were angels with their wings hidden beneath their heavy clothing. Not once had I ever observed a nun eat, drink, or use a toilet.

The nuns were often referred to as 'Brides of Christ,' and came from a variety of backgrounds. Most had a vocational calling from God to enter the religious life early in their lives.

Others entered the convent as young novices to appease their parents. In Catholic Ireland, families with children who entered the religious life to become nuns or priests were held in high esteem. As young men and women, they dedicated their lives to God and the Church, by taking vows of poverty and chastity. The religious orders the nuns entered were all different. Some joined specific orders where teaching and medical assistance were required. This enabled the nuns to provide essential services for the communities they lived in.

As I grew older, I realized that all nuns wore habits, regardless of their religious order. Not all of them followed the same principles of supervising young children in their care.

The Good Shepherd Nuns I encountered in Waterford were a mixture of praise and poison. Divided into three separate groups, they were assigned to specific roles and duties. One group supervised the fallen girls at St. Mary's, while another took care of the children at St. Dominick's School. Many other Good Shepherd Nuns didn't play any part in either of these areas. They lived and worked in the confines of the convent and were only ever seen in church.

Standing together in small groups, the Good Shepherd Nuns looked like a colony of penguins. Their heads were adorned with long, black flowing veils. They wore cream-colored habits that consisted of a long tunic, scapular and coif. The coif covered the entire head, neck, and part of the face and forehead. It also held together a square headdress that rested on the forehead. The wimple was white and lay over the chest like a large, curved bib. From the swish of the habit around the ankles, I saw their dark brown or black laced shoes worn over long white stockings. Not a strand of hair was ever seen, except for the hair on the brow. The only exposed part of the body was the hands and half the face.

Another small group of older nuns at the Good Shepherd's were known as the Magdaline Nuns. Unlike the standard habits of the Good Shepherd Nuns, they wore an identical style of habit, but the color was dark brown.

They never appeared to mix with the nuns in beige-colored habits and were hidden in an isolated section of the church to attend mass. They never spoke, but prayed and sewed all day. Although they were called the Magdaline Nuns, they were not the nuns in charge of the girls at St. Mary's. It was the nuns in the cream-colored habits that supervised those girls.

Some of the nuns were young with pretty features. Others were old and infirm. It wasn't just their odd attire that made me uneasy, but the stern and often unwarranted strict discipline they imposed. I discovered early in my youth that the Good Shepherd Nuns in all outward appearance looked the same, but their personalities were vastly different.

They had an established hierarchy. The nuns at the top of the pecking order were the operators, administrators, and educators. Others worked in the kitchens, laundries, bakeries, or sewing rooms. A few were too old to work and retired. The nuns on the lower level were known as 'skivvies.' Depending on their level of education, expertise, or talent, they were assigned to a particular set of duties. The head abbess was addressed as the Reverend Mother Superior or simply, The Reverend Mother. I rarely saw her, but when I did, I had to bow my head in reverence as I passed her in the hallways.

Most of the Good Shepherd Nuns I interacted with were civil and pleasant. However, others were unreasonably harsh and cruel. It was their hands I feared the most. Being on your best behavior simply wasn't good enough, forcing me to keep my guard up at all times. These sinister nuns vented their internal angst by using verbal intimidation or by corporal punishment. It was a method they practiced to suppress an individual at any given opportunity. Some took immeasurable pleasure in dishing out their choice of physical punishment.

The most unforgiving nuns at St. Dominick's were Mothers Regina, Philomena, Maria, Scholastica, and Concillio. They were the ones that lashed out the most. We knew these nuns by the choice of weapons they used. They chose their hands, nails, fists, rulers, scissors, rosary beads, whips, or sticks to punish unwary individuals.

Mothers Colette, Dolorous, Gabriella, Ignatius, and Gertude were kind and unintimidating. They had a gentle way of using kind words to speak to me. Their line of work didn't require them to have direct dealings with us unless we were sent to help them out with chores. They worked in the church, kitchen, and bakery. Mother Gabriella often supervised us on the playground and never lifted her hand or said an unkind word to us.

As young, vulnerable children, we were cognizant of the kind nuns, and the ones who were not. The nice nuns had a clearer understanding of young children's temperaments, and were considerate of the predicaments we found ourselves in.

Shortly before I left St. Dominick's, Mother's Enda and Gemma arrived. Both nuns were younger and had a more practical approach in dealing with us.

Mother Teresa was the head nun in charge of the St. Dominick's girls when I first arrived in 1960. She was always kind to me, but I never quite understood why she was often unreasonably cruel to the older girls.

A terrifying story circulated about Mother Teresa when she locked an older teenage girl in the storeroom. The storeroom was on the third floor, down the hallway from the teenage girl's dormitory. The room was without windows, and the punished girl was left there for two days. The only person she saw was another teenage girl who helped Mother Colette in the kitchen. She delivered her food to eat. The girl told her she wasn't sure why Mother Teresa put her there, but said the nun walloped her about the head with her hands tied behind her back.

Many of the girls were aware that I was Mother Teresa's pet, and her unusual favoritism toward me didn't go unnoticed.

One Sunday morning when I was eleven years old, I witnessed the cruel and callous side of Mother Teresa. Her assault on a lovely girl named Ann was exceptionally hideous. Ann was about sixteen years old. She had short, black, wavy hair, blue eyes, and her young teenage figure was very voluptuous. Mother Teresa figured her punishment was serious enough to shame her in front of her peers.

We were gathered in the Section Room waiting to line up for benediction. Suddenly, Mother Teresa barged into the lower section. She had a dark and angry look on her face, and ordered all but the youngest of the children to go to the Recreation Room. When we got there, Ann was seated on a wooden chair at the front of the room with her head lowered. She was wearing a large beige cardigan and a shiny navy skirt decorated with red roses. Once we were all assembled, Mother Teresa told Ann to put her hands behind the back of the chair. Then she stepped behind her and knotted the sleeves of her cardigan to prevent her from escaping. Standing in front of Ann, Mother Teresa repeatedly slapped her across the face with all her might until she finally stopped. With each swat, Ann's head bobbed from side to side.

Tears and mucous streamed down Ann's face and onto her skirt, and she had no way of cleaning it up. Being one of the younger girls in the room, I was standing at the front. I was so horrified by what I was witnessing, I had to cup my ears and my eyes, so I didn't have to hear or feel Ann's pain. Ann's sister was also one of the onlookers. I briefly opened my eyes to search for her. She was standing only a few feet away from me wearing a look of horror on her face.

When she was done punishing her, Mother Teresa turned to look at the audience of girls. Her face was beet red and wet with sweat. "Now let this be a lesson to all of you. This is what happens when you do what she has gone and done," she said.

I wondered what awful thing Ann had done to be so demoralized and beaten in such a way, and I never did find out. Up until that time, Mother Teresa was my anchor. Within days, Ann disappeared from St. Dominick's. Following that incident, a part of me never fully trusted Mother Teresa again.

On New Year's Day in 1964, she showed her stripes a second time.

New Year's Day was always a happy day at St. Dominick's. However, that day, something must have been truly disturbing Mother Teresa.

After lunch, I waited in line with the girls outside the locked Section Room. It was customary to go there on New Year's Day and find a small gift on a table with your name on it. Waiting patiently for the door to open, we were excited and noisy, guessing the gifts that awaited us inside.

Mother Teresa appeared out of nowhere and flew into a rage when she heard how boisterous we were. She hollered for us to be quiet. Then in anger, she made us line up, and show the back of our hands. Frightened by her outburst, we immediately got in line and obeyed. She had a ruler in her hand, and rapidly moved down the line whacking the backs of both hands of every girl she approached. As she drew closer to me, I scrunched my face and squeezed my eyes in preparation for her ruler to come down on the backs of my hands. When it was my turn, she pushed both my hands aside, and moved on to the next girl. Then she continued whapping the remaining line up of girls. In my confused mind, I thought she spared me because of the dreaded look I had on my face. But I knew all the girls were equally as terrified of her hitting them as I was. It puzzled me why she would hit them, but not me?

After that onslaught, I felt ashamed and awkward knowing most of the girls had seen her brush my hands aside. There was no doubt in my young mind; Mother Teresa was clearly being unfair, and it did not go down well for me with some of the older girls.

That same day, two girls passing me on the cloister shoved me up against the wall and called me Mother Teresa's pet.

"How come she likes you more than us. Is it because you are a country mug from County Tipperary, like she is?" the younger one of the two asked.

The jibing and name calling from the girls continued for several more days. It was wrong of Mother Teresa to open me up to such criticism from my peers and expose my fragile ego. I was fortunate in knowing that many of the girls believed her actions were not my fault. As the time passed, they forgot about the incident and their attention shifted elsewhere.

I had lived at St. Dominick's four years when Mother Teresa gathered us up one Monday evening and told us to proceed to the Recreation Room. She wasn't angry but looked somber as we assembled and stood facing her. "I brought you here this evening because I have an announcement to make. I am being transferred to another Good Shepherd Convent in Cork, in two weeks. You will have a new supervisor who will be taking over my duties. Her name is Mother Philomena."

Listening to what she said was devastating news not only for me, but also for many of the other girls. Despite her shortcomings, Mother Teresa's departure from St. Dominick's was not the news we wanted to hear. A few girls approached me after her announcement and asked me how I felt about her departure. I brushed it off because I wasn't going to reveal to them how crushing this news was for me. That night, when I crawled under the bedcovers, I cried myself to sleep. I knew I was about to lose another crucial anchor in my life, and my guess was correct.

Mother Philomena's personality was very different than Mother Teresa's. Shortly after arriving, word spread that she suffered from rheumatoid arthritis. Because of her condition, she was often cranky, impatient, and cruel.

Mother Philomena was taller than Mother Teresa. She had a small chubby and round face, with a ruddy complexion. Her front teeth were tiny, gapped, and yellow. Initially, she was pleasant, but once she settled in, her true colors surfaced. She frequently dished out unfair punishments without rhyme or reason. Many of us secretly complained about her and blamed her rheumatoid arthritis for her irrational behavior.

One Saturday afternoon, I was helping Mother Ignatius in the kitchen. She had recently taken over Mother Collette's job, and I was sent there to help her clean up after lunch. Nellie had also been sent to help. She was working in the scullery, with a big pot of peeled potatoes, and was removing their eyes. She was almost finished with her task when she spotted a hedgehog. It was hiding under an old porcelain sink opposite from where she sat. Knowing I was in the kitchen, she snuck inside to signal for me to follow her outside to show me what she discovered.

As soon as I had the opportunity, I slipped outside and found Nellie crouched down looking under the porcelain sink. I got down on my knees beside her and looked for the hedgehog. It was rolled in a ball and tucked in the corner of the sink. Both of us were desperate to retrieve the hedgehog and hold it. We attempted to lure it out by making silly vocal sounds and tickling it with a small stick. Although we weren't having any luck, we remained on the ground absorbed by the discovery. What we failed to notice was Mother Philomena making her way through a side door of the cloister. Both of us jumped when we saw her standing over us. Nellie excitedly showed her the hedgehog's hideout, believing she would be as equally happy to see the hedgehog as we were.

But we could not have been more wrong. Instead, she had a scowl on her face, and questioned why we weren't doing our kitchen chores. Next, she lifted the silver scissors that hung from her leather belt and hit both of us on the top of our heads with the ring ends, back and forth. I put my hands to my head to protect myself, and the hard metal rings came down on my hands. She had absolutely no interest whatsoever in the hedgehog. When she was done scolding us, she sent us back to the kitchen to continue with our work.

Later, Nellie and I talked about how deflated we were by Mother Philomena's heartless cruelty and why she didn't like the hedgehog. The following day, the two of us compared the lumpy bruises Mother Philomena had inflicted on our heads.

After each school day, the secondary school girls were required to go to the study room to complete their homework. The study room was at the far end of the cloister and Mother Philomena supervised us from a desk at the front of the room. I usually sat at a table just inside the study room door with three other girls. From where I sat, I had a good vantage point of Mother Philomena. Occasionally, she had a small stack of letters for the lucky girls who received them. At the end of our studies, she generally handed them out, and I eagerly waited to see if one of them was for me.

Often when I completed my homework, I sat and secretly watched Mother Philomena handling the envelopes of the letters. She had a habit of picking up one and used the corner edge to remove trapped remnants of food from her gapped teeth. Then she would blow the food particle out of her mouth, and wipe away any remaining residue on the envelope on her apron. Seeing her doing this always repulsed me.

When I did receive a letter, Mother Philomena waited for me to open it, and tell her who it was from, before allowing me to read the content of the letter. While opening the letter, I surreptitiously inspected the edges, hoping it wasn't my envelope she used to floss her teeth.

I usually received letters from my family at Christmas and close to the end of the school year. Nanny always wrote to let me know when she was coming to pick me up over the summer break. My grandmother had terrible handwriting and spelling and it was never easy to read. Sometimes Mother Philomena took the letter from me when I struggled to read it. After reading it, I wondered how she was able to read it so quickly. Despite it being close to the end of another school year, I sometimes had to wait until July or early August before I was released to spend time with my grandmother.

On weekdays in the summer months, Mother Philomena used a rotary system to assign the secondary school girls to work in the convent kitchen after the nuns ate their lunch. At fourteen years, I fell into that category. At first, when she chose me to go, I went over to the convent with another girl. Our job was to wash and dry the dishes by hand, then sweep and scrub the kitchen, pantry, and scullery floors.

I never saw any of the nuns eating lunch, and only ever met one of them. She was in charge of supervising our work, and wheeled trolley loads of dirty dishes and cutlery from the nuns dining room for us to wash.

At first, I didn't mind going to the convent and took the job in stride. Two Mondays later, the rotation of girls ceased, and I was sent to the convent alone. After she sent me five days in a row doing all the work by myself, I sulked and complained to my peers about it. I didn't dream of asking Mother Philomena why she decided to send me to do the work on my own. I remembered how the nun who supervised me complimented me on my good work and asked me for my full name two weeks earlier. Feeling proud that she was singing my praises, I guessed she told Mother Philomena.

The following Monday when Mother Philomena told me to go to the convent again, I surprised myself by telling her how unfair I thought it was that I had to go there. This was the first time I rebelled against authority, and I believe Mother Philomena was equally taken aback by my audacity.

Then she grabbed my ear and marched me down the hall to her office and closed the door behind her. Standing in her office, I waited to see what form of punishment she was going to dish out. I was aware I wasn't going to get away with speaking my mind to her. Limping to her long grey cupboard, she pulled out a thick wooden stick. "Is this what you want me to use on you? Are you going to go over to the convent and clean up or not?" she said.

Staring at the wooden stick she intended to use on me, I nervously agreed to go, and left her office. I guessed the nun who oversaw my work, and smiled so sweetly each time I saw her, must have told Mother Philomena to only send me over to the convent. I no longer liked her or trusted her and thought she was sly.

When my work was completed that day, I walked my usual route back along the polished cloisters. Reaching the door that took me to the cloister of St. Dominick's, I stopped. Opposite was a small door which led outside to the expansive grounds of the Good Shepherd Convent. I looked behind me to make sure I wasn't being watched. Then I nervously fumbled with the doorknob with the intent of running away, but it was locked. Feeling hopelessly defeated, I took a deep breath and let the tears fall from my eyes. I waited there until I was able to pull myself together again. Then I turned to face the brass door handles of the St. Dominick's church and said a prayer to the Blessed Virgin. I was so upset and was still reeling from the fact that I stood up to Mother Philomena. Once I calmed down, I continued my journey along the shiny cloister to St. Dominick's. As soon as I opened the door, Mother Philomena was on the other side waiting for me. "I wondered when you were going to show yourself. I hope you did a good job in the kitchen today. Now, you can take yourself up to the dormitory and remain there for the rest of the evening," she said.

I couldn't believe she was still cross with me after I had carried out her orders. Feeling angrier than ever with her, I stomped off toward the dormitory stairs in a temperamental huff. She limped along following me, warning me that I better watch it, or I will get what's coming to me. When I walked up the stairs to the Big Girl's Dormitory, she stood at the bottom watching me. Once inside, I sat on the side of my bed and aired my frustrations by screaming as loud as I could in the confines of the dormitory walls. I remained there without any supper for the rest of the evening.

After lunch the following day, I waited fearfully to see if she was going to send me to the nuns' kitchen again. My greatest dread was how I might react if she was going to force me to go. When the time to go there arrived, Mother Philomena gathered the girls outside the refectory. Eyeing me closely, she chose two different girls to go the convent instead of me. I felt a great sense of relief that she hadn't asked me. I knew if she had, and I disobeyed her, that she had the power to change my life in an instant.

Fate saved me that day. Had the church side door been unlocked, and I had run away, I am not sure how my life would have unfolded.

Although I personally didn't know of any girl who ran away, it was a well-known fact that girls who had escaped, were returned by the Gardaí. For some, they were shipped off to reformatory schools. This was far worse than my situation. These places were nothing more than disguised slave labor factories.

Mother Maria was menacing and in a league of her own. She not only struck us, but also played accusatory mind games wearing deceiving smiles.

If you didn't know Mother Maria, she looked like a nun that could easily be trusted. She was young and very pretty with dark brown eyes and straight white teeth.

My first introduction to her was when I was fifteen. I had just returned from spending time with my grandmother when she approached me. I wasn't aware a new nun had joined St. Dominick's, so when I saw her, I waited for her to introduce herself to me. Instead, she stood and looked at me waiting for me to introduce myself to her. "It's obvious you don't know who I am, but I know who you are. In future, show respect to your superiors," she said.

I blushed with embarrassment not knowing what to say, because I had no clue what her name was. Staring at me a few seconds, she turned on her heel and walked off. I was stunned by her unlikely manner.

She especially showed her deviousness when five young boys aged four to seven were admitted for the first time to St. Dominick's over the summer.

That year on my return, Mother Philomena told me I had to clear out my bedside locker in the teenage dormitory because she was putting me in charge of taking care of the boys.

The boy's bedroom quarters were at the far end of the corridor, opposite the Big Girl's Dormitory. This room was divided into six separate cubicles. I was assigned a slightly bigger cubicle than the boys, located next to a sash window. At fifteen years old, I observed how innocent and obedient the boys were living under such rigid rules. The only fear I had in taking care of the boys was that Mother Maria also supervised the boys.

Each morning, she woke us up at seven. I helped get the boys out of bed and had them kneel for morning prayer. In their sleepy state, they recited The Lord's prayer and a Hail Mary with me. Quite often, the oldest boy wet his bed, and when Mother Maria discovered this, she slapped him on his naked behind. He was petrified of her, and his big blue eyes filled with tears when she beat him. It was upsetting to see how terribly sad and embarrassed she made him feel, and I couldn't do anything to protect him.

She generally left the dorm room while I got myself and the boys washed and dressed. The boys' hair was cut short, making it difficult to flatten their cowlicks. The only way I could keep their hair from sticking up was to dampen it with cold water.

After making their beds, I lined them up outside the bedroom door and then locked it. Keeping to my routine, I held the room key securely in my hand while walking the boys down the corridor where Mother Maria waited for me to hand them over to her. At this point, I also gave her the room key. Joining the girls from the Big Girl's dormitory, I headed down the stairs with them to daily mass.

On several occasions, Mother Maria informed me that I failed to give her back the boy's room key. She mostly asked me later in the day.

"Where is the boy's room key? You never gave it back to me. What did you do with it?"

"But Mother, I gave it back to you this morning before mass."

"Well, I don't remember you giving it back to me; otherwise, I'd have it."

Feeling helpless with her accusations, I had to tactfully remind her I had given it to her that same morning. After accusing me several times, I realized she was cleverly trying to taunt me.

One day in the presence of a group of girls, she accused me again and made them laugh, telling them I wasn't fit to be taking care of the boys. That same evening, when it was the boys' bedtime, she took the key out of her habit pocket and opened the bedroom door. She didn't flinch or have any remorse for what she had so wrongly accused me of earlier in the day. She had a devious way of stripping my delicate ego and making me feel unworthy of myself. But I soon understood that I wasn't the only one she liked to torment. Other girls complained about her too. Like me, they didn't dare challenge the allegations she made against them.

For a brief time, at St. Dominick's School, Mother Concilio supervised the refectory. Looking back, I believe she had an inferiority complex because of her short stature. Her favorite weapon was her whip. She used it constantly, without mercy. Not only would she use her whip, but she also accompanied it with demeaning words to make a girl feel worse about herself.

"Now, who do you think you are, rising above your station? You're not at home now."

She relished seeing girls cower in fear and shield themselves as she struck them. Her whip gave her the power to subdue any girl she considered to be out of line. She was heartless, and without an ounce of compassion for any of us. Then, one day, 'poof' just like that, she disappeared from St. Dominick's. I am convinced wherever she went, she packed her whip in her suitcase to use against any unfortunate soul that crossed her. She was especially intimidated by any girl taller than she.

Mother Scholastica was in her late seventies and one of the oldest nuns in charge of us. She was tall and skinny with a wrinkled snow-white face and hands. The white apron she wore was bleached and starched without a hint of a wrinkle anywhere. She was well-groomed with manicured nail tips, and her brown, laced shoes were forever buffed to a high sheen.

Her bright blue eyes stood out behind a pair of gold-rimmed spectacles she rested on the bridge of her long, pointed nose. Because of her age, she was allocated to doing light duties. One of her jobs was to supervise the return of girls arriving from the three different schools we attended outside the Good Shepherd Convent.

After passing the large wooden doors of the Good Shepherd Convent, we turned right and climbed up some concrete steps beside the convent lodge. The steps were connected to a narrow path which led up to a small door on the right that opened onto St. Dominick's playground. It was on this path that Mother Scholastica waited for us. Quite often the school groups scattered and arrived in dribs and drabs. This was especially true for girls attending secondary school, where classes were often delayed because of after-school studies.

When Mother Scholastica met us on the pathway, she questioned why we weren't together on our return. After explaining the reason for our tardiness, she didn't believe any of us. Instead, she would lean forward from her tall lanky frame and dig her long hard nails into our upper arms. She made sure to squeeze hard enough to make it hurt and leave a bruise. On one occasion when I arrived late with another girl, she had been praying the rosary on the beads that hung from her leather belt. Holding the large cross in her hand, she poked it into each of our chests.

On rainy days, we were required to wear black, rubber Wellington boots while walking to school. Being young teenage girls, it embarrassed us to wear such ungainly boots. Before departing for school in the mornings, some of us sneakily put our regular shoes in our satchels and set out from St. Dominick's in our 'Wellies.' At the end of the footpath, we removed our boots and hid them in a thicket of bushes before changing into our shoes.

The only problem was, we had to switch back into our Wellingtons again when we returned to St. Dominick's.

Sometimes, we were lucky that Mother Scholastica wasn't waiting on that area of the path and catch us making the switch.

One evening when I returned around five, I wasn't so lucky. I was with another secondary school girl when she caught us pulling our boots out of the bushes. She grabbed each of us by an arm and, digging in her nails as hard as she could, she marched us into Mother Philomena's office. When Mother Philomena heard what we had done, she warned us that if we weren't going to wear our Wellington boots going to school, that she would send us off bare-footed if we tried it again. Strange as it was, she didn't react as I thought she might. My only guess was she knew Mother Scholastica had already taken care of that.

Mother Regina was the deputy nun in charge. She supervised the Sacred Heart dormitory and worked in the sewing room when she wasn't teaching plays, recitations, or choir. I marveled at her musical talent and how she played the piano. She taught us lyrics to classical music such as Johann

Strauss's, "The Emperor" and "The Blue Danube" waltzes, that I have remembered ever since.

Despite her beautiful, long, piano fingers, she sometimes used her fists like boxing gloves and liked to hit the head or face of a girl if she found reason to.

It was summertime, and I was nine years old. I was excited when Mother Regina told me I had to get ready because my father was picking me up to spend a few weeks with my grandmother. She took me to the sewing room and asked me to strip naked to try on some clothes. She handed me a white vest and told me to put it on. Then she had me stand back to inspect it. After trying on the first and second vest, I began to feel uncomfortable when she had me try on several more. All the vests I tried on were above my hip-line, making me feel self-conscious. After finally choosing a vest for me, she then gave me a pair of pink knickers to try on. "Now stand back and let me have a look. How do they make you feel down there? Are they tight?" she asked.

I was confused by her question and when I didn't answer her, she called me over to her. Standing in front of her, she touched below my waistline. "I mean there," she said.

I wondered if she was going to ask me to try on several more pairs of knickers like she had with the vests, but she didn't. Without having to test for the size of more underwear, she gave me a fresh frock and cardigan to wear.

The strange incident I had with Mother Regina regularly played on my mind for the next few weeks staying with my grandmother. I never told anyone. Another girl did relate a similar story to me before I left St. Dominick's. She, like me, found Mother Regina's actions very odd.

In springtime each year, students from schools around Waterford County highlighted their talents by performing at The Theatre Royal Concert Hall in Waterford City. This competition lasted a week, with each school choosing a specific theme. The students performed in plays, dance recitals, poetry, or choir. The Good Shepherd Convent also entered the competition and were represented by the girls of St. Dominick's. Mother Regina was in charge of putting on the show. Each year she picked a different theme and prepared most of us girls to take part in the performance.

I was twelve years old when she cast me in the lead role of Snow White, in the musical, *Snow White and The Seven Dwarfs*. She said the reason she chose me was because I had a good singing voice. I was ecstatic that she had selected me for the role because I loved to sing. In preparation for the show, I had to practice my acting role, and memorize the song lyrics and lines. Halfway through the performance, I had to change into a different dress. In the first half of the show, I wore a red dress with a black collar and red sash, and in the second half, a white, lacy dress. On my head I wore a black velvet hair band with a fabric black bow on top. Since I was so skinny and flat-chested, both dresses had to be altered significantly by a Magdalene Nun. I had to go to the convent several times so the nun could make adjustments for my bustline and waistline.

Following numerous rehearsals, we were ready to present the show at the Theatre Royal. Girls who were not participating were allowed to sit in the audience and watch. Being naturally shy, I was both excited and nervous about going on stage the first night. The shows started at seven and were scheduled to finish at nine p.m. Before it began, Mother Regina gave the cast a spoonful of glucose to provide us with energy. I relished the sweet powdery treat and couldn't wait for her to pop it on my tongue.

The show was a success the first evening and the judges asked us back to compete with another school two evenings later. Alas, on the evening we were to return, I came down with laryngitis that progressively worsened throughout the day. On stage, I had to force out the lyrics of every song, some of which were inaudible. Mother Regina, who was in the wings listening, was horrified when she heard me. Because I wasn't feeling well, it didn't help that I forgot to smile as I had in the first performance. Mother Regina, waving for my attention, kept giving me smiley signals. Close to the end of the show, the girl playing the part of the witch was supposed to enter the stage from the right wing to present me with a poisoned apple to eat. My part was to bite into the apple and then fall on my right side. Both of us had rehearsed the part for weeks before.

That evening, the witch entered the stage from the left wing and stood behind me. I had my back to her waiting for her to enter from the right side. When I realized she was behind me, I took the apple, and after biting into it, I fell down awkwardly on the stage floor on my left shoulder and hurt it.

When the show was over, Mother Regina came back to the changing room, and in front of the other girls, she told me how badly I let the school down. She wasn't one bit interested in the fact I felt so unwell. Besides being sick, and sore from my ungainly fall, I felt terrible about the substandard performance I had given.

After my failed performance, Mother Regina's manner changed toward me.

Two weeks later, she escorted me with a group of girls on a bus trip to Dublin City. When we arrived, we had lunch, followed by a viewing of the animals at Dublin Zoo. It was my first time ever seeing live monkeys. Their humanlike fingers and toes fascinated me, and I loved watching their playful antics. After the zoo, we went to a theatre in Dublin to see a stage performance. When the curtain went up, two men dressed in colorful clown outfits appeared. They had a chair between them and one of the clowns turned it upside down. Both sat on the chair and when one of them stood up, the other man fell on the floor. All of us watching the act, including Mother Regina, thought the show was hilarious and laughed until our bellies ached.

The following evening back at St. Dominick's, I was in the Section Room after supper. One of the girls who was with me on the Dublin trip suggested we try the same chair routine with each other. Once we were seated on the upturned chair, she stood up first, and I fell on the floor. We kept playing the game, enjoying how much fun it was.

When it was her turn to sit on the chair, again, I stood up, and she fell down clumsily splaying her legs and bringing her frock up over her underwear. At the same moment, Mother Regina witnessed what happened and became livid with me. She swooped over me and taking my ear, she dragged me out of the room and shoved me into the corner wall outside the refectory. Knowing how much trouble I was in, I covered my face and head with my arms, while she beat me with her fists. I was shocked and deflated by her actions knowing only the day before she watched the clown act as I had and thought it was funny. I couldn't understand why she felt it was okay to laugh at the clown act in Dublin, yet it was wrong for me to play the same trick back at St. Dominick's. In the back of my mind, I knew she held a grudge against me and was retaliating because of the bad stage performance I gave at the Theatre Royal.

In the house of God, these same irrational nuns were meek and pious. Rapt in a solemn trance of reverence, they looked so angelic with closed eyes and their hands clasped together under scapulars. For what were they praying? Were they asking God to forgive them for the cruel treatment they dished out on young vulnerable children?

If it had not been for the nice nuns at St. Dominick's, I would have believed that all nuns were diabolical and had to be feared. Yet, even the cruel nuns sometimes had something to offer.

Despite the fact I left the Good Shepherd Convent terrified of what lay in store for me facing the world as an adult, I took with me the positive things the nuns taught me. Those were good moral values, etiquette, strong organizational skills, and my faith. Looking back, Mother Regina had the most undeniable talent of all the nuns I encountered. Not only could she sew and knit, but her greatest talents lay in the arts. She was an expert with stage drama, recitations, singing and dancing. Had I been raised at home, I would not have had the same exposure to music and drama that Mother Regina introduced me to. If my mother had lived, she no doubt would have encouraged me to enjoy the arts without fear being attached.

*Good Shepherd Nuns and the habits they wore.*

*1962—St. Dominick's children with Mother Teresa—I am first row far right. Marian (friend) is standing, 3rd row from bottom left, second person in.*

# Chapter Ten

# THE SHEPS

If only the halls could talk, they would have many tales to tell.

In the ten years I lived with the nuns at St. Dominick's, three important elements were missing. First and foremost was the lack of good nutrition. Most of us were chronically undernourished and often hungry. The result was that we probably never realized our own growth potential. The food rations were meager, and if you didn't like what you were given, or felt unwell, there was no other choice, you just went to bed hungry. Secondly, in the winter months, we were always cold. The shoes and clothing we wore were not suited for freezing cold temperatures traveling to and from school. The buildings and dormitories were frequently cold to save on fuel.

Another reason for the cold dormitory was to deter fleas from multiplying in warm spaces. Each bed was furnished with one red blanket and two bed sheets to cover up, irrelevant of the season.

Last of all, was the lack of physical nurturing in the absence of a parent. When we were hurt emotionally or physically, we either cried alone or took solace from each other. Fear replaced love and security through the constant threat of spontaneous beatings. Sometimes, it was hard to know when you were doing the right thing. Our precious childhood years of real joy, creativity, and discovery were slapped down.

I was amongst at least fifty girls, ranging in age from two to seventeen years, and all of us hailed from different backgrounds. Some girls had both parents, others had lost one or both. A few had siblings living with them. Outside the walls, we were known as "The Orphans," or "Good Shepherd Girls," but we labeled ourselves, "The Sheps."

St. Dominick's building was on three floor levels and featured numerous windows. Six nuns were in charge of caring for us. Each was assigned a particular role, in the capacity of their expertise.

On arrival at St. Dominick's, I had to adapt to a new protocol of how to correctly address nuns and priests. I had to be specific and could never be informal or familiar with a nun or a priest. At home, I understood that mothers and fathers were called parents, and sisters and brothers were siblings. But now, these titles took on a whole new meaning. I was required to address a Good Shepherd Nun as 'Mother,' an Ursuline Nun, where I attended day school, 'Sister,' a priest 'Father,' and an unordained priest, 'Brother.'

Four years later, The Good Shepherd Nuns changed their titles from 'Mother' to 'Sister.' This sudden change came as quite an adjustment for many of us. On a few occasions, I forgot to use the new title 'Sister', and each time was reprimanded for being impolite.

At six and a half years, I quickly gained a reputation for being Mother Teresa's pet and I can only guess it was because she knew I spent time in hospital suffering from malnutrition. Also, I hailed from the border of Co. Waterford close to where she came from in the south region of County Tipperary. One older girl was bold enough to say Mother Teresa liked me because she fancied my father. She said she noticed how Mother Teresa blushed on the rare occasions that he came to visit me.

The first morning I had breakfast at St. Dominick's, I was served a boiled egg and toast. Mother Teresa had asked Mother Colette to prepare me an egg for breakfast daily because I was extremely thin. "You're all skin and bones. We will have to put some meat on your bones," Mother Teresa told me.

I felt strange being the only girl in the refectory served an egg, when the others had to eat porridge for breakfast. While nibbling on it, I shyly eyed the girls at my table. I soon realized that it wasn't just the girls at my table who were watching me, but also the girls seated at nearby tables.

One morning after breakfast, an older girl approached me while I was getting ready for school.

"Everyone is sayin' you're *Mo Teesa's* pet and you're always hanging out of her apron strings. How come you get to have a boiled egg for breakfast, and we do not?" she asked.

I didn't know how I should respond to her. In my mind, I also believed it was unfair. Besides, I never liked being the center of attention. After several weeks, the morning egg service finally ceased, and I was no longer the object of jealousy amongst my peers.

One November evening in 1962, I discovered my birthdate. As a young girl, my father often mentioned to me that I was born in November, but never told me the actual date. In my family, birthdays came and went without any recognition or celebration.

After supper that day, we went upstairs to the second floor where there was a much smaller recreation room. Mother Philomena took her seat at a table at the entrance of the room. In front of her, she had several letters to hand out. Curious to learn if one of them was for me, I stood around her table beside a girl named Elizabeth. Mother Philomena looked at Elizabeth. "Do you know today is your birthday. You are eight years old now. I have a letter here for you," she said, holding what looked like a birthday card for Elizabeth.

Elizabeth eyes lit up when she heard it was her birthday. After Mother Philomena wished her a happy birthday, she then looked at me. "And tomorrow is your birthday, November 14. You'll be turning nine years old," she said.

Like Elizabeth, I was over the moon when she told me. I had no idea what my birth date was until then. Thereafter, I made sure to remember my birthday when it came around each year. I even paid close attention to other girls when they found out their birthdates. Sometimes, I gave them a gift of a makeshift doll. It was basically a doll's head I made with a small handkerchief. I used some paper to stuff it, tied a string around the neck and drew dots for the eyes and a half-moon shape for the mouth.

For many of us, birthdays came and went with nobody to acknowledge the occasion. I only believed my true birthdate when I saw it handwritten on my birth certificate.

The year I turned ten, a girl in my dormitory section gave me a small doll. She had two dolls her aunt had given her, and she gave me the smaller one of the two. I called my doll, Lucy.

She was skin toned, about five inches tall, and made of rubber. Her hair was straight, short, and blonde. She had blue eyes that opened and closed with sweeping long lashes. Lucy was the first doll I ever owned, and I nurtured and treasured her with all my might. At night before I went to sleep, I set her on my bedside locker and whispered to her.

I had my doll for nearly a year, when I took it on a coach trip with me to Clonea Strand one day in late August. The weather was warm and sunny that day. Before I went in for a swim with some of the girls, I left Lucy safely wedged between two rocks full of limpets. When I got out of the water again, I looked for Lucy, but she was gone. At first, I thought some of the girls were hiding it from me, but they swore they hadn't taken it. I was so upset about losing my doll, that I cried on the bus all the way back to St. Dominick's.

That day, other families were on the beach. I believe someone found it, and thinking the doll had been abandoned, took it.

On Christmas morning in The Sacred Heart Dormitory, there was much excitement when we woke up and looked to see what Santa Claus had left for us. At some point during the night, one of the nuns hung a Christmas stocking on the knob at the foot of our beds. Some girls woke up before the wake-up call and scampered around their sections to see what they got. The stockings were manufactured, netted and flat, and didn't hold a lot. One year, I found a yo-yo, a whistle, and a chocolate penny wrapped in gold foil paper.

When I was thirteen, several of us were given a pair of adjustable solid metal roller skates that had to be strapped over our shoes. Mother Philomena told us they were donated to us from a charity in Dublin. Although it was very cold on the playground, we were allowed to try them out. Once I got the hang of how to use them, I didn't feel the cold, and enjoyed skating back and forth in them.

After Christmas morning mass, all of us went to the Recreation Room to be entertained by a group of men from Dublin. We called them "The Dublin Men." They came to St. Dominick's every Christmas morning and were full of warm smiles. They spent two hours showing us magic tricks and performing Christmas Carol sing-a-longs with us. The leader of the group was the most energetic, and the image of Danny Kaye. He was skinny with thick, wavy, sandy blond hair that he kept swept over the side of his head. From the television images we had seen of Danny Kaye, we were all convinced it was him, except for his thick Dublin accent and his constant use of the word, 'youse.'

When lunch was over, we assembled in The Study Room. Mother Philomena sat at her desk with a pile of brown paper parcels in front of her. I always felt confident one of the parcels would be for me and I watched and waited while she handed them out. Usually, I got a gift from Nanny and Aunt Pat and Uncle Sean at Christmas. Nanny's gift routinely arrived in a stuffed white envelope. Inside, I found a Christmas card and handkerchief. The hankie was white with an embroidered multi-colored letter 'N' in one of the corners, and surrounding it, were tiny colorful flowers.

Each year, Aunt Pat sent me a fairly large parcel with a different colored handmade, cable-knit cardigan inside. It was accompanied by a card and a long, newsy letter about England and the new additions in her family. I carried her letters around with me for days after Christmas, reading them word for word, over and over again.

One year, I was surprised to find the parcel she sent me was tiny. When I opened it, I was thrilled when I found a matching fountain pen and pencil set. It was maroon colored and had my full name engraved on both pens. It was a novelty for me having my name spelled out on the pens. I proudly showed them off to the girls at both St. Dominick's as well as the girls at The Ursuline School. Fearing I might lose them, I hid them in my satchel until it came time to use them.

On Christmas Day in 1967, I was disappointed when I didn't receive any parcel at all. Even Mother Philomena was taken aback. After she handed out the parcels to the girls

WARD OF THE COURT

who received them, she instructed the rest of us to go to her office. Sitting on her desk, she had a selection of prewrapped gifts, and handed one to each of us. When I unwrapped mine, I found a large, red spinning top. Even though I was grateful for the present she gave me, I was puzzled as to why I hadn't received my usual gifts from my grandmother or Aunt Pat. I felt certain Aunt Pat would never have forgotten me. I truly missed her gift and the newsy letter she sent with it each year. A few days after Christmas, Nanny's handkerchief gift arrived. Weeks later, I heard that all UK mail had been temporarily put on hold, because of a foot and mouth disease outbreak. For all of Mother Philomena's faults, she made sure none of us went without a gift on Christmas Day.

New Year's Day was celebrated in a similar way to Christmas Day. We dressed in our Sunday best, and after two masses and lunch, we piled into the Section Room. The Section Room was divided into three pastel-colored compartments and set up with tables and chairs. Depending on our age group, we were assigned a table with our names displayed at a place setting. It was fun going around the tables searching for our names. All morning, we talked about nothing else, and waited in anticipation of what gifts we might be receiving. Usually, the toys were small, like yo-yos or puzzle books. One year, I got a pocket-sized crossword book and pencil. I enjoyed trying to figure out the puzzles and believe it was that gift that gave me a lifelong passion for doing crossword puzzles and word games.

I was ten when I learned to ride a push bicycle. The bicycle was donated to the school by a Mr. O'Neill, who was an advocate for St. Vincent's De Paul. When it was brought out onto the playground, there was great excitement. The bike was mid-sized and navy colored, and you had to be ten-years and older to learn how to ride it. However, Mother Teresa attached a three-foot-long sturdy string to the back of the bike saddle and put an older girl in charge of holding the string as we rode around on the playground. She was instructed to pull on it if we went too fast or if we got in the way of other girls on the playground.

The first time I got on the bike, the girl overseeing my progress tugged on the string when she thought I was going to run into another girl. The bike wobbled and I toppled off, grazing my knees and elbows. I didn't get back on the bike again, fearing the same outcome. I wasn't the only girl who fell off because of this dangerous practice.

A pretty girl named Margaret was learning to ride the bike one day when she had the string pulled on her. She fell off the bike and broke her two front teeth and was badly grazed. Because her teeth were so badly broken, she had to have the remainder of her teeth pulled. Sadly, at age thirteen, she had to be fitted with false teeth that were nothing like her original permanent teeth.

Weekends were different than weekdays at St. Dominick's. On Saturday mornings, we were given an extra hour to sleep in, because we didn't have to attend mass that day. Once breakfast was over, we had to return to our dormitories to do our chores. We changed our bed linen every fortnight. When that came around, a big white sack was dropped off at the door of St. Dominick's by a girl from the Magdalene Laundry.

After checking the seams of the mattress for fleas, we remade our beds with freshly laundered linen. After that, we dusted and swept our sections, and took turns scrubbing the toilets and the row of hand sinks at the front of the dormitory. This took over an hour to complete. Next, we lined up again and went back down downstairs to the first floor to polish the cloister and hallway.

The cloister ran from the Refectory to The Study Room and had an attached hallway. Before polishing the floor, the older girls applied a thick layer of hard wax that quickly dried into a film of large beige swirls. Mother Regina was in charge of supervising our work. She handed out two square pieces of red polish cloths and two pieces of twine to about thirty girls ranging in age from nine to sixteen.

After placing the polishing cloths under our shoes, we gathered up the four corners, and tied them snuggly around our ankles. As soon as we were ready, we began the polishing routine. At first it was a struggle to move our feet over the hard stiff wax, but once we broke through, we glided back and forth like performing ice skaters. The polishing of the cloister and hallway continued until both floors were buffed to a glossy shine.

An hour after lunch on Saturdays, we had a weekly bath. The bathroom was located on the ground floor a few doors down from the refectory. Inside were three bathtubs, three foot tubs, and four wall sinks. Mother Cyra tended to our bathing. She selected older girls to bathe the youngest children first. They began by washing their hair. This was followed by a foot bath, and then a full body bath.

Due to the short supply of hot water, the bathwater was only changed four times during the bathing process. Our bathing time was limited to fifteen minutes in the bathtub. Quite often, when it was my turn to bathe, the water was lukewarm, and a buildup of black, greasy scum had already formed around the bathtub. I got lucky a few times, and waited my turn while the tub was filled with fresh water.

The same rule applied when using bath towels. After numerous uses, they were changed only four times for fresh ones. Sometimes when I got out of the tub, I had to dry my body off with a saturated towel from the previous users. The bathing rotation went on for up to two hours and didn't finish until all fifty of us were washed.

Mother Cyra also checked our heads for head lice and for the length of our hair. If she saw our hair was below our ears, she cut it. Up to the age of thirteen, our hair was kept short above our ears to prevent the spread of head lice. All the girls younger than thirteen had similar looking hairstyles. The only difference was, she gave some girls fringes and others had their hair parted on the side and tied up with ribbons or clips to hold it in place. However, having short hair didn't necessarily stop the continual infestation of head lice. Mother Regina's keen eye was often the first to detect if any of us had head lice.

Once an infestation was discovered, she lined us up, and doused each of us with a louse-killing solution. Then she ran a fine-tooth comb through our hair to pull away any nits or lice that might be stuck to the strands of the hair. With a white paper on a table in front of us, she tapped the toothcomb onto the paper. If she found live ones, she had us squish them on the paper with our thumbnails. Strange as it seemed, I found it thrilling to hear the crackling sound of a nit or lice being popped! When she was done, she shook DDT powder on our heads to quell another infestation.

The majority of us also suffered from tooth decay. This was due to a lack of proper dental hygiene and from the poor diets we consumed. It was only when a toothache became unbearable, did we visit a dentist. Each time I was sent to the dentist, I had a tooth extracted. Thankfully, it was always my back molars that were pulled. The practice of having our cavities filled was not yet in vogue. By the time I left St. Dominick's, I was missing seven molars. Many girls ended up having missing teeth or had to wear dentures years later.

On Sunday mornings, we were awakened at seven a.m. for mass. Following mass, we had breakfast, followed by a second mass. With second mass over, all teenage girls were required to go to The Recreation Room for, 'Instruction Class,' given by Mother Philomena. Then Mother Regina took over, and we had choir practice and returned to the church once more for benediction. Once lunch was over, we had the afternoon free to socialize with each other.

On the first Sunday of each month, we filed into the refectory after the first mass, and found a clear liquid at the bottom of our white teacups. This solution was called a 'Dose' and was given to us to ease constipation. Before taking our seats, we were instructed to stand behind our chairs and drink the liquid as soon as the 'Grace Before Meals' prayer ended.

I hated having to swallow that liquid. Although it didn't have an odor, it had a poisonous bitter taste and made me gag with every sip. Some older girls were used to the routine, and cleverly figured out ways to avoid having to drink the 'Dose.'

When the nun's back was turned, they carefully spilled the liquid into the center of their rolled-up serviettes. The first time I experienced this putrid stuff was under the beady eyes of Mother Concilio. She came to every table checking the bottom of our cups and stood waiting for those who hadn't yet drank it, to swallow it. Once all our cups were empty, only then did she allow us to take our seats for breakfast.

Within hours of ingesting the 'Dose,' most of us were in the throes of explosive diarrhea. Soon, a line formed to use one of the three toilets at the far end of the cloister. Each toilet stall was provided with square strips of shiny waxed paper that hung from a piece of twine attached to the stall wall with a nail.

One Sunday when I was about thirteen years old, I stood in line with the girls, desperate to use the toilet. As I inched forward, word spread that the stalls were out of waxed toilet paper. A loud grumble rippled down the line when we heard this. I was the fourth in line waiting behind a girl named Molly. When she heard the rumor, she temporarily left the line and took measures into her own hands. She returned carrying a Bunty magazine. She tore out some of the pages, before passing the remaining part of the magazine along the line for the rest of us to use.

When a toilet became available, Molly stepped inside. After using the toilet, she flushed it, and quickly ran out when she saw the toilet bowl overflowing, hence causing a messy flood on the lavatory floor. What she did annoyed the rest of us because it made our hopeless situation even worse. A girl who was next in line threatened Molly with a fist and called her an 'ammatan' as she crossed her legs in an effort to control her bowels.

Mother Ignatius heard about the clogged toilet and came from the kitchen to inspect it. When she saw the smelly mess on the floor, she flew into a furious rage. Spit flew out of her mouth, and her face turned crimson red, while demanding to know who caused the overflow. We pretended not to know and looked at her, blankly. "Whoever did this is going to have to clean it up," she shouted angrily, with so much force that it made her top false teeth fly out of her mouth, and slide across the floor before hitting the wall next to the far toilet. Mortified by what had happened, Mother Ignatius quickly ran to where her false teeth lay and scooped them off the floor and slipped them in her habit pocket. Without her false teeth, she didn't look at all like herself.

A girl behind me couldn't contain herself and got a fit of the giggles after witnessing what happened. Looking at Mother Ignatius, I saw her face was contorted and her top lip fell back under her nose. Although I was bursting to get to the toilet, I also sniggered at the whole spectacle. The girl behind poked me in the back, as if to say, 'are you seeing what I'm seeing?' I didn't want Mother Ignatius to think I was laughing at her, so I sneakily brought my hand over my mouth to stifle my laughter. But the nun was no fool. She knew what we were doing and rushed toward us. In a practiced swoop, she raised her hand and adeptly swiped the two of us across our faces. Then she turned on her heel and walked off, leaving the floor flooded in the same way that she found it. After she left, we silently and desperately waited a turn to use one of the two remaining stalls.

Up to that day, none of us had ever seen Mother Ignatius lose her temper and be that angry with us. She was normally very pleasant, but this unfortunate incident had obviously upset her, and especially because it occurred in front of all us girls. Although she vented her anger upon me and the other girl, I truly felt for her.

I never learned what the wretched liquid 'Dose' consisted of, except that it was a laxative. It caused disruptive, "gut-wrenching" havoc to all our digestive systems for at least twenty-four hours. With the approach of another first Sunday in the month around the corner, the thought of having to ingest another 'Dose' was sheer misery.

After lunch on Sundays during the winter months, we went to The Recreation Room. Mother Teresa and Mother Regina took turns supervising us. Sometimes they took out a turntable record player and played a selection of vinyl 45's singles records. After stacking several records on a silver pin, the records automatically dropped one by one from the pin and played. Then they were flipped to the "B" side. Sometimes, the stylus gathered dust, causing it to jump off the liner notes and scratched the record. When this happened, some older girls were given the job of carefully cleaning the vinyl with a soft cloth to remove the scratches. Besides listening to traditional Irish folk melodies, we also heard records sung by Helen Shapiro, Brendan Boyer and the Royal Showband, Dermot

O'Brien, Dickie Rock, and other artists. Those days were scarce, but we enjoyed dancing and jiving with each other for the afternoon. Hearing some of the songs for the first time, I hung on to every lyric.

In the refectory, we were served breakfast, lunch, and dinner. Most weekday meals were repeats of what was served the day before. For breakfast we had a bowl of gruel-like porridge, a slice of bread and a cup of tea. I was introduced to cornflakes on Sunday for breakfast two years before I left St. Dominick's. The cornflakes were a welcome treat all of us looked forward to.

For lunch, we had a serving of mashed potatoes, stringy mutton, and chopped cabbage. I never liked the smell of cabbage, and the mutton had a sour odor. Besides the smell of cabbage, twice I found a slug cooked inside, putting me off eating the rest of my meal. Flies were another problem in the warmer months and often ended up being cooked with exposed food. Once while eating a portion of mashed potatoes, I found a dead blue bottle fly.

It was very rare that we were told off for leaving food on our plates. Sometimes when the younger children didn't have an appetite, the older girls at the table ate what was left on their plates.

When barley soup or stews were served at lunch or supper, they came with a slice of bread. The only problem was we had to grab the bread from the tray at the front of the refectory. The stews consisted of mutton with carrots and potatoes added.

At lunchtime on Saturdays, we were served fried sausages, or liver and onions. These items were also served with a slice of bread and a cup of tea. I detested having to eat the liver. The main reason for this was that I had seen how slimy it looked before it was cooked. As a young teen, Mother Philomena often sent me to the kitchen to help Mother Ignatius. She had me put the livers in a huge basin and gave me instructions on how to dip them in flour before frying them. Prior to seeing how liver looked in its raw state, I ate it without knowing any better.

Sunday meals were my favorite. For lunch we had a thin slice of boiled bacon, or roast pork. That was served with a small portion of mashed potatoes, turnips, or marrowfat peas. A dessert of either tapioca, semolina, or red jelly and custard followed the entrée. I loved eating the puddings because they usually had a spoonful of strawberry jam decorating the middle. The jam especially helped when eating tapioca. I never cared much for the sensation of the bubbly pearls in the tapioca or the grainy semolina pudding, but once I mixed the jam into both, they tasted better.

For Sunday supper, we were given two slices of white toast and a hard-boiled egg. No matter what we were served for Sunday supper, the grub was a delightful change from the stringy tough mutton and cabbage served to us on weekdays.

Because the Sunday evening meal was so popular, we bartered with each other for a multitude of favors. "If you give me your hairclips, or medallion necklace, or musk perfume, etc., I'll let you have my boiled egg on Sunday."

For a brief time when I was a preteen, we were encouraged to drink voluminous amounts of milk. Milk was plentiful and became a priority in our diets. The more glasses of milk we drank at mealtimes, the more praise we got. This gorging of milk had us compete with girls sitting at our tables. One day, I bragged about drinking seven glasses of milk.

Sometimes, we drank so much milk it sickened our stomachs. I am not sure why milk was all of a sudden a matter of concern in our diets. My only guess was the dentist must have complained about our dental health, prompting Mother Teresa to increase our milk intake. By the time I hit my teen years, the milk emergency ceased.

As the seasons changed, so did our routine.

One sunny Sunday afternoon when I was fifteen, Mother Philomena asked me to assist the grandfather of a new girl named Bernie. It was late July, and Bernie's granddad was taking her on a day trip to Tramore beach. Bernie suffered many disabilities, and I was sent to help her grandfather.

I was glad when Mother Philomena picked me to go, because I had never been to Tramore beach. I only heard about the place from my school pals. They often went there in the summer months with their parents. On Monday morning after a day trip to Tramore the previous day, they arrived at school showing off the pink and white rock sticks they bought. The center of the rock stick had the word 'Tramore' infused in red lettering that went all the way down to the bottom. At recess, they sucked on the rocks until the stick formed a tapered point and snapped off.

When Bernie's grandfather arrived to pick her up, he came bearing a multitude of new clothes and gifts for her. Mother

Philomena introduced him to me and told him I would be his helper for the day. He shook my hand and gave me a big grandfatherly smile, with his perfectly straight white teeth. In my eyes, he was quite old. He had balding grey hair, a sun-tanned face, and a fat waistline.

Bernie was eleven years old and had difficulty walking, talking, and keeping her eyes focused. She constantly flayed her arms and whacked herself in the face. For some unknown reason, she took a liking to me. I believe it was because I often combed her hair and fixed it with clips and ribbons.

On the drive to Tramore, I sat in the backseat, and Bernie sat in the front. Her granddad's car had a nice, new smell, and was adorned with shiny chrome knobs and cushiony, brown leather seats. Gazing out the window, I was thrilled when I saw the horizontal line of the sea in the distance, knowing we were drawing close to our destination. Tramore was thronging with people when the car pulled into a spot close to the promenade. I helped get Bernie out of the car and held her hand while her grandfather took us to a kiosk for some ice cream. He treated both of us to a "99"—ice cream cone with a Cadbury's flake on top. Bernie squealed with joy when her granddad handed it to her. While we ate it, we sat on the promenade wall absorbing the hustle and bustle around us. I was tempted to go down to the sandy beach and dip my feet in the wavy water, but Bernie's granddad wasn't offering to take us there.

We watched happy children in beach togs heading down to the water's edge with their parents. A few of the children carried buckets and spades and built sandcastles under their parents' guidance.

Not long after, Bernie's granddad walked us back to his car. I stood waiting for him to open the back door so I could climb into the back seat, but he told me to come and sit in the front seat. "There's enough room for you and Bernie up here," he said.

I obeyed and squeezed in beside him and Bernie. I was expecting him to start up the engine and leave Tramore and head back to the Good Shepherd Convent. Instead, all three of us sat in our seats looking at the people and the view of the sparkling Irish Sea. Taken by surprise, I felt his hand on my thigh. I quickly pushed it aside and brought my knees together. He laughed when I did this and placed his hand on my thigh once more. I aggressively shoved his hand away and showed him an angry face. Then he stopped, and the grin on his face disappeared. He looked at me with an ugly grimace and told me to get out of the car and return to the backseat. I hastily leaned over Bernie, opened the car door, and hurriedly climbed over her before making my way into the backseat. He didn't speak a word to me or Bernie on our drive back to The Good Shepherd Convent. When we arrived, I noticed how he slipped back into his charming mode when he saw Mother Philomena.

In retrospect, I was glad I had shown the courage to make this deplorable man stop what he was planning to do to me. He must have figured I would tell Mother Philomena about him if he kept it up. But I knew better than to tell Mother Philomena. She would never have believed the flagrant allegations I was making against such a fine man. He definitely had her wrapped around his finger. My secret was safe until it was time to confide in someone I could trust.

Two Sundays later, I witnessed another girl heading off with Bernie's granddad for the afternoon. I wished I could forewarn her that he might take advantage of her innocence.

Mother Philomena thought she was doing us a favor sending us off with this pedophile. After that incident, whenever I saw him paying a visit to see his granddaughter, I noted how he had the nuns swooning over him. He fooled them with his charming personality and his excessive wealth.

Looking back, Bernie's grandfather's attempted actions toward me and no doubt other girls, led me to believe he must have also been molesting his disabled granddaughter when she lived with him. Then one day, like many girls, Bernie suddenly disappeared from St. Dominick's. I never heard where she went, and only hoped she would end up in a facility better suited to manage her disabilities and wasn't returned to live with her grandfather.

Besides the Good Shepherd Convent, the nuns also owned a massive house in Clonea Strand, Co. Waterford. In the summer months, they routinely took turns to enjoy a holiday there. The house was impressive and sat perched atop a cliff overlooking the Irish Sea. It boasted eight bedrooms, each with its own fireplace, several bathrooms, a large kitchen, and a gracious sitting room. This serene location was truly a relaxing place for them to unwind.

Before opening the house for the summer months, Mother Philomena chose several teenage girls to travel with two nuns on a minibus to get it ready. She sent me there twice, and both times the weather was warm, sunny, and clear.

My job was to dust, clean, and polish the floors. Although the work was fairly hard, I enjoyed going there. During my break, I stood at the top of the cliff taking in the smell of the salty sea air while admiring the sweeping views of the Comeragh mountains behind me.

The nuns also owned an acre of vacant land on the left side of the convent. On the first dry Saturday in July, Mother Philomena had the teenage girls go out into the field and pull the overgrown thistles. I was sent to do that job for a number of years.

Before getting started, each of us were given an apron to wear over our frocks, and several strips of newspaper. The paper strips were used to kneel on, and to wrap around the bottom of the thistles before pulling them out of the ground.

Lining up in rows of six at the top of the field, we put a strip of paper on the grass and got down on our knees to start our task. With such little protection, it was difficult working around the thorny, purple-headed thistles. The thistles were stubborn and hard to pull up by the roots. It took what seemed like hours working our way to the bottom of the field on our knees. By the time we were done, my fingers were sore and chafed, and were full of numerous tiny thorns that stuck under my skin. In the dormitory that evening, those of us with the same problem, shared small safety pins to pry the thorns out of our fingers. This was a job all of us hated doing.

On a few occasions, a number of families from around the Waterford and Kilkenny areas offered to host girls from St. Dominick's to spend Sunday afternoon with them. The host family picked the girls up around eleven a.m. and returned them again at four.

One Sunday, a family named the Comerford's took me out to spend time with their family. They lived in Mooncoin, a village on the outskirts of Waterford City. They were friendly and full of kindness and observed very quickly how painfully shy I was. Without forcing me into conversation, they gently encouraged me to relax in their company.

When I arrived at their home, I was introduced to their children and invited to join the family for Sunday lunch. I was served a delicious Sunday roast, with mashed potatoes and peas. Before returning to St. Dominick's, they stopped at a sweet shop in Waterford and told me to pick out something I would like. I chose some white and red clove rock sweets. Sitting alone in the back seat of the family car I opened the small paper bag of hard-boiled sweets and sucked on some. I was glad I had a chance to enjoy them because Mother Philomena took the remaining sweets from me after the host family dropped me off. She said it would not be fair for me to have sweets when the other girls didn't have any.

Tuesday evenings were spent rehearsing for upcoming stage plays and recitations. A music teacher named Mrs. McGrath was hired to help Mother Regina prepare us for the performances. Mrs. McGrath was pretty with long blonde hair she kept tied up in a French roll. She taught a variety of Irish step dances for *Feis le Cheile*, (Irish festival) competitions. These competitions were held on a Sunday in mid-June. Girls from the County Waterford area dressed in colorful Irish dance costumes and wore soft or hard dance shoes to show off their talents in dancing the Irish jigs, reels, and hornpipes. I was selected to join a group and did the 3-hand reel and slip jig. Our group won silver medals for coming in second place doing the 3-hand reel. After that performance, the Feis competitions ended at St. Dominick's.

For a few years in mid-April, Mrs. McGrath also showed us how to do the Maypole dance. This festive dance was a celebration to mark May Day, the first of May. Depending on the weather, the dance was performed on the first Sunday afternoon in May.

The Maypole was painted red and the spindle at the top of the pole was painted white. It stood at least fourteen feet off the ground and was made of wood. A multitude of colorful ribbons were attached at the top of the flat circular spindle and draped several feet from the high pole.

Mrs. McGrath divided us into two groups, "A" and "B." Group A danced around the Maypole clockwise, and Group B danced on the outside of group A, counterclockwise. The dance steps were four forward and four back, and were simple to learn. But the braided patterns we created with the ribbons were intricate and impressive. To unravel them again, we reversed the direction of the dance to bring us back to where we started. This Maypole dance was fun and left me with cherished memories of those days. Like the 'Feis' competitions, that also came to a sudden end in my early teens.

Walking to and from school in the winter months caused me to develop painful chilblains on my fingers and toes. The main culprit behind this frost bite was the lack of properly insulated coats and shoes. Although I wore mittens that were attached with two strings to my coat, my legs were barely covered with a light pair of knee-hi bobby socks.

I remember one very cold year when I was thirteen. I had grown out of the shoes Mother Cyra had fitted me with earlier that summer and a large hole appeared where the ball of my foot rested. This allowed the cold and moisture to seep into my shoes. On severely cold mornings, my fingers and toes became red, swollen and cracked. As soon as I arrived at school, I had to warm my hands and feet against the school radiators before classes began. This helped to ease the soreness and stinging. However, as they warmed up, the skin on my fingers and toes began to itch and the tips of my fingers formed tiny blisters.

Mother Philomena was mindful of my problem and had a doctor prescribe me a small green pill that I swallowed before mass each morning. Thirty minutes after ingesting the pill, my body temperature rose and I became highly flushed. This strange and uncomfortable sensation lasted for about a half-hour. I was always in a church pew when this occurred. The girls around me, knowing I was given the little green pill, watched, and waited for the moment when my face and body turned beet red. They quietly snickered and poked each other to look at me, and I laughed with them, finding it equally as strange.

Once the warming sensation of the pill wore off, my whole body shivered, and goosebumps appeared like a bleached rash on my arms and legs. The shaking and shivering lasted an hour and abated just in time to head out to school and face another cold winter's day.

By the time I turned sixteen, the chilblains became less bothersome, and Mother Philomena ceased giving me the medication. I am not sure if it was because I had grown out of getting them or if it had anything to do with being provided with better shoes to wear.

Television was initially introduced at St. Dominick's when I was nine years old. The date was November 22, 1963. Mother Teresa had the maintenance man set up a black and white television in the study room for us all to view. On the screen, we saw emerging grim images of President John F. Kennedy's assassination. The same broadcast aired repeatedly.

That day was a sad occasion for Ireland and the world. President John F. Kennedy was an icon to the Irish people, and they solemnly mourned his untimely passing. The Irish were proud that America had chosen one of their own for president of The United States. His ancestral roots stretched back to 19th century Ireland. Following his death, most Irish households displayed a framed picture of the deceased president in their living rooms and kitchens.

Since the introduction of the television, we were permitted to watch shows on Saturday and Sunday evenings. The youngest children were allowed to stay up until eight, and the teenage girls, until ten o'clock. That extra time was fulfilling, and we got to view some terrific shows.

Although RTE was the only channel to broadcast, most of the shows were American. Some of my favorite shows were, *I Dream of Jeannie, Get Smart, The High Chaparral, The Virginian,* and the *Black and White Minstrel Show.* Irish TV programming was slowly evolving, and began to air shows like Daithi Lacha, The Riordans, Wanderly Wagon and School Around the Corner.

The nine o'clock news was the last programming of the evening. The news reader was Charles Mitchell, and when he finished, he disappeared off the screen and was replaced by a bright narrow line left in the middle of the screen. In a matter of seconds, that too disappeared and the TV shutdown for the night.

Prior to the novelty of TV, we were sometimes rewarded with seeing a movie musical on a Sunday afternoon. The intended movie was on a huge film reel that was transmitted onto a white screen from a large projector. The first movie I saw was The *King and I,* featuring Yul Brenner and Deborah Kerr. This was shown in Technicolor while others were in black and white. Jeanette MacDonald and Nelson Eddy were in *Maytime*; Shirley Temple in *Animal Crackers*; Deanna Durbin in *Springtime*; and Sonya Henie figure skated on ice.

I was completely engaged by the big screen movies as well as television. I especially loved the musicals and memorized all the lyrics and melodies I heard.

Music was a form of escape. It was soothing and transported me to a better place mentally, away from the harsh realities behind the high stone walls of St. Dominick's with its nefarious nuns.

*Clonea Strand—1963.*

*1962—St. Dominick's girls 'Springtime' musical
play at Theatre Royal.*

*1964—St. Dominick's girls 'Mikado' musical play at
Theatre Royal.*

*Clonea Strand with nuns summer home on cliff-top.*

*One of the long cloisters from nun's
convent to St. Dominick's.*

## Chapter Eleven

# THE CHURCH

A massive church was the centerpiece of the the Good Shepherd Convent. It was divided into three, partitioned, tall sections and used for three separate groups of residents that lived behind the walled institution.

The partition on the far-left side of the church was called St. Mary's church. This was where the young women of the Magdalene Laundry sat. Although they were kept hidden from us, I sometimes saw them when they stood at their altar waiting for the priest to serve them Holy Communion.

St. Dominick's church was on the right side. It was at this church I spent a quarter of my youth. Both St. Mary's and St. Dominick's churches were mirror images of each other. Each had about twenty dark brown pews, two confession boxes at the rear, and ceramic plaques showing the stations of the cross lined up between colorful stained-glass windows.

The center of the church was reserved for the Good Shepherd Nuns and boasted the largest altar. The nuns sat in individual wooden stalls that lined up in a row on both sides of the nave. The nave was empty except for an oversized area rug, with a red pattern. This rug spread out over a large portion of a glossy red and black tiled floor.

Adjacent to the left side of the altar, was a side annex. This section was much smaller and had a small opening with an alter rail that faced the main altar. Here was where the Magdalene Nuns sat. They were also referred to as the Sisters of the Poor. They rarely showed their faces and never mixed with the nuns in the center of the of the church. The only viewing of them was when they knelt two at a time at their small side altar rail to receive Communion. Although they were referred to as the 'Magdalene Nuns,' they were also part of the Good Shepherd order, but they never monitored the ladies at St. Mary's.

At seven thirty each morning, a Parish Priest named Father O'Gorman celebrated the Latin mass from the center altar. None of us understood him, but mimicked and responded when he made the sign of the cross and said mass.

Facing the altar, he kept his back to the congregation. Above his head was a huge gold-plated sanctuary lamp. It was suspended from a high vaulted ceiling and hung from three long brass chains. Burning inside, was an eternal flame. It was always lit and represented the presence of Jesus. It flickered and glowed continuously inside a red protective glass and gave the appearance of winking all through mass to keep us from falling asleep.

As I got older, I liked to sit in a pew closest to the front of the church. That way, I knew I was away from the watchful eyes of Mother Philomena. She sat at the back of the church to watch the younger girls.

When we entered the pew, we were required to genuflect, and again after we left the pew.

One Sunday morning when I was fourteen years old, Mother Scholastica stood in for Mother Philomena. Inside the church, she lined us up along the pews and stood watching us as we entered them. When it was my turn to step into a pew, the girl in front of me accidently stepped on my foot. I quickly rubbed my foot in my shoe and not paying attention, I followed the girl into my pew without genuflecting. Mother Scholastica, observing this, reached in and dug her long pointy nails into my arm. She pulled me out of the pew and made me genuflect before going back in to kneel.

The pews were stocked with missals that were written in Latin. Many of the missals had loose pictures of Jesus, Mary, Joseph, angels, and the saints inserted between their pages. To kill the monotony at mass, some of us traded the Holy pictures with each other. When mass ended, we secretly showed off our winnings, before putting them back in the prayer books again.

Not only was I getting a religious education from the Good Shepherd Nuns, but also was receiving it from the Ursuline Nuns where I attended school.

As soon as I arrived at the Good Shepherd Convent, I prepared for confessions and my First Holy Communion. Both the Good Shepherd Nuns and the Ursuline Nuns tested me on my knowledge of the catechism. On the day of my First Communion, I was escorted to The Ursuline School by a nun from the Good Shepherd Convent. I was the only girl from St.

Dominick's to make My First Communion with The Ursuline pupils in my class that day. Apart from making my First Holy Communion with my classmates, there were also a few boys from the local Christian Brothers school who joined us and made theirs.

Walking back to St. Dominick's after making my Holy Communion, I slipped and fell crossing the road because of the slippery soles of my white patent shoes. The fall knocked the veil off my head and soiled my communion dress. I complained of having pain on the right-side of my shoulder and was sent to bed for the remainder of the day.

Years later, I discovered the pain I complained about that day was from a fractured clavicle. An English doctor told me during a physical that I had an old fracture that healed itself. The pain was long gone and there was no need for surgery.

The Bishop of Waterford confirmed me in the Waterford Cathedral when I was thirteen. I was supposed to make my Confirmation when I was twelve, but due to a bout with scarlet fever the previous year, I had to wait another year. Once again, I was the only girl from St. Dominick's taking the sacrament of Confirmation.

Standing outside the cathedral for a group photo after the Confirmation mass ended, happy parents and relatives plied their children with gold crosses, necklaces, and money. I stood beside the Good Shepherd Nun watching them. Returning to St. Dominick's I was glum. My own family were never around to celebrate such momentous occasions with me.

My youth was filled with fear and prayer. Whether at school with the Ursuline Nuns or the Good Shepherd Nuns, I was frequently reminded to never lose sight of God.

In religious education classes at St. Ursuline School, I was taught to love God and fear the devil. God was good; Satan was evil. Having God in my life, I was protected. Without Him, I was sure to burn in the flames of hell forever. Religious pictures of God and the Blessed Virgin Mary were awarded to well-behaved students in class, and during the annual retreat.

In the school Catechism book, Satan was depicted as a long, thick, green serpent in the Garden of Eden.

"You see what happened to Adam and Eve in the Garden of Eden when the devil tempted them. They should have listened to God," was one such lesson in religious education class.

In other pictures, Satan, was shown as a crimson human-like figure. He had a long red tail with large red wings and curved black horns that protruded from the black hair on his head. In his left hand, he held a three-pronged fork and tongues of blazing red fire danced around his clawed feet. In my pre-pubescent years, I often stared up at the sky hoping God was looking down to protect me from the devil. God was everywhere, but so was Satan. He was lurking in the shadows waiting for a chance to tempt me. I didn't want to disappoint God and feared Him as much as I feared the devil invading my life.

At school, it was considered wrong to write with the left hand. The left hand was the hand of the devil. When I first learned to write, I automatically picked my pencil up in my left hand. Although I was without a doubt left-handed, I had to switch the writing tool to my right hand. After lots of practice, I finally grasped the technique and consequently became ambidextrous.

In my early-teens, I shared a church task with a girl named Breda. Our job was to take care of the altar rails before and after mass. We both carefully took the altar cloths out of a white linen bag and placed them on the long, grey, marble altar rail. They were then tied with white strings to an equally long brass bar. Following that, we stood on one of the two marble steps, and rolled out a long runner carpet. The carpets were used to kneel to receive Holy Communion. Lining up outside our pews, ten girls, five on either side, knelt and waited for the priest to drop the eucharist on their tongues.

As soon as mass ended, Breda and I returned to the altar to remove the altar cloths. After folding them neatly, we put them back in the bag, and then rolled up the runner carpets into big balls. While performing our duties, the girls watched us from the pews. Some of them secretly placed bets on which one of us would finish the job first. Breda and I were required to work in unison, but we also competed with each other. Knowing some of the girls had placed bets on us, we speedily rushed to be the first to finish. If I finished before Breda, I gloated with pleasure, returning to my pew. I looked forward to attending mass because of this job, and because I had a bird's eye view of the other sections of the church.

One morning after mass while finishing my work on the altar, I was caught off guard when I saw a nun laying prostrate on the nave of the carpeted floor. Her arms and legs were splayed, and I wasn't sure what she was doing. I paused for a few moments to watch her. Afterwards, when I conveyed what I had seen to Breda, she told me the nun was surrendering herself to God to ask for God's grace and forgiveness.

Quite often at mass, the older girls fainted in their pews. Rumors circulated that they had low blood sugar levels because they hadn't eaten, or because they had their monthly periods. Sitting beside an older girl in the pew one morning, I noticed her face turning extremely pale. When she stood up to get in line for communion, she collapsed in the aisle of the church. Mother Philomena called for another girl to help pick her up.

Then the girl was immediately laid flat on her back, and her legs lifted above her hip-line to bring a blood supply back to her head. When she recovered, she sat in her pew for the remainder of the mass.

Father O'Gorman was the assigned Parish Priest at the Good Shepherd Convent. He was tall and handsome with pale blue eyes and wavy blond hair. Apart from the two workmen who did janitorial work at the convent, he was the only other male we saw on a regular basis.

One late Autumn evening, when I was fifteen, Mother Philomena sent me with three other girls to help Father

O'Gorman stuff religious brochures into envelopes. It was around nine o'clock and dark outside when we finished. All three of us walked with the priest to a side door to bid him goodnight. One of the girls opened the door to let him out, and when she did, I stood at the doorstep and looking up saw a huge full moon glowing amongst thousands of twinkling stars. Father O'Gorman stepped outside, and we followed him. Gazing up at the moon, I innocently made an offhand comment. "Look at the moon, Father. It's huge and beautiful."

The other three girls who were with me were equally as impressed with the fall night sky as I was. Father O'Gorman looked up at the moon but made no comment.

A few days later, I was called into Mother Philomena's office. She questioned me about what I said to the priest that evening. I was confused by her question and told her I didn't remember what I said to him.

"Is it the last shower you think I came down in? That's not what Father O'Gorman told me. He said you were making romantic suggestions to him," she said.

I was stunned with disbelief by her untruthful accusations. Then I remembered the sight of the beautiful moon and tried explaining to her what I said. But Mother Philomena wasn't believing anything I told her. Instead, she went to her cupboard, took out a drum-like stick, and whacked it across the backs of my hands.

"Now get out of my office and mind who you are talking to the next time," she commanded.

At that moment, I wanted to run away as far as possible from St. Dominick's. In anger, I stomped out of her office, angry with the lies Father O'Gorman had told her about me.

After that, I lost all trust in Father O'Gorman. I was especially careful in what I told him at confession box. His lying about me to Mother Philomena affected me badly. At school for the next few weeks, I found it hard to concentrate on my secondary school studies.

Father O'Gorman heard confessions at five o'clock every Monday evening. Girls who made their First Holy Communion aged seven and up, lined up to tell the priest sins they committed since their last confession. As pious young girls, we really didn't have any sins to tell him. Because I couldn't think of any sins I committed, I literally repeated the same ones to him every week. As soon as I entered the confession box, Father O'Gorman opened a small wooden door. It showed a silhouette of one side of his face behind a dark screen. Kneeling, I faced him and voiced my sins to him.

"Bless me Father for I have sinned. It's two weeks since my last confession. I laughed and talked in the church."

Father O'Gorman blessed me and usually told me to say three Hail Mary's and a Glory Be to The Father, for my penance. I never worried about telling him the same sins until he lied to Mother Philomena about me. After that incident, I changed my sins around a little by telling him I wasn't paying enough attention in church and played with some of the holy pictures in the church pews. It was hard trying to come up with creative ways to find new sins to tell him. I suspected if I continued telling him my old sins, he might tell Mother Philomena. As

I grew older, I wondered if he confessed his own sins to other priests.

Sunday mornings after breakfast, all teenage girls went to The Study Room for religious instruction. Mother Philomena sat at her desk at the front of the room and touched on various subjects, such as stories from the Bible and challenges we might encounter when we left the Good Shepherd convent. One Sunday, she explained the difference between employers and employees, and the line of work we might end up in when our school days ended.

"Maybe some of you might want to become nuns. That's a good choice for any girl who thinks she might have a calling," she said.

She scanned the room, and out of the blue, she pegged me as a good candidate to be a nun. I almost leapt out of my seat when I heard her mention my name, and instantly blushed crimson. I didn't know whether I should be honored or quake in my shoes by her surprising assumption. I sat silently wondering why she singled me out of all the other girls to become a nun. I started thinking it was because I correctly answered her Bible quiz a few weeks earlier.

On another occasion, a visiting priest told me I had the look of becoming a nun. That evening, I studied my face in the mirror, trying to figure out what it was about my face that led this priest, a total stranger, to think I might be a nun one day. I was aware that most young girls who entered the convent had a calling, a vocation, to become a nun. I never wanted or imagined myself being a nun, and the thought of it haunted me. Thereafter, I made a concerted effort to never allow that to happen.

When Mother Philomena's instruction ended, Mother Regina took over. She lined girls seven years and older to rehearse for Benediction before lunch. She divided the choir into three separate groups, based on our vocal range, and referred to each group as firsts, lowest range; seconds, mid-range; and thirds, high. She put me into the thirds section because I was able to hit the high notes.

All the hymns she taught were sung in Latin. She began by playing the melodies on her piano one line at a time, and then had us repeat each line back to her while she sang the lyrics with us. I enjoyed going to Benediction, but had trouble pronouncing the Latin words, and didn't know what they meant.

*"Panis Angleicus, Tantum Ergo"* and *"O' Salutaris Hosita,"* were hymns she mostly had us sing at Benediction. With all three sections of the choir singing in unison, each hymn sounded beautiful and melodic, despite the fact we slaughtered all the lyrics.

Prayer retreats were held in April at St. Dominick's. Girls twelve years and older had to remain silent for three days. The Good Shepherd Nuns used these three days when the regular school days were out on a spring break. The retreat days were a special time to reflect and to fully connect with God, through prayer and confession. From the moment we got out of bed, the only time we used our voices was when we prayed together and in the church. This was a very challenging three days for all of us to adhere to.

Throughout the day we were supervised by different nuns and were reminded continuously to remain silent if we accidently slipped up and spoke to each other. Ironically, the only real place we could converse was in the church.

After supper, we went to the church and listened to a visiting priest talk to us about the Bible. Then he quizzed us on what he told us. When he was done, he had us all stand up and bellow out the lyrics of, *"I am a little Catholic."* On the third day of the retreat, he heard each of our confessions. Just like Father O'Gorman, I gave him the same rundown of sins I never committed. It was pure relief when the retreat ended.

The Ursuline School I attended also held a retreat. That retreat lasted only one day. Although our classes continued, the nuns kept us busy with reading materials, and left large encyclopedias on the classroom tables for us to read.

Skimming through the encyclopedias, we found medically related colorful pictures showing naked men and women. As curious teenage girls, we considered them to be very naughty. If any one of us found a picture of interest, we poked each other to look at the picture. When the nuns' backs were turned, we discretely giggled amongst ourselves.

I was eight years old when news of the Cuban missile crisis reached Ireland.

This international crisis threw the Good Shepherd Nuns into a panic. Mother Teresa gathered us together and told us to go straight to the church and pray, should there be a nuclear fallout. Black and white leaflets on what actions to take were circulated throughout the Good Shepherd Convent. Even some of the cloister windows leading to the church were covered in black paper.

To scare us even more, each of us were given fabric scapulars to wear around our necks and rosary beads to pray with. The scapulars were brown with a string attached. They had a double-sided square picture of The Blessed Virgin and child on one side, and a script which read, "Whoever dies in this scapular, shall not suffer eternal fire," printed on the other side. At mass, we prayed to God to keep ourselves and John F. Kennedy safe from nuclear war. My eight-year-old mind manufactured my biggest fear. "What if I were asleep when it happened? How would I be able to get to the church on time!"

Thankfully, the world was spared from a nuclear war between the USA and the Soviet Union.

When an elderly nun died, the church bells tolled loud enough to be heard throughout the confines of the Good Shepherd and over the walls on the outside. The death bells had a different sound than the Angelus bells. They were slow with longer intervals of ringing. Regardless of where we were when the bells rang, we immediately got down on our knees and said a prayer for the dead nun. Three days later, we gathered in the church for a long Requiem mass.

One of the death bells was for Mother Scholastica. She passed away after she fell and broke her hip. She was in her mid-eighties and died a week after her fall. The following day, she was taken to the church and laid to rest in front of the large altar.

Mother Philomena allowed some of us to go to the church and pay our respects to Mother Scholastica. When we got there, I watched the nuns file by her coffin. Some touched her clasped hands that were wrapped in white rosary beads. I had never known the Good Shepherd Nuns to show such affection. With reverently bent heads, they earnestly grieved for the loss of their friend.

When it was my turn to view the coffin, I saw the nun's eyes were closed, and her face was white and full of wrinkles. Copying what the girl ahead of me did, I sheepishly put my hand on the dead nun's lily-white hands, but quickly pulled back when I felt how freezing cold they were. Although this was the same nun who dug her nails into me, my eyes welled up with tears and I was filled with emotion when I saw her laying in her coffin. I think the finality of life and death struck me once again.

After a late stage performance at the Theatre Royal one Saturday evening, those of us who participated were allowed to remain in bed the following Sunday morning. I was fifteen years old at the time and sleeping in the teenage dormitory. Instead of going to mass at the Good Shepherd Church, Mother Philomena allowed us sleep in until eight that morning, and sent us out to a church outside the grounds of the Good Shepherd Convent.

The mass was due to start at nine a.m. and an older girl was given the name and address of the church we were to attend. Not knowing any different, we ended up going to a Protestant church of the same name, where a nine a.m. service was taking place.

When we returned to St. Dominick's, Mother Philomena asked about the mass. When we told her all about it, she almost keeled over when she discovered we had attended a Protestant service instead of a Catholic mass. She allowed us to eat some breakfast, and quickly sent us back out to find the correct Catholic church for a later mass. Before leaving, she reminded us not to take Holy communion because we had already broken the fast.

Some of the secondary school boarders and day pupils in my class at the Ursuline School left the classroom when it was time for a Religious Education class. By the end of my first year in secondary school, I realized those girls were Protestants. This was my first inkling of how religious denominations divided us.

At age thirteen, I received the much-honored Pioneer Pin. This pin was a symbol of taking a vow to abstain from drinking alcohol for life. Although we were often warned about the dangers of alcohol, and how the devil cleverly tempted people to drink, that day, I wore my Pioneer Pin with pride, vowing to never touch alcohol.

The abstinence from alcohol worked perfectly for me until I arrived in Dublin a few years later.

One evening, I was in the center of Dublin with my co-workers. We entered a pub on O'Connell St. and not knowing what to drink, I opted to have a Babycham. The ad I had seen on TV featuring a cute yellow deer was truly what tempted me to try it.

"Everyone Loves Babycham, the Genuine Champagne!"

The smiling yellow deer, the sparkling glass of champagne and the catchy jingle, were enough for me to forget all about my Pioneer Pin.

Despite all the forced religion I was subjected to during my years at The Good Shepherd Convent, I am still devoted to my faith.

*First Holy communion—1961 back row.*

## Chapter Twelve

# THE NURSERY

One feature of St. Dominick's we all enjoyed was looking through the nursery window. The nursery was on the second floor close to the Sacred Heart Dormitory. The room was huge and had a large square window. This nursery wasn't for babies, but for beautiful dolls. The dolls came in all sizes. Some had red, rosy cheeks and all were made of porcelain. Apart from the baby-sized dolls, they all had real human hair. Most of the dolls had curly hair in either black, brown, or blonde colors. Their eyes were blue or brown and opened and shut; bigger dolls showed sweeping, long eyelashes.

Each doll had its own special place in the nursery. Some stood tall while others sat on rocking chairs or were displayed in cribs or metal beds. The beds were adorned with colorful covers and underneath were white linens and lace. The big dolls wore silken styled dresses with colorfully designed trims on the hems and at the wrist cuffs. Some wore black or brown leather shoes or boots over lacy white socks.

The walls of the nursery were painted in pink and mint green, and the floor was fitted with a plush pink carpeting. No one knew who owned the dolls, but a rumor amongst the girls said that they belonged to some of the Good Shepherd Nuns residing in the convent. The nursery door was always kept under lock and key. Over the years, only a selective number of older girls were sent there to carefully dust around the dolls and the decorative white ledge encircling the nursery walls.

Sometimes, I stood outside the nursery window and gazed at the dolls. I was desperate to pick one up and hold it. Out of the blue one day, Mother Teresa allowed my friend Breda and I to go inside and look at the dolls. She reminded us not to touch their hair or drop them, because they broke easily. Inside, I gently picked up two of the dolls I had so often admired through the nursery window. I treasured the moments I had to play with them. Soon, other girls were allowed inside the nursery. I don't know what gave Mother Teresa the change of heart in allowing us inside to enjoy spending time with the dolls.

Soon after, the dolls suddenly disappeared out of the nursery window. The room was turned into a six-bedded nursery where current and incoming female toddlers could sleep under the supervision of an older teenaged girl. Girls from the Big Girl's Dormitory were sent to the nursery each morning and evening to help get the toddlers up and dressed before they headed over to mass. One girl remained with the toddlers until mass ended.

The beautiful dolls just vanished without a trace and wherever they went was a total mystery to us all.

## Chapter Thirteen

# THE SACRED HEART DORMITORY

For my first six years at St. Dominick's, I slept in the Sacred Heart Dormitory. This dormitory was where girls twelve and younger slept and was also referred to as 'The Small Children's Dormitory.'

The Sacred Heart Dormitory was located on the second floor at the top of the stairs. It was divided into four pastel-colored sections, two on the right and two on the left, and were separated by a long, wood-paneled corridor. All the sections were furnished with eight, cream-colored, cast-iron single beds, a wooden locker beside each bed, and a small chair sat at the foot of the bed. The section on the upper left had a mixture of beds and brown wooden cots for the smaller girls until they were moved into the nursery. This was also the section where the toilets and fire escape were located.

The long corridor had large glass panels. This allowed easy viewing for Mother Regina, who oversaw us. Below the glass panels were pale blue panels. After about eighteen months of sleeping in the same bed, I was moved to a different section with girls in my own age group.

Mother Regina had a strict rule about getting dressed in the mornings and before bedtime. We were only allowed to sit or stand on the right side of our own bed to change our clothing. Once we removed our outer garments, we then had to slip our nightdresses over our heads and then remove our underwear. After that was completed, we put our clothes neatly on our chairs, to have them ready for the following day.

As a newcomer at the 'Sacred' dormitory, I was given a bed in the lower right section. I learned the proper way to remove my clothes from copying what the other girls in my section did.

While I slept there, a new girl named Rita was transferred from another section to sleep in the spare bed next to me. When we got ready for bed the first evening, she sat on the floor on my side of the bed. Believing it was okay for her to do that, I didn't say anything to her. With the small amount of space between us, we bumped into each other while changing out of our clothes. Rita got impatient, removed her underwear, and momentarily sat naked beside me. She was about to put her nightdress over her head when Mother Regina caught her.

"What do you think you are doing sitting there on the wrong side of your bed. You are supposed to change your clothes on your own side of the bed," she told her, wearing an angry scowl.

Rita looked up at her, not knowing what to say.

Next, Mother Regina reached over and yanked her off the floor, scooping up her nightdress in the process. Dragging her by the arm out of the section, she ran her out of the dormitory stark naked.

It was still dusk outside when Rita returned to her bed. As she climbed in, I could see she had been crying because her eyes were red and swollen. Turning her head away from me, she hid under the bedcovers. After Mother Regina left the dormitory, I whispered to Rita. "What happened to you?"

At first, I thought she was sleeping or couldn't hear me. Laying silently, I captured a movement and the silhouette of her hand, lifting her bed sheet. I waited a few seconds and asked her the same question again. In a low voice, she said Mother Regina took her down the corridor to Mother Teresa's office. When she got there, she was made to lay across the seat of a chair while Mother Teresa caned her on the buttocks.

"Were you naked?" I whispered.

"Yes, and she really hurt me. When she was done, she told me to get up and put my nightdress on."

I gasped with what she told me, and quietly sympathized with her and tried to imagine what it must have been like for her. The next morning, when we got up, I saw her touching her sore behind. While getting dressed for school, she stayed on her own side of the bed. After that, both of us were careful to only change out of our clothing on our own side of the bed.

Before turning off the dormitory lights each night, Mother Regina gave a final walk through each section. In my second year, I was moved to the section on the upper right side. While Mother Regina was checking my section, she stopped by my bed. I was lying on my belly and had one arm over my head, and the other was tucked under my chest. I looked up from the position I was in when I saw her standing over me.

"What are you doing to yourself," she asked.

I was puzzled by her comment and remained on my tummy. Then, she suddenly yanked the bedcovers off me, and demanded to see where I had my other hand. I pulled it out from under my chest to show her. "In future, keep your hands out where I can see them, and stop laying on your stomach like that," she ordered.

Complying with her command, I immediately rolled over onto my back and faced her. I liked sleeping on my tummy and made every effort not to lie on it thereafter.

Mother Colette was St. Dominick's kitchen cook. She slept in a room called a cell. Her cell was on the other side of the dormitory, directly behind the hand sinks. A large opening separated the hand sinks and in the middle of them was a large, square, glass window with a wide windowsill. The window was hinged and opened and closed like a small door. Behind it, hung a small beige curtain. Before drifting off to sleep, I often saw Mother Colette peeping out from behind the curtain. In my mind, I felt sure Mother Regina instructed her to spy on us so she could report back any disturbances she heard throughout the night. Sometimes, after Mother Regina left the dormitory, a few girls tip-toed to each other's beds, and sat whispering. Whether Mother Colette was aware of the girls' movements or not, she was kind enough to never inform Mother Regina.

A girl named Ann Vee was appointed to help Mother Regina in the dormitory. Ann was older than all of us preteens and slept in the right upper section of the dormitory.

Her job was to lead us in the morning and evening prayers as we knelt by our beds, and to supervise us in the line-up to wash at the hand sinks. Mother Regina gave her full authority to hit us if we got out of line.

Every morning, Mother Regina promptly entered the dormitory at seven. Pacing up and down the long corridor she clapped her hands and shouted until all of us were out of bed.

After the morning prayer, we filed out of our sections and lined up in the corridor in bare feet and skimpy nightdresses. We were tired and while we waited to wash, we shivered in our bare feet. We were especially cold during the winter months.

Mother Regina supervised the front of the queue, and Ann, the back. If either one of them spotted us sneaking a quick nap against the partitioned wall, we were whacked across the head, shoulder, or back. I was a victim of this punishment a couple of times. The sudden blow hurt more when it was cold because I had just crawled out from under warm bedding.

Several of the girls had problems with bedwetting. They were supplied with a strip of terracotta colored rubber lining to use under their bed sheets. For some, the lining shifted as they slept. This caused some girls to not only wet their bed sheets and nightdresses, but also soak their mattresses.

While lining up in the corridor, Mother Regina checked the backs of the suspected girls' nightdresses. When she discovered girls with wet nightdresses, she pulled the unfortunate bedwetters out of the line one by one. She hit them anywhere above the shoulders and sent them back to strip their beds and air dry their sheets and mattresses. With the shame of their bedwetting accidents on full display, some girls sobbed and others looked clearly upset, while carrying out the nun's commands.

Nellie, who sat with me at the same dining table, was a bedwetter. She dreaded the mornings when she woke up and found her bed wet. It frustrated her a lot, and she asked me one day what she could do to make herself stop. I didn't know what to tell her, since I didn't share her problem. Even though we had the same diets and drank the same liquids, she had a problem that I was lucky to escape.

Mother Regina particularly enjoyed disgracing Nellie in front of the non-bedwetters, and Nellie hated her for it.

Despite Mother Regina's persecution toward her, Nellie retained her quirky sense of humor and loved getting up to mischief.

Early one evening, when I was close to twelve, Mother Philomena sent Nellie and me up to the Sacred Heart dormitory to put away some freshly laundered blankets and sheets. Inside the dormitory, there were two large storage closets in the lower left section close to the entry door. Each closet had two long double doors, with three levels of storage space for pillows, blankets, and bed linen. This was also the same section that Nellie slept in.

When everything was put away in its proper place, we closed the wooden latches across the doors to keep them shut. Before leaving, Nellie stood at one of the sash windows in her section and called me over to have a look outside.

Peering out the window, I saw a small semi-flat section of a roof. It had a narrow gully-like dip that connected the dormitory and kitchen roof tiles together. I looked at Nellie and saw she was wearing a mischievous grin. Turning to me, she told me she fancied climbing outside to see what it was like to stand on the roof and asked me to join her. Next, she brazenly opened the window wide enough for her body to squeeze through. Then she hopped up on the radiator and sidled her way outside. I felt apprehensive about following her, and initially stepped back because I was scared. When she saw I wasn't following her outside, she came back to the open window and begged me to join her.

Building up some confidence, I nervously stepped up on the radiator and climbed out onto the roof. To maintain my balance, I steadied myself and leaned against a flat concrete surface for support. Below me, I could see part of the gravel yard and the laundry building where Mother Cyra worked. Realizing how high up we were, I didn't dare budge from my spot, and I wished I hadn't followed Nellie out. Standing there, I quivered at the thought of what might happen if we got caught.

Nellie, on the other hand, was fearless. Unknown to me, she had another plan up her sleeve. She carefully moved away from me and balancing herself, she stood in an upright position. My eyes widened when I saw her pull her knickers down around her ankles, and crouching low, she began urinating. I watched a large volume of her urine flow down a narrow channel, where it then toppled over the edge of the roof. Shocked by her audacity, she turned to see my reaction and laughed, while I remained glued to the same spot.

Mother Ignatius, who was working in the kitchen, heard the noise above her and came outside to check. I froze when I saw the top of her black veil moving about in the yard below me. After sensing something had fallen on her head, she raised her hand to feel the top of her veil. Then she spun around and stepped back to look up onto the roof.

In the final moments of Nellie squatting to empty her bladder, she remained in a crouched position while struggling to pull her knickers up. Mother Ignatius kept up her search to see where the liquid had emerged from. Luckily, she couldn't see me or clearly see Nellie because of the angle of the roof.

"Who's up there? Answer me," she asked.

When she didn't get an answer, I watched the top of her veil slowly disappear from the yard. I knew we were surely in trouble. Feeling panicked, I pushed myself away from the wall, and cowardly climbed back inside the window. Within seconds, Nellie scurried in behind me. Back in Nellie's section, I was in a quandary thinking of what we should do.

Nellie hastily shut the window behind her and told me we should clear out of the dormitory before we got caught. Grabbing my arm, we ran to exit the dormitory door, but stopped when we heard footsteps traveling up the stairs outside.

"Quick, we better hide in the blanket closet," she said with an anxious concern in her voice.

Unlatching the first closet, we pushed back the red blankets and pillows, and in a flurry of seconds, we swiftly climbed in. Nellie stretched out and tucked herself into the corner of the closet, and I laid down opposite her with my feet against her left shoulder. Once we were settled, both of us stuck out our hands to close the closest doors, but they both came ajar again. In our panic, we had forgotten about the latches that kept the doors closed. Realizing if Mother Ignatius saw the doors were opened even slightly, our hideout would be discovered, Nellie devised a different plan.

"Grab the end on your door, and pull it in to close it. Keep holding it, and I'll do the same," she said.

She was talking about the thin overlay of wood that ran along the bottom of both closet doors. Each of us pulled a corner of the closet door nearest us and held them tightly to keep them closed. Then, we buried ourselves deep beneath the thicket of blankets and pillows and remained dead still.

Within seconds, there was a rattling sound of the dormitory door being opened, and heavy footsteps followed. Laying in the dark holding my breath, I guessed it was Mother Ignatius. My body began to shake and my heart pounded in my chest waiting for her to swing the closet doors open. But the footsteps hastily fled past the closets and abruptly stopped. I figured the nun was looking at the window we had just climbed in. A squeaking sound echoed in the closet when the window was opened. A few moments later, the window was aggressively slammed shut. "Nellie Murphy, are you in here? I'm warning you, you better come out wherever you are. You're in big trouble now."

I recognized Mother Ignatius's voice. Holding still, I remained rigid under the pile of blankets. I thought my shaky hand would make a noise outside the closet door or that I would accidentally let go of the door. Finding no sign of Nellie on the roof, Mother Ignatius called out her name again and then rapidly crossed into the next section where the toilets were. Nellie, realizing this, nudged the side of my leg. With barely enough air to breathe, we listened to every step the nun took. As her footsteps grew fainter, I thought she was checking the fire escape or was in the right upper section where my bed was. Nellie gave me another nudge. When I brought my head out from under the blanket, she signaled for me to get out of the closet.

Gently letting go of the doors, both of us stealthily slipped out of the closet. Nellie adeptly latched the doors while I stood anxiously looking around me for Mother Ignatius to appear. Time was running out and I was petrified that we were surely going to get caught. With the dormitory door only steps away, Nellie and I tiptoed over to it. Without bringing attention to the noisy doorknob, Nellie turned it slowly and quietly. Once she opened it, we quietly and swiftly stepped outside onto the corridor. Closing the door deftly again, we both headed down the stairs outside the dormitory door.

Once we were at the bottom of the stairs, we made a dash to the door that led to the playground. Feeling elated by her daring challenge, Nellie calmly opened the door and both of us snuck outside to mingle amongst the other girls. While I stood beside them, I secretly prayed we hadn't been noticed. I felt sure Mother Ignatius or Mother Philomena was going to burst through one of the playground doors at any moment and nab Nellie and me. I hung around with the girls, before moving off to look at the flower beds. I pretended to inspect a white peace lily, while carefully keeping an eye on the playground doors.

With every minute that passed, the less tense I became. Before long, the bell rang for supper. Mother Philomena was in the refectory as I entered with Nellie and said nothing to us. Strangely, Mother Ignatius never confronted Nellie about her suspicions.

Later on that evening, Nellie and I talked about our daring feat, and how glad we were Mother Ignatius had never reported us. We felt sure she knew it was Nellie when she called out her name in the dormitory. We wondered if it was because she didn't have real proof it was Nellie she saw on the roof, or was it because she liked Nellie and often referred to her as, "Little Nellie of Holy God?"

The legend stated, Little Nellie was born in Waterford, on August 24, 1903. She was a revered child who dedicated her life to God after losing her mother to TB. Nellie's father, who was in the Royal Artillery, was unavailable when his wife died. With no one to take care of Nellie and her sister, they were sent to an orphanage in Co. Cork, run by the Good Shepherd Nuns. The nuns were harsh and cruel, but their scorn and irritation changed when Nellie told them she was having conversations with God after her mother contracted TB.

The 'Nellie' Mother Ignatius spoke of, was obedient and pious. The Nellie I knew at St. Dominick's, was good and kind, but also whimsical and mischievous.

Both of us were lucky to get away with our bold antics that day. Disobedient girls were often sent to The Reformatory School in Limerick for insubordination or other bad behavior. The Reformatory School was also run by the Good Shepherd Nuns but employed a far more draconian system of rules than St. Dominick's.

One evening, as I got ready for bed, an older girl named Mary asked me if I would do her a favor. She slept in the same section as me, and sneakily washed an underslip and a pair of lacy knickers someone had given her. Knowing I wasn't a bedwetter, she asked me to put her under slip between my bottom sheet and mattress so it would dry out while I slept on it.

When I woke up the following morning, my nightdress was damp. I was aware Mother Regina might see it, so immediately I pulled Mary's slip from under my bed sheet and gave it to her. After morning prayers, I stood in line waiting to wash at a sink. As I got closer to where Mother Regina stood, she noticed the damp circle on the back of my nightdress. Grabbing my upper arm, she dragged me back to my bed to check my sheets. Noting they were damp; she gave me a push against the metal bedframe that rammed against my bony spine. "What have we got here, another bedwetter? Take off that sheet and air your mattress. Make it quick. You haven't got all day," she said, without an ounce of empathy.

She deliberately shoved me against the bedframe to hurt me. I was so cross with her, I wanted to push her back, but controlled my anger. She already knew it was the first time I supposedly wet my bed. How was I supposed to explain to her that I hadn't? I certainly wasn't going to snitch on Mary because she would have been in worse trouble. Lining up for mass a half-hour later, Mary told me she was sorry she got me in trouble. She told the girls the true reason why my bed was wet. Her relating this to them, relieved me of further embarrassment and gave me peace of mind.

The Sacred Heart dormitory had frequent flea infestations. Once the bite marks were observed on any of our limbs, our sheets had to be removed and the folded seams of our mattresses checked for the fleas' hideouts. If a live flea was found, we were instructed to roll and squish it between our index finger and thumb, before drowning it in a cup of cold water. That way, we were told, they could not jump out and escape. Anytime I found a flea, I showed it to Mother Regina and felt like I had scored a victory.

Before making our beds, we had to shake DDT powder on our mattress to kill any fleas we might have missed. For the next two nights, the bottom blanket and sheet had to be rolled back and left untucked. That practice left our feet sticking out of the end of our beds when we stretched out. It was particularly uncomfortable in the winter months when the fleas were most active. I never liked sleeping with my feet poking out below the bedcovers because it made me restless for the whole night.

The winter months brought a host of miseries to the majority of us sleeping in the dormitory. We got head colds, the flu, tonsillitis, stomach viruses and other childhood ailments.

One night, I woke up feeling nauseated, and when I couldn't get to the toilet in time, I vomited on the floor beside my bed. For the rest of the night, other girls woke up with the same problem. I wanted to sleep after I got sick, but it was impossible. With so many of us being sick, I had to bury my head under the bed covers because of the vile stench of vomit wafting throughout the dormitory.

The next morning when Mother Regina came into the dormitory to get us up, she must have smelled the vomit, and told us to remain in our beds. After opening some windows, she left the dormitory. When she returned a few hours later, she arrived with four metal buckets, and four large spoons, and placed one in each section. As we began to recover, she had us get up and scoop our own vomit off the floor and put it in buckets. While cleaning up my own mess, I felt queasy, and retched with every scoop. But I was lucky I only had my own vomit to clean up. She had the eldest girl in each section clean up after the younger girls. Once the floor was clean, she allowed us to get dressed and go to the refectory for tea and bread.

Inside the refectory, we discovered some girls in the Big Dormitory had also been sick. A rumor spread that day that Mother Philomena and Mother Regina were so mad at us for vomiting, that they were going to serve vomit to us for supper.

That evening in the refectory, waiting for supper, we pensively watched and waited to see what Mother Colette was going to give us to eat. Soon, she came out of the kitchen carrying a tray of bowls. Inside each bowl was some grey curdled glop, topped with a half-stewed apple. When Mother Colette placed a bowl in front of me, I got a strange sour smell from the contents. The second she left our table, I pushed my bowl aside. Mother Philomena supervised us that evening. After we had all been served, she got out of her chair, and using her walking cane, she walked between the tables and saw none of us had eaten. Oddly, she never reprimanded any of us. This led most of us to believe the rumor to be true.

In the Recreation Room after supper, we stood in small groups, quietly discussing how disgusting the food looked. One girl said it was gruel, but we didn't agree with her because of the strange smell it had. We never heard what the curdled mush was in our bowls that evening.

As young children of the 1960s, there was no escape in catching our share of contagious diseases. Most of the diseases we contracted were brought back from the day schools we attended. If one of us came down with a contagious disease, within days, the rest of got it. We were familiar with measles, mumps, rubella, and chicken pox outbreaks. In the first two years of living at St. Dominick's, I contracted the measles, and rubella, but escaped getting the mumps.

Several times I developed styes in both my eyes. One morning when I woke up, my left eye was swollen shut. Overnight, a large stye had formed along my lower eyelid.

When I tried to open my eye, it throbbed with pain. Following my usual routine, I waited in line in the corridor to have a wash. Because I wasn't feeling well, I rested my head in my hands. Unbeknownst to me, the line had moved forward, and I held up the girls behind me. Ann Vee ambushed me from behind, and whacked me across the back. I hollered from her sudden attack.

Mother Regina was at the front monitoring the girls, and hearing me yelp, she walked back and pulled me to the end of the line. While telling me off, she noticed my eye, and looking at it suspiciously, she asked me to open it. When I couldn't, she ordered me back to bed. I remember how relieved I was being able to crawl back under the bedcovers again. For the next two days, I stayed in bed until the stye popped and the swelling went down.

Quite often in the winter months, we headed off to school feeling sick. If an Ursuline Nun observed our maladies, she immediately sent us back to the Good Shepherd's. When we returned to St. Dominick's, we were told to go to bed and the dormitory door was locked. A few times, I was alone in the dormitory recovering. Once I felt better, I got bored. Sometimes, I got up and peeped through the dormitory door keyhole. The door faced a long wooden corridor, and I was able to see the bottom half of any person walking along the corridor. If it was the swaying of a nun's habit I saw, I quickly climbed back into my bed in case the nun was coming into the dormitory.

The Refectory was directly under the Sacred Heart Dormitory. I could always tell when the schoolgirls returned for lunch. After The Grace Before Meals prayer was said, the sound of dragging chairs on the tiled floor echoed in the dormitory. This also meant it was time for me to get my lunch. A kitchen helper usually brought me my lunch. A few times, I was forgotten and had to wait until suppertime to eat.

When more than one of us were out of school sick, mealtimes were always prompt. The food arrived on wooden trays, and I enjoyed this special attention we got. It was fun recovering from an illness with other girls in the dormitory.

Once we were better, we sat on each other's beds and chatted. However, we remained vigilant for the slightest sound, and took turns peeking through the keyhole to make sure we weren't caught. At the first sound of a rattle of the dormitory door, we scampered back to our own beds.

On the morning I was due to make my Confirmation, I woke up and discovered I was covered head to toe with an angry looking red rash. When Mother Regina observed this, she sent me back to bed. Later that morning, another nun I hadn't seen before, came to inspect my rash. After taking my temperature and carefully examining me, she diagnosed me with scarlet fever and said I had to go into isolation.

For the next month, I was kept isolated in the upper left section, where my bed was tucked in a corner outside the toilets. I became tremendously bored, especially in the daytime, when I was alone.

While I was recovering, two middle-aged maintenance men, named Tom and Terry, came to the dormitory to repair a broken sash window. From my bed, I watched them busily working on the chord while Mother Regina supervised them. As soon as she stepped away, Tom, the older of the two, turned from the window to chat to me. He told me that he had a daughter about my age and asked me if I had a mammy. I told him my mother died when I was four. Then he went silent, and I saw him bless himself, before he continued doing his work.

At the time, I thought it odd that he blessed himself. I believe both men observed many unhappy girls both at St.

Dominick's and St. Mary's, while doing janitorial work at the Good Shepherd Convent. It must have pained them having to compare our lives to the lives of their own children growing up under very different circumstances.

Shortly after I recovered from the scarlet fever, I was moved to the 'Big Girl's' dormitory. I was disappointed that I never got to make my Confirmation with my class that year and had to wait another year before making it. The sacrament of Confirmation signaled a passage from childhood to teenagehood. It was also a time when many of the girls started their menstrual flow. Although I had reached my teen years, I still had to wait several more years before I fell into that category.

*Picture of the window I climbed out is at a right angle and above the kitchen below.*

## Chapter Fourteen

# THE BIG GIRL'S DORMITORY

The Big Girl's Dormitory was on the third floor, with the same pastel-colored sections as The Sacred Heart Dormitory. The only difference was this dormitory had six sections instead of four. Each section had six metal framed beds that lined up in rows of two. Three toilets were situated in a small room off the middle section on the right-hand side. The eldest girls slept in two beds at the top of the section, and the youngest slept in the lower two beds. In my first year there, I was given a bed in the left lower section inside the entry door. I never liked sleeping in the two lower sections because they were wide open and were without paneling. The other four sections had far more privacy. Getting dressed in the mornings and evenings, Mother Philomena sat on a chair in the right section, facing the section I slept in.

Mother Philomena's cell (bedroom) was outside the dormitory door, facing the stairs. Her cell window looked out over the hand sinks. It was mid-sized and square and had a white curtain that hung on the inside of the window. After Mother Philomena left the dormitory in the evenings, I often saw her shadow moving about in her cell from the glow of her bedroom light. Sometimes, the curtain moved, and she peeked out onto the dormitory before switching out her bedroom light.

The first thing I heard at seven each morning was the clinking sound of a metal key turning inside the dormitory door. Those of us who slept in the lower sections were the first to be roused from our slumber. Once the door was unlatched, Mother Philomena swept into the dormitory clapping her hands and used her high-pitched voice to awaken us.

"Wake up. Wake up. *Tis* time to get up," she shouted, banging on the glass panels with her cane, while limping up and down the long, polished corridor.

A chorus of muffled groaning echoed through the confines of the dormitory as her clapping and bellowing shook us awake. It was always a paralyzing struggle for me to suddenly open my eyes and climb out of my bed. However, by the time she walked back down the corridor, I was up, and, kneeling by my bed, waiting for her to start the morning prayer.

One girl in the upper section found it very hard to get out of bed. Hearing Mother Philomena's voice prompted her to sink deeper under her bedcovers. This irritated Mother Philomena. She entered her section, stripped off the covers, and waited for her to get out of bed.

After morning prayer, we lined up with our face towels and wash bags, waiting for an available sink. Our washbags were equipped with a facecloth, a toothbrush, and a small tube of Colgate toothpaste. Using toothpaste to brush our teeth was a novelty. Quite often, I ran out, or my toothbrush went missing. When that happened, I used my forefinger to clean my teeth with the beige carbolic soap placed on the hand sinks.

Most of the girls in the teenage dormitory had already started their monthly periods. Sometimes, girls younger than me woke up in a panic when they discovered they had blood on their sheets.

After prayers one morning, a girl approached Mother Philomena with blood on the back of her nightdress. I felt sure she was going to be in trouble. When she showed Mother Philomena, I was surprised when she called for an older girl to take care of her. The older girl supplied the girl with a sanitary belt and several white sanitary towels.

Every week a large white bag of freshly laundered terry toweling sanitary pads were delivered to the teenage dormitory from the Magdalene Laundry. Girls expecting to have their periods were allowed fifteen towels for the five days of their cycle. They wore them by folding the towels in doubles or thirds and used a waist belt with a metal clip at the front and back, to hold the towel in place. Most of the towels were covered in old bloodstains and were as stiff as a board. The older girls, more familiar with the set-up, searched the bag looking for newer and softer towels. Quite often the girls complained of having stomach cramps on the first day of their cycle. Others fainted in the church pews. Being a very late bloomer, I never had to experience wearing those sanitary towels, nor did I have to suffer from the period pains some girls had to endure.

As young teenagers, we were cognizant of our rapidly changing physiques. We fussed more about our hair and how we looked. Some girls spent longer than usual preening in front of the horizontal mirror above the sinks. They back-combed their hair to look fashionably taller and pinched their cheeks to give them a rosy glow. Others were particular about their budding bust-line. They squeezed the cups of their bras to exaggerate their busts and brought them to an attractive line behind their clothing. I admired and envied those girls because they looked so mature and were far more developed than me. At fifteen, I was still flat-chested and nowhere near ready to wear a bra. I yearned to know what it was like to wear one, believing it was something mysterious and sensual.

One day that desire grew stronger. Lying in bed that night after the lights were turned off, I decided to try on another girl's bra when I figured she was asleep. The girl was named Una. I slept in her section and my bed was directly below hers. Getting ready for bed that evening, I watched Una lay her clothes on the chair at the end of her bed, and carefully noted where she put her bra.

After the lights were turned off, I waited a while to ensure she and the other girls in my section were asleep. Then I stretched my hand through the wrought iron bars at the head of my bed to reach for her chair. Tapping her clothes lightly, I poked around in search of her bra. Once I found it, I sneakily pulled it back through the rungs and slipped it under my bedcovers. I removed my nightdress and pushed it aside. Lying flat on my back, I placed Una's bra over my flat chest. Then I took the two sides and stretched them behind my back. At first, I struggled to clasp the hooks and eyes together. When they were finally hooked, I was elated. I tenderly brushed my hand over the fabric of the bra cups, but they were empty and flat. I waited to experience that unique sensation I thought would come with wearing a bra, but it never happened. When my experiment was over, I quickly removed Una's bra and quietly returned it under her clothing.

The following morning, I surreptitiously watched her getting dressed under her nightdress. When she lifted her bra off the chair, I hoped she didn't notice that it had been tampered with. When she was finally dressed in her school uniform, I felt relieved, for I knew my secret was safe.

When I returned to St. Dominick's after one summer's break, I was given a different bed in the upper right section of the dormitory. As much as I disliked being back at St. Dominick's, I was happy to secure a bed in that section. This was also the section where my friend, Breda, slept. However, my time there was short-lived, because when I left for a few weeks the following summer, Breda was given my bed. On my return, I was moved back to the lower section on the right-side. I was very disappointed that I was once again sleeping in one of the lower sections and felt like I had been demoted.

A few months later, around two in the morning, all of us were awakened by a piercing shriek. Seconds lapsed before there was a second scream. The shrieking echoed from a girl in one of the two upper sections. Mother Philomena, hearing the disturbance, flung open her cell window wanting to know what was happening.

Moments later, there was another scream, "It's a burglar. It's a burglar," a girl hollered.

Mother Philomena yelled from her cell window for someone to turn on the dormitory lights. I sat up in my bed, shaken and confused. When the lights came on, I saw Mother Philomena. She had her head poking through her cell window and was wearing a white bonnet.

Then, the sound of several feet came galloping down the dorm corridor. I saw Breda leading the way followed by three girls from her section. She stood by my bed, trembling and sobbing, saying there was a burglar in her section.

Mother Philomena urgently rushed into the dormitory. She had changed into her veil and began questioning the girls. Through tearful eyes, Breda told her she was disturbed from her sleep when she felt someone tapping her shoulder.

"I opened my eyes and saw a man looking down at me. He whispered for me to be quiet. I screamed with fright, and he then put his hand over my mouth. I tried biting his hand, but he pulled it away. When I screamed a second time, he ran away from me and climbed out the window," she said.

Mother Philomena turned on her heel and headed up the corridor to confirm Breda's story. Breda and the girls, still trembling, held onto each other, and followed her up the corridor.

Inside the section, Mother Philomena found the window beside the fire escape wide open. The rope pulley used to open the window was wrapped around one of the lifting hooks. Mother Philomena guessed that the man climbed in the window with plans to kidnap Breda.

It was now around two-thirty. Mother Philomena, comprehending the reality of what happened, told Breda and the girls to remove the blankets and pillows from their beds and take them down to sleep on the floor of the two lower sections. Breda was still disturbed by the incident and began weeping loudly. After removing her bedding, she dropped her blanket and pillow on the floor beside my bed. She told Mother Philomena she was frightened the man might come back and grab her if she was on the floor by herself and asked her if I could sleep on the floor with her. With Mother Philomena's permission, I removed my own blanket and pillow, and laid down beside her.

Once we were settled, Mother Philomena announced she was leaving the lights on in the dormitory, then she headed back to her cell. For the remainder of the night, none of us slept, because we were too hyped-up and scared. Breda continually repeated the story of her scary experience to the girls in our section. She was truly traumatized, and jumped and screamed at every sound she heard, which petrified us more. The fear was strong enough that it prevented most of us from going to the toilet. The dark night, and the uncertainty of where the 'Boodie Man' was hiding, forced us to wait until daybreak.

Laying beside Breda, it dawned on me how it might have been me the man was trying to kidnap. If I had been given back the bed that Breda now slept in, he most certainly would have tried to kidnap me.

The window the intruder climbed through was closer to another girl's bed than Breda's, yet, he hadn't disturbed that girl. She only woke up when she heard Breda screaming. In her sleepy state, she watched the man jump up on the windowsill beside her bed and climb out the window. Why he hadn't tried to kidnap that girl, instead of Breda, was a mystery.

The following day, the girls in the Big Girl's Dormitory were kept out of school. As we descended the stairs for breakfast, we saw a crowd of people gathered outside the walls of the convent on the road opposite College Street. Watching us making our decent, they looked up at the large window facing the stairs and began pointing. Word about the kidnapper at St. Dominick's spread like wildfire in the local community. People were curious to learn who it was and if it might be someone they knew.

The Gardai arrived early to initiate a full investigation. Breda and the girls in her section were interviewed. They took photographs and fingerprints around the window where the man made his escape. For the rest of the day, we moped around in small groups, tired and shook up from a lack of sleep. The

'Boodie Man' had terrified all of us and we didn't dare walk anywhere alone.

Days later, when I returned from school, I heard one of the girls had been escorted off the convent grounds. I was shocked when I heard who it was. Apparently, she was part of the reason for the break-in. Her name was Dettie. She was timid and pretty and was one of the most unlikely of girls to be accused of such an unsettling incident.

Rumor had it that Dettie befriended a teen boy she met on route to her school. Her bed was in the midsection of the dormitory, and apparently, she had no idea this boy was attempting to steal her away that night. Perhaps he took pity on her when she told him about her life at the Good Shepherd Convent and wanted to rescue her from it. However, that night, the boy climbed in the window, entered the wrong section, and tried to kidnap the wrong girl.

We heard Dettie was sent to a Reformatory School in Limerick. I was sad when she left. I always knew Dettie to be quiet and naïve, and found it hard to believe that it was her fault.

It took several weeks before dormitory life returned to its normal routine. Some girls woke up having nightmares; others took to sleepwalking up the corridor at night. The girls who slept in the two top sections were allowed to sleep on their mattresses and bedding in the lower sections. Even Mother Philomena softened and continued to leave the lights on in the dormitory all night. I took the liberty of keeping my mattress on the floor beside Breda's. Those of us who hadn't seen the 'Boodie Man,' conjured up images of a huge man with big hairy hands and missing teeth. In our minds, we believed he could snatch us when we least expected it. But this was merely a young boy who was truly infatuated with a young girl.

Sadly, after leaving St. Dominick's, I lost touch with Breda. I believe if I hadn't been moved to the lower section that year, and the intruder tried to kidnap me, it would have surely affected my mental health.

Weeks after that episode, I suddenly woke when I heard the floorboards behind my bed creak. Laying perfectly still, my stomach was knotted in fear, and I quietly snuck deeper under my bedcovers. The footsteps got closer and circled around my bed. Then, the floorboards at the bottom of my bed creaked. They appeared to pause there, until they moved off and fully disappeared. I remained under the covers wide awake, for the rest of the night. Although I was well under the bedcovers, I longed for the daylight and the sound of the dormitory key twisting in the knob of the dormitory door.

When I heard a girl in my section getting out of her bed to use the toilet, I slowly sidled out from under my covers. Daylight had broken and the sun was streaming through the window. As the girl climbed back into her bed, I sat up and asked her if she heard footsteps during the night. She told me she hadn't heard anything because, she said, she was sound asleep. Knowing it wasn't a figment of my imagination, I guessed one of the nuns was sent to the dormitory to check on our safety. Thankfully, I never heard any creaking of the floorboards or footsteps after that night.

Years after I left St. Dominick's and journeyed through life, I found it hard to sleep in a room alone. Before climbing into bed at night, I checked under my bed and in my wardrobe, so I could enjoy a safe night's sleep.

## Chapter Fifteen

# THE URSULINE SCHOOL

From the first day I arrived at St. Dominick's, Mother Teresa had already decided on the school I was to attend. She divided the girls into three different groups and sent them out to three different schools. She chose the The Ursuline Convent primary school for me. The other groups were sent to either The Saint John of God's, or The Sisters of Charity. All three schools were located in Waterford City.

The Ursuline Convent in Ballytruckle is on the outskirts of Waterford City. The school was also referred to as St. Ursula's, and consisted of two separate buildings. One building was for educating girls ages four (high babies) to twelve years. The second building, situated on the same spacious grounds, was St. Ann's Secondary School. After breakfast, each school day, all three groups formed separate lines and headed down a long pathway that led outside the large wooden gates of the Good Shepherd Convent.

The walking distance from the Good Shepherd Convent to The Ursuline School was about a mile, and Mrs. Kenny was our school escort. She lived in a row house in nearby Poleberry, close to the Good Shepherd Convent. She was short and chubby with bowlegs and kept her short, wavy, black hair tied back with a large hair grip. Her two front teeth were yellow and gapped and displayed a furry appearance when she smiled. Because of the wide gap in her teeth, she constantly spat when she spoke. This caused her to dribble excessively, and she had to use her handkerchief to mop it up.

Every morning before nine o'clock, our group of fourteen set off for school with satchels on our backs. Mrs. Kenny held the youngest girls' hands and walked at the back of the group while keeping a keen eye on the rest of us. If we strayed too far ahead of the group, she shouted for us to come back and stick together.

Mrs. Kenny was nice to all of us. Returning to the Good Shepherd's after school, she often stopped at her house and gave us hard boiled sweets from the large glass jar she kept on her kitchen counter. By the time we reentered the gates of the Shepherd Convent, all evidence of her treats were well gone.

Sometimes, I walked with her at the back to keep her company. I learned early on that I could never walk too close to her because she bumped into me. She had an unusual gait because of her bowed legs. This caused her to waddle from side to side, and her coat to swish and sway around the calves of her legs. Because she walked on the outsides of her black laced shoes, the heels were worn down to scarcely nothing.

On our journey to school, curious locals often stared at us and teenaged boys bumped into some of the girls as they took the same path to school. It was clear that a few of them had crushes on certain girls. One January morning, the snow was coming down heavily and lay thick on the ground. The boys, knowing our school route, waited to ambush us and launched a volley of snowballs at us. Some of the girls made snowballs and threw a few back at them. Mrs. Kenny, losing control of our group, gave chase to them with her bandy legs.

Arriving on the grounds of the Ursuline, our group split up, and Mrs. Kenny left. The younger girls headed for the primary school building, and the older girls to the secondary school. Both buildings had cloakrooms as you entered. Before going to our classrooms we were required to hang up our coats and change out of our day shoes and into our indoor shoes.

The Ursuline Nuns were less rigid than the nuns I lived with, although they followed the same religious principles. They were addressed as 'Sister' and wore entirely different habits than the Good Shepherd Nuns. Their habits were dark grey with less layering and were ankle length. The sleeves were long and fitted and a black leather belt was worn around the waist. A stiff white collar rested at the neckline and a small wooden cross hung from a brown string, and sat at the mid-chest. On their heads they wore a shoulder-length black veil with a blue and white trim that encircled the veil like a headband. Their hair was kept hidden under the veil. Close to the time I was leaving, they began to show more hair on their foreheads. Without a doubt, The Ursuline Nuns had a much easier time getting dressed in the morning, because of the simpler habits they wore.

The uniform I wore at primary school had a different style and color than the uniform I wore in secondary school. This color was royal blue. It had a gymslip with four large pleats at the front and back, a royal blue wool cardigan, a royal blue waist sash and necktie, a white button-down shirt, beige knee-hi socks, and brown lace-up shoes.

The teachers in primary school were mostly nuns, except for two lay teachers. The lay teachers wore modest clothing under an open black gown.

About twenty girls were in my class and all of them were day pupils except for me after my friend Marian left. Initially, we were the only two girls in the class from Good Shepherd's. After she was gone, I felt like an absolute outsider. Those feelings were strongest when the day pupils' parents dropped their daughters off for school and picked them up when school ended.

I had my own wooden desk where I stored my books in a compartment under a heavy lid. The desk had an inkwell on the upper right corner, where a small white ceramic inkpot was placed. Every Monday morning the teacher filled the inkpot with ink. The top of the inkwell had a rectangular metal sliding plate that protected the ink from drying out. At the end of the school day, it was our job to ensure the slide was pushed over the top of the inkwell. The ink stayed in the holder until Friday afternoon. Then any remaining ink was emptied into a large blue jar. Each pupil had to rinse and wipe their own inkpots before putting them back in the inkwell where they remained over the weekend.

Sister Rosario was my First-Class teacher. She taught the class how to write in cursive using a pen and nib. Before she began, she handed each of us a sheet of lined paper, a square of blotting paper, and a wooden stick with a nib attached. Then she asked us to pick up our pens in our right hands and copy the large cursive letters she had written on the blackboard in between the lines of the paper. Using our left hands, we placed the blotting paper over the letters to soak up any excess ink.

The moment I first used a pen and nib, I knew I was left-handed. Following the nun's orders, I picked the pen up in my right hand, but automatically switched it to my left hand. Sister Rosario usually walked around the classroom observing our work. When she saw me writing with my left hand, she had me switch the pen to my right hand.

"You must follow my instructions, dear. Watch what the other girls are doing, and use your right hand to write your letters," she said.

Using my right hand was a challenge. I instinctively knew I should have been using my left hand.

Mrs. Cox was one of the lay teachers who taught the fourth class. Besides teaching elementary level education, she also taught Irish (Gaelic). Before she began her class, she had all of the class address our names to her in Irish. *"Cad is ainm duit?"* (What is your name)? The same applied when any of us needed to go to the toilet. But first, we had to raise our right hands in a salutary style, while seated at our desks, and then find the correct words in Irish, to ask: *"An feidir liom dul amach go dti an leithreas le do thoil."* By the time the words were phrased in the right context, the desire to go to the toilet would often pass. I was ambidextrous by the time I started her class, and even forced myself to use a scissors and pick up my eating utensils with my right hand.

Out of the blue one day, I relapsed, and Mrs. Cox caught me. She was teaching the class about the four seasons of the year and had us write them down in our jotters. Without thinking, I picked up my pencil and began writing with my left hand. When Mrs. Cox saw me, she rapped me on the knuckles and told me to put my pencil in the correct hand to write. After that, I perfected my ability to only use my right hand when writing.

The other lay teacher was younger and wore more fashionable clothes than Mrs. Cox. She was very pretty with big brown eyes, and wore make-up. In the warmer months, she liked wearing colorful pretty skirts and blouses. Because of her short stature, her pointy black stiletto heels gave her extra height, especially when she stood on the dais to teach. I often dreamt of being a teacher like her and to be able to wear the same fashionable clothing.

Well before I entered fifth grade class, I heard about the notorious nun who made disobedient pupils wear a dunce's hat. She occasionally used her ruler to discipline us, but she got better results when she made us stand in the corner of the classroom wearing a dunce's hat.

She kept the dunce's hat on a table in the corner of her classroom. It was tall, white, and conical with a long, pointed tip. The front of the hat had a large letter D written in bold black. The nun had us wear the hat for several minor offenses. The unfortunate pupil was made a victim of ridicule. Some girls wore it more often than others.

When forgetting to hand in my homework to her one day, she called me to the front of the class and had me wear the dunce's hat. When I placed it on my head, it was too big for me and slipped off my forehead and fell onto my nose. Standing in the far corner of the room, I could hear the girls snickering and felt my face turn beet red. Once my time was up in the corner, she allowed me to remove the hat and reminded me not to forget to bring in my homework when it was due.

The fear and shame most of us felt about wearing the dunce's hat at the beginning of the school year changed by the end. By then, most of the class had worn it, making it an honor, not a punishment.

We were given an hour's break for lunch each day. Most of the day pupils had lunch at the school canteen, while all the Good Shepherd girls had to return to St. Dominick's to have lunch.

One afternoon when I was in sixth class, I returned to the Ursulines ten minutes early. I walked over to two girls from my class who were playing a game of marbles. They knew I liked playing the game at '*elevenses*,' and asked me to join them. They had already eaten lunch in the small canteen at the rear of the playground, and with some extra time to spare before classes, they decided to play a few games.

They used the small gutter with a down spout at the side of the building to roll the marble into. When one of the girls rolled the large marble, called a *Taw*, it bounced off the concrete gutter and spun into a small grassy patch near the canteen. Because it was my turn to play next, I immediately jumped up to fetch the marble. As I walked on the grass to look for it, I noticed how lumpy the tufts were, making it hard to see where the marble landed.

The girls were eager to continue playing and joined me to search for the marble.

A misty rain began to fall, and one girl suggested we should give up. Just as I was heading back to the playground, I spotted a bright, shiny object. I bent down to pick it up, and discovered it was a two-shilling Irish coin called a Florin. The girls dashed over when they saw me pick it up. The marble game was soon forgotten, and we began looking for more coins. Before long, the three of us were on our knees pulling at the tufts of grass, and we found numerous other coins buried in the soil. At first it was hard to see what type of coins they were because they were covered with mud. I let the rain fall on mine, and after scraping the mud away, I saw that most of them were shiny Irish pennies, called Pingins. We were so thrilled with our find; we lost all sense of time. In our excitement, we talked about what we were going buy with the money on our Confirmation Day.

When we couldn't find any more coins, we counted what we had. I counted seven shiny Pingins and one Florin.

We got nervous when we noticed the playground was empty and decided to go to the classroom. Clutching our coins, we ran across the playground, and saw a nun walking towards us. She had a rainhat over her black veil and wasn't at all happy to see us on the playground in the rain.

"What are you lot doing out there in the rain. You are supposed to be in the classroom."

"Sister, look at what we found in the grass," one of the girls piped up while showing her a handful of muddy coins.

Glimpsing them, the nun's eyes widened, and her face tensed.

"That's not your money. That's called stealing. Hand me that money now," she demanded.

She cupped her hands as we handed over the money to her. Holding the money, she pushed the playground door with her foot to open it. Inside the hallway, she told us to follow her, and promptly marched us into the head nun's office. The head nun was sitting behind her desk when we got there. She had a look of shock on her face when she saw how dirty and wet we were. Standing in front of her, I was terrified. I felt sure she was going to report me to Mother Philomena.

Placing the coins on the head nun's desk, the nun who took us to her, gave her a run down on where she found us and the reason she confiscated the coins from us. The head nun quizzed each of us individually about how we came upon the coins. After all of us repeated the same story to her, she told us to never take anything that doesn't belong to us. She made each of us apologize for what we had done. Then, she sent us to the bathroom to wash our hands before we returned to the classroom.

For the rest of that day, and days later, I lived on my nerves waiting for Mother Philomena to call me into her office to punish me. Thankfully, the Ursuline Nun never reported me to Mother Philomena. The Ursuline Nuns were aware who the girls from the Good Shepherd Convent were, and I believe that's why she never reported me.

I was months away from starting secondary school, and glad my flow of education wasn't disrupted by what I had done.

## Chapter Sixteen

# ST. ANN'S SECONDARY SCHOOL

I was thirteen when I entered St. Ann's secondary school, a part of The Ursuline School. St. Ann's was later renamed St. Angela's.

All our classes began and ended in prayer. Throughout the day we had a rotation of nuns and lay teachers teaching different subjects each lasting one hour, with one class dedicated solely to religious education.

In secondary school, I was not only amongst day pupils, but also with Ursuline boarders. The boarders were easy to identify because of their distinguishable uniforms. They wore bright red cardigans, grey pleated skirts, white button-down shirts, red neckties, beige knee-hi socks, and brown shoes. In contrast, day pupils wore maroon pleated skirts, pale blue button-down shirts, maroon ties, and cardigans, as well as beige knee-hi socks, and brown shoes. A few years later, the day pupils' uniform changed to look the same as the boarders. Both uniform styles had blazers with the school crest attached to the pocket. They were worn during cold weather or on special school occasions.

Classes were mostly held in the main building, but as the school's enrollment increased, newly constructed prefab buildings were installed on the same grounds as the school. The classrooms were divided into four sections, A, B, C, D. The boarders were assigned to classrooms A and B along with a handful of day pupils. All remaining pupils sat in classrooms C and D. As an outsider from the Good Shepherd's, I was automatically placed in classroom D. Being the only girl in the class from the Good Shepherd's, I felt awkward and out of place amongst the day pupils and boarders.

In my first year at St. Ann's, I had a lay teacher named Mrs. Bryan. She taught Irish (Gaelic). As much as I liked her, I didn't feel she did her best in preparing us for the necessary Gaelic to pass exams. She had a happy marriage and spent most of her time talking about her husband and children. The good part was, she never got angry with the class and barely gave us any homework to do.

Sister Clotilde was my English teacher. Although she was quite elderly, she was a superb teacher. She had a special way of engaging the class and encouraging us to read. She generally dedicated the last fifteen minutes of her class to reading part of a classic story from one of the volumes of books she kept on a shelf behind her.

Her love of stories instilled a passion in me for books. She recognized early on how much I enjoyed them and frequently praised me when handing out class results. Her English class was one of my favorite subjects.

Sister Paul was another one of my English teachers. She was very strict, and her teaching style was different than Sister Clotilde's. If a pupil disturbed her while she spoke, she made her stand outside the classroom door. She never smiled and most of us were scared by the way she stared at us from the top of her oversized eyeglasses. She constantly criticized my handwriting, saying it was too *scrawly* for her to read. A few times she had me rewrite my compositions before she accepted them.

"Your penmanship is not acceptable. It's far too mature for someone of your age. Slow down when you write to make it more legible for me to read."

Despite her intolerance of any form of disobedience, I believe she helped me focus on my studies and improve my handwriting.

I began learning Spanish in my first year, but the following year, Spanish was replaced with French. Our French teacher was a young petite nun. She had a large overbite that caused her to spit and whistle when she spoke French. This made it difficult to learn the language because of the way she mispronounced the words. Being young teens, this made us giggle. She was very self-conscious of her problem, and blushed when some of the girls requested she repeat herself.

One day in her class, I witnessed an incident that led me to discover that nuns were mortal beings. That revelation came when the French nun fell off the chair behind the dais. She sprawled out on the floor in an unladylike manner. Her veil flew off her head, in the process, showing her shorn hair. Thankfully, she wasn't hurt, but it was embarrassing for her to say the least. Feeling ashamed, she stood up, replaced her veil, and left the classroom.

Soon the head nun came to investigate what caused the nun to fall. She presumed her fall was a result of a class pupil loosening one of the chair legs. She wanted to know who had been around the dais and chair between classes. I raised my hand because I had hung around the dais with two other girls. I was taken out of the class with the other two girls. After proclaiming my innocence, I was allowed back into the classroom. One of the girls I had been with turned out to be the culprit and was expelled from the Ursuline School.

The French teacher was very sweet and certainly didn't deserve to have her dignity stripped in such a manner, and especially in front of a classroom of teenage girls. Justice would have truly been served if it had happened to one of the heartless Good Shepherd Nuns.

The domestic science teacher taught sewing and cooking. On the days she gave cookery classes, she requested that all pupils bring in their own supplies. Before the end of class, she handed out a list of ingredients to bring to our next cooking class. I enjoyed her cookery classes, but cringed when I ended up being the only pupil in the class without the required ingredients.

Every time I was given a list of ingredients, I handed it to Mother Philomena well in advance of my next class. Once, she gave me cake flour to bring to class, but that was only one ingredient along with a list of others. In the beginning, I thought Mother Philomena had simply forgotten to give them to me, but when she continued overlooking my requests, I knew she had no intention of supplying them. On the days

I was due to bring the ingredients to school, I was tempted to approach Mother Philomena, but cowered out for fear of landing myself in trouble for being so forward.

At the school kitchen, I felt humiliated standing with my classmates without the required ingredients. The domestic science nun understood my situation and had me pair up with other girls to share their supplies. In one of her classes, she brought in her own supply of Seville oranges. That day she showed us how to make a batch of marmalade jam. After cutting the peel into thin strips she had us use lots of sugar to remove the bitterness from the orange. When the jam making was completed, she had us all sample it, and it was delicious.

Somehow, when it came to my sewing class, Mother Philomena allowed me to have the required material I needed. When I gave her that list, she told me to go to Mother Regina for my supplies. Mother Regina worked in the sewing room at St. Dominick's and had lots of extra scraps of fabric. She gave me enough to make both a skirt and an apron. Without completing both items, I would have failed my domestic science class. By the end of the school year, I had hand sewn a colorful apron and summer skirt with a zipper and buttons. I felt proud showing them off to the girls at St. Dominick's.

Mrs. Sullivan was a lay teacher and taught third-year geography. I was fourteen when she arrived in the classroom one day carrying a cactus plant. She broke off a piece of the cactus leaf, gave it a squeeze and showed the class the juicy liquid it held inside. She explained how a cactus plant can survive in the desert with little or no rain. Suddenly, her lesson somehow morphed into her telling the class about the facts of life. "Do any of us know the difference between a cow and a bull? A hen and a rooster? A mammy and a daddy?"

Most of us easily related to farm animals because of our proximity to the countryside. Listening to her, I was puzzled as to why she was connecting people to farm animals. "All of us in this classroom are of the female sex. Most of you have female relatives. Your mothers, sisters, aunts, and grandmothers are all female. The opposite to the female sex is the male. Here you have your fathers, brothers, uncles, and grandfathers. Most of you know the male anatomy is very different from the female anatomy. If it wasn't for your mothers and fathers, you wouldn't be sitting here today. It's our mothers and fathers who created us all, with the help of God."

Then she paused to ask the class if we understood what she was saying. When none of us answered, she continued talking. "Two important functions must happen between a male and female for God's creation of new life to take place. Now, raise your hands those of you who have started your monthly periods."

I was sitting in the front row of her class, stunned when she asked this question. I slowly looked around and saw most of the class had raised their hands. Feeling self-conscious, I put my head down. While continuing to explain the role of a mother and father from conception to birth, the class became curiously silent.

"First, the female must release an egg from her ovaries. The egg is then fertilized by the male sperm inside the female's body. A new life will grow inside the womb of the female body. After nine months, a baby is born. Now that's how your mothers and fathers created all of you," she said.

When she finished speaking you could hear a pin drop in the classroom. Some of the girls in my class had a fair knowledge about the facts of life. A handful were as green as I was and were only learning about them for the first time. The subject of sex was never mentioned around the Good Shepherd nuns, and learning about it from Mrs. Sullivan, caused me to shyly blush.

After her class ended, we had a short break. I stood close to my desk with a small group of girls and listened to what they had to say about Mrs. Sullivan's lecture. One streetwise day girl butted in, saying she already knew all about having babies and girls having their periods.

"My mammy told me not to go near any boys because they'll only get me in trouble. See, I have my periods now," she said, pointing to her tiny breasts.

As green as I was at fourteen, I knew what monthly periods were. Hearing what she said made all of us burst out laughing. She got angry with us and fired back directly at me.

"Sure, what would you know about anything? Your chest is as flat as a pancake," she said, walking away from me.

What she said hurt. One of the girls, seeing how embarrassed I was, told me not to mind what she said. "That one thinks she knows it all."

The Ursuline Nuns were very clever in assigning a lay teacher to talk to the class about the facts of life. They had a greater understanding of teenage girls and the dangers they might face if they found themselves pregnant. Ironically, the Good Shepherd Nuns were well-versed in fallen women, yet they never spoke or educated any of us on the facts of life. The word, 'sex' was an unspoken word in our vocabulary.

In math class, I especially liked solving algebra problems, but struggled with other math subjects. One reason I found it difficult to grasp certain math concepts was because I never had any money to spend. To further complicate matters, the old Irish monetary system of half-crowns, shillings, and farthings was preparing for the changeover to decimalization in 1971. The currency conversions coincidently fell in line with the introduction of modern math. Then there was geometry, logarithms, fractions, and long division. Geometry was like another language to me, especially when trying to figure out the Pythagoras theorem.

Each year, St. Ann's School chose a day in early summer for the secondary school girls to participate in Field Day. The event involved a competition where pupils performed in long jumps, running with an egg on a spoon, rounders, sack races, and other events.

While the event took place, we were all required to take turns working at the concession stand. We sold packaged sweets, crisps, Lucozade, fizzy orange, lemonade, and confections. One pupil had the position of handing out the concessions, while the other pupil collected money and made change.

When it was my turn to help, I had no problem handing out the concessions, but froze when I had to make change for them. Money terrified me because I wasn't used to handling it. I dodged dealing with the money by asking another girl to take it.

But that trick ended one year when the nun in charge of assigning our roles caught me. She was supervising the queues when she noticed I wasn't taking the money. She told me off for not following her schedule. "It's imperative you all know how to make change before leaving school," she said.

When I took money from the next pupil in line, the nun stood beside me. She knew I was nervous about making change and had me mentally add up the cost of the goods I was selling, and subtract from the amount of money I was given. Luckily, the concessions were very cheap and the coins I was handed only required making small change. I know that nun helped me to quell my fear of handling other people's money.

Sister Magdalene was our chorus teacher. At three o'clock on Mondays, the class entered the music hall, and she lined us up on the stairs according to our vocal ranges. She had a good knowledge of how our voices sounded from the first day of class. She put me in the high C range because I was able to hit the high notes. Standing in the back row, she frequently looked up and signaled for me to sing louder.

In spring each year, Sister Magdalene put on a themed musical production for the school. She usually picked the boarders for the lead roles, with only a handful of day pupils for smaller parts.

The most memorable musical she staged was *The Student Prince*. For the role of the prince, she chose a pretty blonde boarder. Leading up to the production, there was great excitement in the school where numerous rehearsals were held daily. The show was performed in the music hall for two evenings.

I joined my class to watch the performance on one of those evenings. While waiting for the curtain to go up, we were giddy with excitement. The first person performing when the curtain went up was the girl playing the role of the prince. She was barely recognizable in her regal attire and was made up to look like a boy. Her long hair was neatly tucked under a navy-blue pillbox hat and secured under her chin with a leather clasp. She wore a decorative double-breasted red jacket with gold buttons and epaulettes. Her navy pants had gold and silver stripes that ran down the sides of both pant legs.

She acted and sang her part perfectly, and left the audience spellbound. When the play ended, I walked with a group from my class to congratulate her on a job well done. One day pupil who was not too keen on the boarder refused to acknowledge her presence. Instead, she looked directly at her, and spitefully told her, and those around her, that we were all acting like a bunch of lesbians. Taken aback by the girl's apparent rudeness, one of the girls in the group asked her to explain what she meant. Like me, she didn't understand her remark.

"All a ye should be ashamed of yourselves the way ye were fawning all over her. She's a girl and you're all acting like ye are madly in love with her," she said.

I had never heard of the word lesbian before. The boarder, understandably upset, turned on her heel and moved off from us, while the nasty girl walked toward the door. The day pupil who confronted the girl's remarks, vented her anger with her in a jovial manner. "She's only jealous because she didn't get picked to play the part. Sure, all of us love the lads, don't we girls?" she said.

At school the following Monday, and for days later, the rude girl was ostracized by several of the girls in the class. But she didn't mind. She was brazen and had her own friend, a neighbor, that she preferred to hang out with.

I was given a job on Tuesdays, after lunch, to pick up the altar breads (Holy Eucharist) from the Good Shepherd Convent and deliver them to a nun at the Ursuline. On several occasions I forgot to take them with me, making the Ursuline nun furious. She would suddenly barge into the classroom looking for me. The minute I saw her, I knew I had forgotten the altar breads. I turned scarlet with embarrassment when she showed me up in front of my class. "How is it that you can be so unreliable to once again forget to give me the altar breads. Now you'll have to go back to the Good Shepherd Convent and get them for me," she ranted.

When I returned to the Good Shepherd's, I was scolded a second time by the nun waiting for me to pick them up.

When I entered my teen years, the repressed life I was living compared to that of my conventional two-parent classmates was evident and getting more difficult for me. I found it hard to form friendships with the day pupils and boarders, simply because they knew I lived a different life than they did. I often overheard the day pupils planning to meet up with each other after school or on weekends. Although I sometimes stood amongst them, I was never included. Somehow, they knew better than to ask me, perhaps believing I had my own friends at St. Dominick's.

I sat in class beside a girl named Deirdre. Deirdre was pretty, with long, wavy, dark blonde hair, and sky-blue eyes. When we were on breaks between classes, she often told me about her older sister and her parents.

Then, out of the blue, at the end of class one Friday, she invited me to visit her home. I was shocked that she asked me and didn't immediately accept her invitation. When she asked again before leaving the classroom that day, I agreed to go with her. Whatever possessed me to agree to visit her home I have never been able to fathom. I knew I couldn't join her without first asking permission from Mother Philomena. Once it was confirmed, Deirdre told me she would come with her parents around midday on Saturday to pick me up.

"How will I know where you live?" she asked.

I explained that after entering the grounds of the Good Shepherd Convent on the Cork Road, she had to turn right and walk up a narrow path until she came to a small brown door. There she would have to ring the doorbell, and it would be answered.

Back at St. Dominick's that evening, I made several attempts to tell Mother Philomena about Deirdre's impending visit. I knew if I told her I had already prearranged the visit without her approval, I would be in trouble. Besides, I wasn't even sure that Deirdre would keep her promise to pick me up. Apart from sitting beside her at school, I didn't really know her. As time slipped away, I hoped she had changed her mind about coming. I was also aware Mother Philomena wasn't going to allow me to just take off with total strangers. If Deirdre did arrive with her parents, they more than likely would be turned away.

After completing my chores on Saturday morning, I went out to the playground and hung out with a few of the girls. At noon, the Angelus bells tolled, and I became jumpy waiting for the doorbell to ring. A few minutes after noon, I heard the doorbell ring. I watched Mother Philomena go to the door and open it. Outside, I got a fleeting glimpse of Deirdre with her parents. While Mother Philomena spoke to her parents, Deirdre craned her neck over her mother's shoulder to look at the playground. After a few minutes, Mother Philomena turned around, and scanning the sea of girls, she spotted me and waved me over. Fearing that she might tell me off in front of Deirdre and her parents, I walked over to her slowly.

Deirdre was happy to see me, and excitedly introduced me to her parents. They both shook my hand, as Mother

Philomena stood watching them. "So, you know Deirdre from school?" Mother Philomena asked.

"Yes, we are in the same class and sit beside each other," Deirdre jumped in with a beaming smile.

Mother Philomena looked at me, and in affirmation of what she heard, nodded and smiled.

"These nice people are here because they want to take you out for a few hours today," she said.

Shyly, I silently smiled. I waited for her to ask if I already knew they would be coming to pick me up and was relieved when she didn't. Instead, she tactfully informed Deirdre's parents to have me back at St. Dominick's by four p.m.

Deirdre's house was in St. John's Park. It had a small backyard where I played with her while her mother prepared us lunch. At the lunch table, Deirdre's dad attempted to involve me in small talk while I ate my food. He started by asking about the teachers at the Ursuline, and if I liked them. I wasn't sure which teachers to tell him about but let Deirdre do all the talking for me. Feeling my face blush, I wished he weren't directing so many questions at me. His questioning soon led to a series of inquiries about St. Dominick's and the Magdalene Laundry girls.

"Did I like living with the Good Shepherd Nuns? Did they hit us? I hear they call the Magdalene girls, penitents. Did I ever see them, or were they hidden away?" he queried.

I felt so tongue-tied by what he was asking me, I nervously swallowed a mouthful of food without chewing it. My face immediately flushed scarlet, and I began to cough. Deirdre's mother jumped up from the table to get me a glass of water to wash down my food.

"Leave the poor girl alone and stop asking her so many questions," Deirdre's mother told her husband sternly.

After recovering from my coughing jag, I sensed a change of atmosphere around the table. Deirdre wasn't talking anymore but sat quietly eating the food on her plate. I wondered if she was she going to tell the girls in our class what her father had been quizzing me about?

After lunch, Deirdre's mother gave her money to buy us ice cream at a nearby shop. While eating our ice cream cones, we walked around St. John's Park, and she pointed out the houses where other girls in our class lived. I was happy when we hadn't run into any of them. It was approaching four o'clock when I headed back to the Good Shepherd's with Deirdre and her mother. I felt honored that Deirdre had considered me a friend and invited me to her home. But somehow, I felt more comfortable back at St. Dominick's, being around the girls I lived with. There, at least I would not have to skirt around questions that I couldn't answer.

Whether a coincidence or not, a few days after my outing with Deirdre, I sensed the girls in my class were acting strange with me when I walked into the classroom after lunch. Some gaped at me with half smiles, others eyed me curiously. Sitting at my desk, a girl in front of me turned and asked me if I was okay, with a look of concern on her face. My face reddened, and I pretended not to have heard what she said, while pulling my history book out of my desk like everything was normal. I guessed the girls had been talking about me. And, why not, to them I was the enigma who stepped in and out of their lives every school day.

The end of the school year was fast approaching, and I was only months away from turning seventeen. After finishing my final exams in June 1970, I left The Ursuline School, never to return. Despite the fact I felt like an outsider at The Ursulines, when I am asked which school I attended, I have always been proud to tell people I was a past pupil of the Ursuline Convent. Sadly, after I left The Ursuline School, I never saw Deirdre or any of my classmates again.

The solid education I received from the nuns and lay teachers at St. Ursula's Primary School and St. Ann's Secondary School, without a doubt, left a very positive impact on my life.

## Chapter Seventeen

# TOUCHED BY ANGELS

I met Uncle Sean and Aunt Pat in December 1959 when I was a patient on St. Brigid's ward, in Ardkeen Hospital, Waterford. Weeks before they came, I was admitted to hospital, suffering from severe malnutrition and from physical abuse.

I never remembered meeting my uncle before that time, but noticed he spoke just like my father. Also, he had the same brown eyes and black wavy hair as my dad, but his hair was swept over the top of his head.

Aunt Pat stood beside my uncle wearing a warm smile as he spoke. Looking up at her, I noticed how pretty she was with her curly blonde hair and twinkling blue eyes. Walking to the other side of my cot, she leaned over it, and gently held my swollen hands in hers. "I brought you some gifts I think you're going to enjoy," she said in a sweet lilting English accent.

She let go of my hands and I sat up when she gave me a brown paper bag. Inside I found a Christmas-themed coloring book and a box of multicolored crayons. She asked me what my favorite color was, and when I told her it was red, she took one out of the box and gave it to me. The coloring book had a drawing of Santa Claus, and I began coloring in his suit with my left hand. I tried to make his suit as red as I had seen it depicted in other pictures. Watching me do this, Aunt Pat unlocked the side of my cot and dropping it down, she sat beside me to help. "See, I use my left hand just like you. But we don't need to make Santa's suit so red," she said.

When I finished the picture, she kissed my face and hugged me tight. I immediately relaxed into her warm embrace and wished she would hold me forever. In that moment, a strong bond formed between Aunt Pat and me.

She and my uncle continued to see me for the remainder of their visit to Ireland, and each time, they plied me with kisses and hugs. I became fascinated with Aunt Pat and her English accent. On the last day of their visit, they told me they were leaving for England but would come back one day and see me again. I especially missed Aunt Pat when they left. I wanted her to replace the mother I so sorely missed.

Aunt Pat was in her early twenties when I was first introduced to her. She met my uncle when he worked in her hometown of Essex, in the UK. When they decided to get married, she had to convert from her Protestant faith to Catholicism. This displeased her father so greatly that he refused to give her away on her wedding day. He was even more angry with her when he found out she was marrying an Irish man.

I was made a ward of the court soon after my release from the hospital. When Aunt Pat and Uncle Sean found out about this, they took a special interest in my welfare. Every two years they came to visit family in Ireland with their growing family. On those trips, they came to see me at the Good Shepherd

Convent, or visit me in the summer months when I lived at my grandmother's.

A few times, I was able to travel with them and their children for a week's holiday. Uncle Sean drove a Dormobile, and chose different beach towns along the Irish coast to spend the night.

For Christmas each year, Aunt Pat not only made hand-knit wool sweaters for her own children, but also remembered to make one for me. The sweaters she selected were a different color cable knit, and fitted me perfectly.

One September, when I was ten years old, Mother Regina called me in from the playground and told me I had visitors waiting to see me in the parlor. I was puzzled and wondered who it could be, because I had just returned from my grandmother's house only days before.

I guessed it was someone important because the guests were invited to the parlor. The parlor was a showpiece for special guests when they visited. It was a few doors down from the refectory and the swankiest room in the whole of St. Dominick's. I had been there on a several occasions when my father and other relatives came to see me. Inside were four alabaster pedestals. On top of them were four, long, trailing spider plants displayed in shiny green ceramic pots that rested on the red-patterned tile floor. The center of the room was decked out with six plush cushioned chairs made of a silken cream fabric, and in the middle was an ornate glass and brass coffee table. This room was grand enough for the nuns to impress any visitor.

When Mother Regina opened the parlor door, I saw Aunt Pat and Uncle Sean waiting for me. Aunt Pat had a baby boy on her lap, and her young daughter stood beside her. Her older son sat on a chair next to his dad. I was shocked when I saw who had been waiting for me and got all shy and awkward. Aunt Pat held her hand out for me to come to her. I walked over and she took my arm and pulled me close to her. Mother Regina stood by and watched as my aunt showed her warm display of affection.

Seconds later, the parlor doors opened, and Mother Collette entered pushing a trolley of confections and hot tea. The trolley was brimming with decorative floral plates, filled with biscuits, Swiss roll slices, fairy cakes, and chocolate gateau. Beautiful bone china cups and silver spoons only added to the decadence.

After the nuns left, I relaxed. Sitting on one of the cushiony chairs, I eyed all the confections. Uncle Sean, noting this, stood up and put a selection of them on a plate for me, and another for his children. I sat quietly devouring every morsel while my aunt and uncle made small talk with me. I was almost finished eating when my uncle unexpectedly asked me if I would I like to live in England with his family. It was such an alarming statement that I felt my face blush and tried to swallow a large lump of a fairy cake. While waiting for a response, they both looked at me with soft endearing smiles. "Take your time and think about it. We haven't mentioned it to Mother Teresa or your father yet," my uncle said.

I was filled with excitement at the prospect of living with them and already knew my answer. There was nothing I would have liked more than the security of living with their family in England. Aunt Pat was always telling me stories about England in her letters. Feeling comfortable with both, I nodded my head in consent. Smiles lit up their faces with my decision. "That's grand. Now we will need to let Mother Teresa know, and hear what she has to say about it," Uncle Sean said.

Not long after, Mother Teresa entered the parlor. Aunt Pat and Uncle Sean chatted to her a while, before informing her they had matters they wanted to discuss with her in private. They both hugged and kissed me good-bye, and I left the parlor feeling happy and elated.

For the next few days, I waited for word of my departure, but it never came. When the days turned into weeks and into months, my dream of living in England with my aunt and uncle never came to fruition. Although I continued to get letters from my aunt, there was no mention of me going to England. Two years would pass before I saw them again.

They arrived at my grandmother's house in August 1965 with their three children. I was excited to see them and felt sure this was the year I would be returning to England with them. Knowing my summer holidays were ending, they asked my grandmother if they could take me on a holiday for a few days. My grandmother agreed to let me go and put a small bag of clothing together for me to wear. I was happy to be heading off with my aunt and uncle, assuming they were taking me on holiday to tell me I would be moving to England with them.

Uncle Sean had his Dormobile parked outside Nanny's gate. I hopped in and sat alongside my nine-year-old cousin Shane, and six-year-old Lucy. After a short drive, we pulled into the seaside town of Stradbally, in Co. Waterford. Aunt Pat remained in the Dormobile preparing supper on a little gas stove, and I went outside to play with my cousins. Although they were younger than my twelve years, I had fun running around with them.

The first night in their Dormobile, I watched how my uncle converted the inside space into a sleeping quarter. After unhinging two locks on the roof of the Dormobile, he lifted it up several inches to create more space and rolled out two side hammocks. I slept on one of the hammocks opposite Lucy. The square table where we ate supper now became a double sized bed. First, he lowered the table base, and then put the seat cushions on top of the table to function as a mattress. This was where he and my aunt slept. Cousin Shane slept on a smaller cushioned bench. The following morning, he returned it all back into its daytime place.

On one of those long summer evenings, it was pouring down with rain. Instead of going outside to play after supper, we remained inside the Dormobile. Sitting beside Uncle Sean, I watched him open a tin of tobacco, and drop a portion of it onto a sheet of cigarette paper. Then, he rolled it into a tight tube, and licked the edges to seal it. After lighting the cigarette, he relaxed on one of the cushioned seats. "Tell me this," he said, talking at me.

"Did anyone ever tell you I'm not just your uncle, but that I'm doubly related to you on both sides of the family. I'm sure your Nanny must have told you that anyway."

Not knowing what he was talking about, I said nothing. All I was waiting to hear was when I would be going to live with them in England. In my mind, I wondered why he thought Nanny would tell me about our family relationship. She would never divulge any such information with me. He puffed on his cigarette a few seconds, giving me time to absorb what he said. "I am only a half-brother to your father. His sister, Aunt Cora, who you lived with in Fews, she's my mother."

My eyes widened when he said this because I only ever had bad memories of Aunt Cora. But how could she be Uncle Sean's mother? Despite the fact I already knew she was my father's sister, but it shocked me to learn she was also Uncle Sean's mother. He went on to tell me his mother gave birth to him in her teens and raised him in the family home in Graigavalla, Rathgormack. He lived there with his half siblings until his mother got married. At age eighteen, he left home to join the Irish Army. After serving his time, he left Ireland to find work in England. "So, now you know, I'm not just your uncle, but also your first cousin," he said.

Leaving me with that thought, I wondered why he didn't mention anything about taking me back to England with him.

We stayed in coastal towns for the next few days, and I cherished the time I spent with them. The weather was warm, and I swam in the sea and made sandcastles on the beach with my cousins. I returned to Nanny's after six days. When they left; I bawled my eyes out. Another two years would pass before I would see them, and I perished the thought of ever leaving the Good Shepherd Convent.

Two years before I left St. Dominick's, Aunt Pat and Uncle Sean paid me a final visit to my grandmother's home. It was the summer of 1969. Aunt Pat revealed to me that she and my uncle had talked to my father and Mother Teresa about adopting me when I was ten years old. She said they explained to them how easy it would be for me to adapt to living in the UK with their family. They pointed out how I had the same last name and was only a few years older than their children.

Sadly, their pleas were all in vain. I had been made a ward of the court and was not allowed to leave Ireland. My father no longer had authority over me, and he too disagreed with their plan to take me out of Ireland. He said he wanted me to stay in Ireland because he would need me to take care of him when I finished school.

It pained my aunt and uncle each time they had to leave me behind. On one visit to the convent, Aunt Pat thought about sneaking me out the back door of the parlor. Uncle Sean advised her that if she attempted to do that, they would both be banned from ever entering the convent again and might possibly lose contact with me for good.

Two years later, I left the Good Shepherd Convent, and lived with my grandmother until I secured a job in Dublin. Aunt Pat stayed in touch by sending handwritten letters and Christmas cards.

Later in 1973, when I left for Surrey, UK, to study nursing, I became financially independent. In the same year, Aunt Pat and Uncle Sean moved to Ireland permanently. The kindness my aunt and uncle had shown me in my childhood was forever present in my mind. In one letter to Aunt Pat, I told her I would like to repay her and Uncle Sean for the love they shared with me as a child. I believe she was taken aback when she got my letter. She promptly wrote back and told me she was only doing what she would have done for any child in my situation.

Her letters grew fewer as I moved on with my life. Every two years I changed my address and was living in different countries. When I went to live and work in Amman, Jordan, in 1981, our letter writing to each other ceased completely.

It wasn't until I was on my honeymoon in Ireland in 1985 that I had an opportunity to see them again. After touring around Ireland for a week, I ended up in my hometown of Carrick-on-Suir to see my relatives. None of them had been able to attend my wedding in Chicago, so my cousin, Margaret, and her husband, Michael, planned a surprise wedding party for me. Arriving at their house with my husband, Margaret took us back to her living room, and waiting to see us, were Aunt Pat and Uncle Sean. I was so overwhelmed; I broke down and cried tears of joy. My cousin Margaret had tracked them down in the coastal town of Tramore and couldn't have given me a better wedding gift.

I went to visit Aunt Pat and Uncle Sean's home while I was on my honeymoon. In one conversation with Uncle Sean, I learned who his father was. He told me that my maternal grandfather, was also his father. This was startling news to me. I realized then what he meant, when he told me years before about being doubly related to him. Then a flurry of memories came back to me. One day in particular stood out when he came to visit me.

It was a late August afternoon when he arrived at Nanny's house with Aunt Pat, three of his children, and his mother, Aunt Cora. From the moment my grandmother saw them at her front door, she became awkward in their presence. I figured she was flustered because she felt inferior to them and found it difficult to understand Aunt Pat's English accent. After offering them tea and cake, she never sat down or joined their company. She kept herself busy boiling up water to make them fresh pots of tea. As soon as she saw their cups were half-empty, she filled them up, despite their refusal for more.

After they left, Nanny was visibly relieved. For the rest of the evening, she said very little, but remained quiet and pensive. It had to be truly painful for my grandmother to have to entertain Aunt Cora, knowing she had an affair with her husband.

Sadly, eight years after my reconnection with Uncle Sean, he died of a heart attack. After his death, the bond I had in my childhood with Aunt Pat evolved and grew even stronger. On my annual trips to Ireland, I make a point of visiting her on a regular basis.

Thanks Aunt Pat, for being ever present in my early childhood. You are truly remarkable and left a cherished imprint on my heart.

*1966—Summer Holiday with Aunt Pat and
Uncle Sean in their Dormobile.*

*2009—Aunt Pat.*

## Chapter Eighteen

# MY FATHER

Ever since I could remember, I had an aching curiosity to talk to my dad about my mother. What I really wanted to hear was for him to explain to me why she died so young. Never once had I known him to speak of my mother in conversations with relatives, friends, or his children. On two occasions, while sitting alone with him, I plucked up the courage to ask him, and both times, all I did was make him cry.

I was twelve years old the first time I broached the subject, and he brushed it off, and again when I was fourteen. After the last reaction I had from him, I never brought the subject of my mother up with him again.

Growing up, I had gleaned snippets of information about my mother, and that she died of a heart condition. But the exact cause of her death was never clearly explained to me until I was much older. Once I entered my teen years, I became more eager than ever to learn how she died. One main reason was that my grandmother often said that my father was to blame for her death.

When I stayed with Nanny in the summer, Dad sometimes paid me a visit on a Friday or Saturday evening. He generally arrived between nine and ten when he knew my grandmother had already retired to bed. On rare occasions, he came to visit me on a late Sunday afternoon. When this happened, Nanny was polite and offered him tea or sometimes shared lunch with him.

Gathered around the lunch table with my father, Uncle Johnny, and Nanny, there was often an uncomfortable silence. It was clear, my father was more unwelcome at the table than my grandmother and uncle let on. Because I was so protective of my father, I felt torn. I could see that he was enjoying his food as he rarely had someone cook hot meals for him.

Dad's evening visits were never guaranteed. He only came when the notion suited him. However, on Friday and Saturday evenings, Nanny made sure to be well out of his way in case he should visit. I sensed Nanny's dislike for Dad for a long time. I believe when he did visit me, she ear wigged from the other side of her bedroom door. It wasn't because of the cigarette butts she found thrown into the fireplace, but because of the series of questions she asked me the following morning. "I see *yer fadder* was here last night. What did he have *ta* say to *ya*? Was he smellin' of the drink? What time did he go?"

I was vague with my responses, for the simple reason that my father and I never did have much to say to each other. When he arrived, we mostly made small talk, and after an hour, he got up and left.

Uncle Johnny, (my grandmother's son) was the youngest of her six children. He was still living at home and the only one of her children who remained in Ireland. Each Saturday and Sunday evening, he walked to the village pub in Rathgormack, and didn't return until around midnight. Dad and he sometimes ran into each other at the pub. Although they were cordial with each other, they were more like two ships passing in the night. Uncle Johnny was twelve years younger than my father, and growing up, he must have heard some tall tales about my father from his mother, my grandmother.

On Friday and Saturday evenings, I sat on the fire-stained stool and waited patiently for my dad's impending arrival. I felt jittery with every sound I heard and jumped up from my stool every few minutes to look out the kitchen window, expecting to see his emerging shape coming up over the hill. The loud ticking of the illuminated alarm clock on the kitchen dresser appeared to tease me with every minute that passed. My ears pricked for the familiar thud of his footsteps at the front door. Once ten o'clock came and went, I forced myself to believe something must have held him up that evening that prevented him from coming to see me.

It was just before nine thirty, when he arrived one Saturday evening, in August 1966. Hearing his heavy footsteps at the front door, I quietly called out, "Is that you, Daddy?"

When he confirmed his presence, I opened the door to let him in. Walking inside, he hurriedly threw me a handshake before brushing past me. I immediately caught a distinctive whiff of alcohol and cigarettes from his breath when he greeted me. When he drank, he had a strange habit of lifting his left shoulder while showing a crooked grin. Sinking his hand into the pocket of his brown hound's tooth coat, he pulled out a brown paper bag, and handed it to me. Inside, I found wafers with a small block of Wall's ice cream.

The ice cream was soft and had already begun to melt from the heat of his body. I knew if we didn't devour it soon, it would surely turn into a milkshake. He took a seat at the kitchen table while I opened the ice cream package. I cut two generous slices and placed them between two wafers. Enjoying the creamy slices, both of us sat licking them before they melted. When dad finished eating, he stood up and sat on the wooden stool in front of the fireplace. I cleaned up and took a seat beside him on the same stool when I was ready.

Sitting beside my dad, he asked me the usual run of questions. What had I been up to, and if I had any news to tell him. With little to report, I just shrugged my shoulders and I looked at where Uncle Johnny's thick, grey, forestry socks hung. They were draped over the black hob airing out with dangling scraps of dirt. He usually hung them there when he came in from working at the forestry.

The silence between us broke when dad let out a loud belch. This brought me back to reality, and to what had been playing on my mind since seeing him two weeks prior. I knew if I didn't speak up soon, he would get up and leave, and I would miss my opportunity. His visits were well-timed, so he didn't have to run into Uncle Johnny returning home from an evening at the pub.

Finally, I took a deep breath, and looking down at my hands, I blurted out what had been tormenting me for years. "Daddy, can you tell me how mammy died?"

An awkward silence followed, and I glanced at him to see his reaction. Without blinking, he stared straight ahead at the unlit large round log at the back of the fireplace. Then, lowering his head, he inhaled deeply, and releasing his breath again, a blast of alcohol and cigarettes fumes filled the air. Neither of us spoke while he shoved his hand into his coat pocket and pulled out a pack of Woodbine cigarettes and a box of Friendly matches. He tapped out a wrinkled cigarette from its box, and moistened the filterless end with his tongue. Then, putting it between his lips, he cupped a hand around the cigarette and struck a match to light it. Closing his eyes, he deeply inhaled the cigarette like this was his last one. Suddenly, it was like his whole body had been awakened.

His face scrunched and contorted into odd shapes. Snorting and pursing his lips, I realized he was crying. Large tears dropped from his eyes and onto his trousers. A rising warmth of guilt and shame shrouded me, and I wished I had never gone to that place he avoided. Holding his cigarette in one hand, he pulled a musty grey handkerchief from his coat pocket with the other. A drool of mucus streamed from his nose and his mouth, and he kept swiping it off with his handkerchief. I was so guilt-ridden, I wanted to put my arms around him to console him and tell him I was sorry. But it came to me that he would only push me away, because he never liked a show of affection. I began to panic seeing how I made him cry. "I'm really sorry, Dad. I really didn't mean to ask you about that again," I told him fretfully.

This made him sob even more. Then, holding his cigarette with one hand, he covered his face with his handkerchief to stifle his cries. Taking another deep breath, he slipped it back in his coat pocket. Tears were rolling down his face again. Having no top teeth, his lower lip jutted out, and his top lip sunk under his nose. I was familiar with the strange facial contortions he made when he was under the influence of alcohol, but never while he cried.

Pulling his handkerchief out of his pocket again, he wiped his face several times and took another deep breath. He had stopped crying and dropped his head between his shoulders. While holding his cigarette, I watched the ash growing longer and then fall to the floor. Sucking in another gulp of air, he turned and looked at me crossly with swollen red eyes. "Don't *ya* be *sayin' tings* like *dat* to your *oul fadder. Yer* poor mother is dead and gone, and *deres* no need *fer ya ta* be *askin'* me *aboush* her now," he said.

My jaw dropped with what he said. Then, lurching forward he abruptly stood up and steadied himself. With his cigarette back in his mouth, he walked unwieldly toward the front door. I jumped up to follow him. Gripped in confusion, I was unsure of what to do or say to him. Next, he hastily lifted the latch on the front door and pulled it open. With a look of sadness showing on his face, he looked at me awkwardly. "Good luck now. I'm off. Maybe I might take a ramble ta see ya sometime next week," he said, while stumbling off into the cool, dusky night. He had left me without even as much as a handshake.

Feeling deflated and sad, I locked the front door behind him and climbed into my bed. Telling myself off for what I had done, I knew I should have known better than to bring up the subject of my mother with him again. Laying under my bedcovers, I couldn't sleep. I wondered if he cried walking alone on the hilly trek back to his empty home in Graigavalla. But why wouldn't he talk to me about his deceased wife, my mother? I had to accept that it was too painful for him, or maybe there was something he wasn't telling me?

Growing up, I always felt protective and pity for my father. He had been deprived of a life with his wife and children. Not only was it hard for him to live without his wife, but it was also hard for me not having my mother in my life. In my youth, I nurtured and guarded any amount of information I heard about my mother.

I was in my late teens when a female family acquaintance revealed some disturbing revelations about the life my mother had with my father. She told me that on several occasions, my mother had to flee from my father with her children because of his alcohol abuse. Although he only drank on weekends, alcohol altered his thinking, and made him irrational, aggressive, and confrontational. My mother was growing fearful of him and what he might do to her, and her children in his drunken state.

Returning from the pub one evening, he discovered she had already left the house with the children. He knew where to find her and headed straight to my grandmother's house. When he arrived, the children were already asleep in bed, and my mother was in the kitchen with my grandmother. Dad demanded that she go back home with the children. When she refused, he dragged her out of the house by the hair and told her to wake up the children and take them with her.

This new information astounded me and led me to understand why my grandmother had such a dim view of my father. Her complaints to friends about him being a drunken, irresponsible husband were real. Her main priority was to protect her daughter and grandchildren from him.

Yet, the father I came to know as I grew older, was not an aggressive or argumentative man. Only once had I known him to be confrontational. That was with his younger brother, Morey, and with good reason.

After my mother's untimely death, dad's life was turned upside down in an instant. He not only lost his wife, but also had his children taken away from him. He had been punished enough, and he was indeed a very broken man. A few years after losing his wife, and after his children were declared wards of the courts, he suffered a nervous breakdown.

When sober, he was stable and civil. All the structural training he learned from his five-year stint in the army, during the emergency period in 1939, fell by the wayside. He never remarried and lived out the rest of his days as a lonely man in the confines of an empty house. A home that once echoed with the sounds of children's laughter.

I was twenty-one when I returned to Ireland to visit my father. With little else to do, I offered to do some house chores for him. I washed the floors, and cleaned and polished his windows. I was tidying up the kitchen cabinet when I came across an empty Flahavan's porridge packet. It was rolled into a ball and pushed into the far right-hand corner of the cupboard. Just as I was about to toss it out, my father stopped me. "Wait, *dere's* something in *dere*. Don't go *throwin' dash* away. *Yer* mother's *weddin'* ring is inside *dash* and *ya* might as well have *ish*," he said.

Surprised by what he told me, I carefully opened the package and found her gold ring stuck inside the corner of the bag, amongst remnants of old oat flakes. Holding my mother's ring in my hand, I smiled, and instantly felt a spiritual connection with her. I gingerly inspected the ring before placing it on my ring finger and showed it to my father.

He admired it saying, "it looks as new as *da* day I *putsh itsh* on her finger."

He said he had almost forgotten that he had stashed it there all those years ago.

I removed it from my finger, and looking inside the ring band, I saw it was stamped in 24-carat gold. I had never possessed such precious jewelry. My mother's ring became the most genuine, sentimental piece of jewelry I would own. Fearing I might lose it, I tucked it safely in my handbag.

In all the years I visited my father, I never for a moment realized he had my mother's wedding ring hidden in his kitchen cupboard. If he hadn't been watching me that day, I would most certainly have thrown her ring out, believing it to be a balled-up bag of rubbish.

On my wedding day 1985, my husband not only walked me down the aisle, but also placed my mother's wedding ring on my finger. I have not removed it since. Wearing her wedding ring symbolizes much more than merely being a 24-carat gold wedding band.

1976—My father Stephen.

1974—Dad and me.

1977.

## Chapter Nineteen

# BROKEN HEART

From the beginning, my grandmother was adamantly opposed to my mother's relationship with my father. Primarily, this was because my mam was only twenty years old when they met, and dad was twelve years her senior.

Before marrying my mother, my father had built himself a reputation for being a lady's man. This reputation and the large age difference didn't sit well with my grandmother. However, when my mother gave birth to me, my father's first child, Nanny eased her dislike for him and begrudgingly accepted him as her son-in-law.

My father's nickname was Stevie. It was easy to see why my mother fell for him. He was the epitome of a tall, dark, and handsome man. He had chiseled features, dark brown eyes, and a shock of wavy black hair that only added to his appeal. Perhaps another reason my mother was attracted to him was that he was years older than her, and more of a father figure. At age six, she lost her own father. Her mother had strict control over her, and Stevie was a convenient escape from her tight clutches.

Nanny's own hardships made her bitter and rigid in her ways. At age thirty, she lost her thirty-five-year-old husband quite suddenly, leaving her to raise six children alone. From that time on, life was a daily struggle for Nanny.

Despite the stranglehold Nanny had over her children, her daughter Mary, my mother, fell into a secret romance with the son of a well-to-do farmer. She had been offered a job working as a housemaid at his family's farmhouse. The farm was in Kilsheelan, Co. Tipperary, a seven-mile trek from her home. Barely nineteen, she found herself pregnant with my sister Margaret (Peggy).

The fact she wasn't married to the farmer's son was shameful. This was not only embarrassing for Nanny, but also for my mother. She had to bear the burden of living in the small community of Rathgormack. In rural Catholic Ireland, there was a disgraceful stigma attached to having a child out of wedlock. This brought great humiliation to the family and caused my grandmother to ban my mother from having any further contact with the farmer's son.

My mother gave birth to my sister at a Mother and Child home run by the Good Shepherd Nuns in Co. Cork. Soon after birthing, unwed mothers were required to put their newborns up for adoption. In a strange twist of fate, my mother got lucky. Her baby was born ten weeks premature and was temporarily blind. This allowed her to escape the painful and mandatory separation from her baby. A blind preemie would not be eligible for adoption. So, she got to take her infant home.

Peggy was four years old when my mother married my father. Against my father's wishes, my mother brought Peggy to live with her. Less than a year after my mother and father's marriage, I was born. Brothers Thomas and Johnjoe soon followed, and were a year apart. Sadly, my mother only lived five years into her marriage with my dad.

I often heard Nanny speak unkindly about my father to her friends. Most of her friends were female, with a handful of male pals. I rarely sat in on their conversations but was often within earshot. After initial pleasantries with Nanny's friends, I made sure to make myself scarce. When it was raining outside, I would remain in my bedroom, otherwise, I sat on the door stoop.

Three of her friends were sisters. They lived in a *boreen* close to her house, in Knocknacreha. The sisters never arrived together, or on the same day. They chose a different day of the week and arrived on Nanny's doorstep in the early afternoon. Because of their isolated existence, they longed to hear the latest gossip from my grandmother. All three of their personalities were very different. One was extremely timid and always arrived wearing Wellington boots and long dark clothing.

The three sisters had a brother named Paddy. He usually made an appearance on a Friday evening, and commonly took a seat on the wooden chair at the left side of the fireplace opposite Nanny. She chatted very little with him, unlike his sisters. Paddy's grooming was impeccable. He wore the same heavy brown trench coat, over a navy pinstriped suit. Attached to the inside pocket of his suit jacket was a silver pocket watch with a long-rolled gold chain. When there was nothing more to talk about, he tapped one of his shiny polished brown shoes on the stone floor and hummed a tune (to himself) while admiring his pocket watch. Sometimes, while sipping on the tea Nanny gave him, he smoked a Sweet Afton cigarette, and with one inch or less left to smoke, he squeezed the tip of the cigarette to extinguish it. Then he put the remainder of the cigarette back in the Sweet Afton box. Once his visit was over, he thanked Nanny, and headed off into the night, to a place no one ever knew.

As little as my grandmother had to offer the sisters, she routinely welcomed them with a slice of cake and cup of tea. Dal was the eldest of the three and the best dressed. She considered her visit to my grandmother to be a grand outing. She arrived on Tuesdays wearing a brown felt hat, a white lacy blouse, a fitted brown pencil skirt, and skin-toned stockings with seams running up the back. To finish off the look, she wore a pair of polished shoes with two-inch heels.

I was thirteen and sitting outside on the door stoop when Dal arrived one Tuesday. Following my customary greeting with her, I remained seated, while she went inside to my grandmother. With the front door ajar, I could hear both of them exchanging stories about people they knew. Soon, the conversation switched, and I heard Nanny griping about my dad. "Sure, Mary shouldn't have gone off *marryin' dat oul'* fool. He never was any good and is *nothin' butsh a womanizin'* drunk. *T'was* he who killed her."

"Ah now, Nora, don't *ya* be *goin' sayin' tings* like *dat. Dats* a *holy fright fer ya ta* be *sayin' dat* he killed her," Dal said. "Sure, *am'nt* I right to be *sayin' dat. Da* doctor told him not *ta* be *givin'* poor Mary anymore *childer'* after she had *da* first two, and he did anyway."

I listened in disbelief to what Nanny was telling her friend about my father. Her words about him were very disturbing for my prepubescent ears. Fearing she would continue bashing my father, I quietly stood up and stealthily walked off to the side of the house. I wasn't sure if Nanny was aware I had been eavesdropping. Once out of earshot, I fled to the corner of the half-acre and threw myself on the grass, trying to make sense of what I heard.

I watched and waited until Dal left, then went back inside. My grandmother was seated in her usual spot by the fireplace, and seeing me, she asked where I had been. I fibbed and told her I was in the half-acre searching for eggs in the ditches but couldn't find any. What I wanted to ask her was if what she said about my father was true. Not wanting to cause disharmony between my Nanny and me, I decided to wait for the weekend. I hoped my father would visit me and I could ask him if what Nanny had said about him was true.

On Friday that same week, he surprised my grandmother and me and arrived around four-thirty. Standing at the front door, he announced that he finished his job at the forestry sooner than expected, and passing Nanny's house on his push bike, he thought it was a good time as any to stop in and see me.

Nanny barely acknowledged his presence, except to offer him a cup of tea. She sat and listened while he sipped on his tea and chatted with me. An hour later, he got up to leave. I followed him outside to say goodbye. Opening the large metal gate, I stood behind him, knowing he would hop on his bike and head for home. When he was about to exit the gate, I spoke. "Daddy, Nanny is telling everyone that you're no good, and it's your fault mammy died."

As soon as I said it, I felt a weight being lifted off me. Holding the sliding lock of the gate, dad froze in his tracks.

He slowly turned and looked at me without reacting. Wearing a furrowed frown, he lifted his stare and gazed off into the distance. A few moments of silence passed before I heard him mumble under his breath. "Well, is that what she's *doin'* now? *Goin'* around *sayin' tings* like *datsh aboush* me?"

I knew what I said hurt his feelings and noticed his eyes welling up with tears. I could tell he was embarrassed that I saw him like this. Turning away from me, he walked outside and latched the gate. With a sad looking face, he got up on his bike, and waved me goodbye. I stood at the gate watching him disappear out of sight, wishing I had kept what I heard to myself.

I didn't see him again until the following Friday. This time he arrived an hour later than the previous week. Again, Nanny was taken by surprise. Sitting with both my father and grandmother, I felt like a traitor, and full of guilt. They exchanged only a few words with each other, and I responded with shrugs and nods when dad spoke to me.

Dad wasn't even halfway through drinking his cup of tea when Nanny unexpectedly stood up and went outside. He put down his tea and got up to follow her. As soon as they were gone, I stood inside the front door to hear what they might be talking about. But their voices weren't audible, because they had walked around to the side of the house. Fearing what the outcome might be, I snuck back to my bedroom.

After dad departed, Nanny angrily barged into my bedroom. *"Whash* are *ya goin' an tellin' yer fadder aboush* me? Don't *ya* be *listnin'* to *whash* I do be *tellin'* to people, and *den go' runnin'* off *tellin' yer fadder.* We don't want any trouble *ousha* him. Do *ya* hear me?" she said, before storming out of the room and slamming the bedroom door latch shut.

Knowing I had stirred up trouble between them, I sat on my bed wondering what to do. Part of me wanted to believe what Nanny had said about my father was true. A flurry of thoughts crowded my mind. I was aware my father drank at weekends but found it hard to accept that he caused her death. Family members and neighbors had been telling me for years that it was her heart that killed her. Now I had gone and upset my grandmother too. She might be so angry about this that she will tell dad that she doesn't want me staying with her anymore. She was still heartbroken that she lost her daughter so young, but it saddened me when she told her friends stories about my father that I believed were untrue. I already felt lost by not having my mother in my life and didn't want to have to let go of my father too.

Following that incident, Dal came to visit Nanny. Nanny told her about the confrontation she had with my father. "Do *ya* know *whash h*e told me? *Datsh* I should keep me *moush shush,* after *da* young *wan* told him *aboush whash* I said *aboush* him. Well, I'll tell *ya,* I was well able for him. I fired back and told him, I will in me eye do *whash* you tells me to do, keeping me *moush shush*. If it wasn't for *meself takin'* in *da* young *wan*, I wouldn't ever *lesh* him in under *me* roof."

Even after the confrontation Nanny had with my father, it didn't stop her character assassination of him. In fact, in future conversations with certain friends, she continued to fan the fire on their visits. She was livid with my father for following her out into the yard that day and telling her off for the scandalous lies she was spreading about him.

Many years later, after Nanny passed, I returned to Ireland from London on a week's holiday. Midway into my visit, I drove from Rathgormack into Carrick town to see my Uncle Jimmy and Aunt Maura. Uncle Jimmy was my father's oldest brother. Growing up, I often spent time with them, their daughter Margaret, and my brother, Johnjoe. Following my mother's death, my aunt and uncle adopted my brother. Aunt Maura and Uncle Jimmy were very wise and practical, and I always enjoyed talking to both of them.

Sitting in front of the Aga with Uncle Jimmy that day, the conversation of my mother arose. I related to my uncle what Nanny often told her friends about my father. He confirmed that none of what Nanny said about my father was true. He said my mother was involved in a freak accident four years before she met my father and filled me in on the whole story.

It happened one summer's day, when my mother was in her teens. Nanny sent her on a two-mile trek to fetch a gallon of milk from the local creamery. After a short walk, she met a local dairy farmer on his horse and cart. He was heading to the creamery with six churns of unpasteurized milk and seeing my mother carrying an empty gallon, he offered to take her there. My mother agreed to go with him. While she climbed up on the cart the farmer said he would hold her gallon. When she passed it to him, the reflection of the shiny metal in the mid-morning sun bounced off the gallon and shone directly in the horse's eyes. This momentarily blinded the horse, and he lifted his front legs high into the air. When my mother saw this, she stepped back out of harm's way. Within a split second, some of the farmer's churns of milk came toppling down off the cart; one of them knocked my mother to the ground. The farmer fell off the other side of the cart but was fortunately unhurt.

He got up and ran to my mother's aid, where he found her pinned beneath a heavy churn full of milk. He removed the churn and sat with her until she recovered. She told the farmer she was in a lot of pain and put it down to bruising on her chest. Feeling embarrassed, my mother stood up, brushed off her clothing, and continued walking to the creamery.

When she returned home, she never told her mother about the accident. She knew it would worry her and she would be scolded for accepting the farmer's offer to ride with him to the creamery.

As time passed, her health deteriorated. When she was pregnant with me, the doctor discovered she had fractured ribs on the left side of her chest. Following the fall, she was never medically treated for her cracked ribs and consequently developed chronic, deteriorating heart and lung disease. On November 14, 1953, she was in labor with me and struggled to breathe. She showed distinctive signs of peripheral cyanosis, and her ankles were seriously swollen. After I was born, the doctor advised her not to have any more children. However, in the next two years, she gave birth twice, to my brothers, Thomas and Johnjoe. These pregnancies proved to be even more debilitating.

After Johnjoe was born in May 1956, her condition worsened. She was advised to remain in the hospital for observation. This lasted six weeks. She was only discharged when her condition appeared to improve.

Back at home, she grew frailer. In late November 1957, she was once again hospitalized and placed on strict bed rest. It was suggested that she needed bed rest in preparation for surgery to repair her fractured ribs. Around noon on January 8, 1958, a ward nurse placed a lunch tray on her bed trolley. She evidently sat up awkwardly to eat her lunch and suddenly slumped over on her side and died. Her death certificate stated that she had bicuspid, tricuspid and mitral valve stenosis, and died from a pulmonary embolism, as a result of her broken ribs.

This was the first time I had been given a full and precise account of my mother's death.

While my mother waited for her surgery, she wrote several letters to my father. He kept all her letters safely in a biscuit tin at his home. On every one of my visits home to see my father,

I took down the biscuit tin and read her letters word for word. Each time I read them seemed like the first, and I memorized every word. Her opening line of each letter read, "Dear Stevie. How are you and my dear children? Tell them mammy misses them and will soon be home from the hospital to see them."

A friend of my mother's in Rathgormack told me my mother was full of good humor and was very witty. She also said how terrified she was to tell her mother about the accident with the churn. "Her mother would have killed her, if she had known she took a ride in the cart from the farmer," she said.

I believe if my mother had received proper medical attention after the accident, she most likely would have been spared such an early death. If she hadn't died of a broken heart, my family would have been complete, and life for my siblings and me would have been altogether different.

*1948—My mother.*

## Chapter Twenty

# COVER UP

Before setting foot inside the graveyard, my grandmother gruffly nudged my shoulder with her forefinger as a signal to pause. I gazed up into her striking blue eyes, and then watched her close them, before blessing herself in reverence of this sacred place.

I was standing with Nanny outside a four-foot, wrought iron gate that straddled between two ivy-covered pillars. Flecks of curled-up paint on the gate showed tell-tale signs that it was once green. This was the entrance to an ancient, fourteenth-century church graveyard in rural County Waterford. As my grandmother labored to lift the gate over the mounds of overgrown grass, it squeaked under duress until it was freed from its rusty hinges.

I wasn't expecting to go there that July day.

After Sunday mass, Nanny usually stood around chatting with her friends and neighbors. I never liked her doing that because I was hungry after keeping the fast to receive the Holy Eucharist. Furthermore, she often made me the topic of her conversation. But that Sunday she cut her conversation short and headed for home. "We'll go off home now, and after we have a bite to eat, we'll take a ramble down to the graveyard to say a prayer for your poor mother," she said.

When we set out, the weather was warm. The earlier rains gave way to bright clear skies, making our journey pleasant. I was no stranger to the old graveyard. Since my mother's passing, I had gone there on many occasions with my grandmother. Walking inside the gate, a strong smell of damp moss wafted from the ground. The wildlife was astir everywhere, masking ghosts of the past beneath the earth. Swallows swooped and dove like toy airplanes. Crows cawed, and bees and butterflies hovered over the wildflowers, while rabbits scurried into their warrens for safety.

Walking behind Nanny, I obediently kept pace with her, trying to avoid the murky pools of water that surrounded the soggy, lumpy grass. I was wearing a pair of black, second-hand, lace-up boots that Nanny's kindly neighbor had given her for me. They were shiny and new looking from the wax polishing I gave them the day before. I took extra care not to soil or spoil them by walking around the clumps of grass.

Today, my grandmother didn't take her usual walk up the grassy hill to my mother's grave. Instead, she stopped walking and turned left to face a half-acre of rich, green grass. Walking closely behind her, I almost bumped into her, but caught myself in time.

"Look *dere*," she said, pointing to the green pasture. "*Dat's* where your poor *oul'* grandfather is buried, down there somewhere. Poor Johnny. Sure, he was a grand man all the same. May God rest his soul," she said, blessing herself a second time with a sign of the cross. And I copied her.

Looking up at her, I saw she was transfixed on a particular patch of green grass. I didn't understand what she was talking about and didn't want to question her. I knew my grandfather passed away years before I was born, but had never known where he was buried, until now. At twelve years of age, I was acutely aware not to ask adults about the death of another. Death in Ireland was both sensitive and secretive and was often talked about in hushed tones when I was in adult company.

Yet, standing on this green grass, I felt a strong urge to ask her if this really was where my grandfather was buried. But how could it be? There was no headstone like those on the hillside where my mother was laid to rest. In front of me was just a pasture of lumpy, emerald-green grass and nothing more.

She finally lifted her trance-like gaze, and swiftly turned her back on the land. Ignoring my presence, she stood a moment, unraveled the black shawl she was wearing, and pulled it closer to her bosom. Then she glanced my way, and, with a directional nod, she had me follow her up the hill to where the remains of my mother lay amongst centuries-old graves and headstones.

My grandmother's name was Nora. I called her Nanny and got to know her when I stayed with her for several weeks during the summer months. She was short and stocky, with striking blue eyes, and kept her long, grey hair tied in a bun at the base of her neck. In contrast to her beautiful eyes, her face was deeply wrinkled and weather beaten because of the hard life she had lived. A fiercely independent woman, Nanny was tough and undemonstrative, and her country ways only added to her oddity. This made me feel uneasy being around her. Never once had I known her to shed a tear or lie in bed because she was sick.

She lived in a three-bedroom cottage on a half-acre of land, without electricity or plumbing and eked out a living selling eggs to neighbors and friends from the hens she raised.

When I entered my teen years, I grew more self-conscious and felt embarrassed to be seen with her in public. This was partly due to her strange lifestyle, and partly, because of the generation gap between us. Unlike her contemporaries, Nanny wore bizarre, dark clothing that made her look like she was off to attend a funeral. Winter or summer, she wrapped herself in a black woolen shawl when she went out. The shawl had tiny, black tassels that trailed along the edges and covered up her long dark skirts. Underneath her skirts she wore thick grey stockings that were rolled up to her mid-thigh and held in place with garters. The garters were hidden under the long legs of her elasticated interlock knickers. She frequently used these elasticated legs of her knickers to stash the cash that neighbors gave her for the purchase of eggs. This was only a temporary hiding place until she got around to banking the cash in her money box. Her money box was small and black, with red and gold trim. She kept it locked and hidden high up in the rafters of her bedroom and only took it down before she went to bed. Before heading to bed, she would slowly count her money on the windowsill, until she was satisfied it was correct.

Occasionally, her knitted stockings came loose and dropped around one of her ankles. This became a matter of urgency for her. Pausing from her work, she hoisted up her skirts and lifted her lily-white leg onto a kitchen chair. Then she rolled the stocking back under the leg of her knickers until it was at the top of her thigh. Checking the garter, she knotted it tighter before securing it back in place.

While in the house or around her half acre, she wore a battered pair of black lace-up boots, and kept a newer, identical pair of boots in a box under her bed. She only brought them out on Saturday to wax and buff with Kiwi polish in preparation for Sunday mass.

The highlight of her week was attending the nine o'clock Sunday mass at Rathgormack's Church of the Sacred Heart. Before leaving, she put a half-crown coin in one of the little, brown offering envelopes she had been provided with. The priest often announced from the pulpit how much the locals gave, and to save herself the embarrassment of not giving, she never left the house without the brown envelope with her name printed on it. When she arrived at the church, she sat on the right side where the females sat. Nanny, making sure that I was noticed, had me walk down the center aisle with her until she found a space for both of us. When mass ended, some of her friends were generous and gave me money to buy sweets.

Nanny's true pride and joy were her hens. She had eighteen of them, and they came in a variety of breeds and colors. Besides her hens, she had a big brown rooster with a black feathered tail. He strutted around her yard by day and slept at night in the henhouse with the hens. At five every morning, he woke me up with his repeated loud calling. 'Cock-a-doodle-dooo.' This was also my grandmother's wake-up call.

Nanny never gave her hens proper names. To her, they were just black, brown, white, and speckled. Yet, she knew the black Silkie hens laid white eggs, the speckled Sussex hens, pale brown eggs, the white Leghorns, white eggs, and the Rhode Island red hens, dark brown eggs. What was important to Nanny was not so much the breed of the hen, but the color of the eggs they produced.

She allowed her hens to wander and forage freely around the perimeter of her property. Because of this practice, many of them took the opportunity to nest in the ditches around her half-acre. Her hens loved her, and followed her everywhere when she was outside. Some even strolled into the kitchen after her, until she chased them out.

Her neighbors were fussy about the color of eggs they ordered. It made Nanny anxious when a neighbor requested a large order of eggs in a specific color.

One summer morning, her neighbor, Kitty, dropped in and placed an order for a half-dozen brown eggs. She told Nanny her daughter was visiting her with her grandchildren, and she wanted to make them scrambled eggs on toast for breakfast. Fearing her hens wouldn't produce the requested eggs, for the rest of the day, and the following, Nanny had me running back and forth to the henhouse every time a hen announced the arrival of a newly laid egg. 'Buk, buk, ba, buk buk.' The sound of their call was music to her ears.

Believing I missed one of the brown hens' nesting spots, she double-checked the henhouse and the half-acre ditches. She was disappointed when a black hen made a fuss about laying a white egg. "*Osha wisha wisha*. Now, *whash* am I *goin' ta* do if *da* half dozen brown eggs aren't ready *fer* Kitty?" she complained.

The day Kitty was due to pick up her eggs, she directed her attention to me. "Why don't *ya* go *outsh agin ta da* half-acre and look in *da* ditches *ta* see if one of *da oul hins* laid an egg there," She'll be here any minute, and I only have *da* four eggs *ta* give her."

Despite the fact I had checked several times that day and the day before, I obeyed her and ran outside to look for any new openings in the ditches. Taking my time, I kept coming up empty. I rounded the corner of the half-acre, and carefully pulling back some briars, I found not only a brown egg but also two white eggs in different nesting spots. Proud and excited with my treasures, I lifted the hem of my frock and gently laid the eggs there. When I showed my grandmother, a big toothless smile spread across her face. Lifting the brown egg out of the hem of my frock, she held it up to the light to inspect it. "Well, I hope *tis n't* an *ould wan ya* found. *Dat* would be a wicked *ting for* Kitty. Now, *dere's* no need *ta* go *tellin'* her *ya* found *da* brown one out in *da* half-acre, or she *mightn't* take *itsh* off me," she said.

Right before Kitty arrived, a brown hen presented Nanny with the last brown egg she needed. When Kitty picked up her order, Nanny happily handed her the eggs, and told her to make sure and let her know if all the eggs tasted good. Kitty never complained about them, making my grandmother happy.

She feared the brown egg I found might be old, or even an unhatched chicken.

Before dusk each evening, she called her hens into the yard to give them a final feed and a head count. "Here chick, chick, chick" she repeated, until they came running from all directions to her.

While she had their full attention as they pecked at their feed, she picked up certain hens and physically checked them to see if they were due to lay an egg the following day. Holding the hen in the crook of her arm, she rotated its body so the hen's head was behind her and the rear end in front. Then she inserted her middle finger up the hen's oviduct canal to feel for an egg.

The first time I caught her doing this, I was disgusted. Nanny had her back to me, and the hen faced me with a wide-eyed look of confusion. Hearing my reaction to what she was doing, Nanny turned around, still holding the hen, and angrily told me to go back inside, because she said, I was frightening her hens.

I soon learned this was her evening ritual. When she finished inspecting them, she shooed them into the henhouse, along with the rooster. Some of the hens knew the score and flew up onto one of the three wooden roosts. Giving them a final headcount, she locked the henhouse door for the night. She knew the sly fox would soon be snooping around her property once darkness fell. This was her only way to protect not only her hens, but also her livelihood.

After tending to her hens, she frequently had feathers stuck to her fingers. Knowing where her fingers had been, I quietly watched and waited to see if she was going wash her hands. Sometimes, she filled the metal basin with water and washed them. Other times, she absentmindedly forgot and went into her bedroom with dirty hands.

She had a mental record of her hens ages. When they got old and no longer laid eggs, she either sold them, or unbeknownst to me, she used them for a tasty meal. I was with her in the front yard one day when she mentioned one of her brown hens was slowing down. The next day, I noticed the hen she talked about the day before was missing.

That afternoon, she filled a big, black, cast-iron pot with water and hung it on the hob over a blazing fire. At some point, she dropped the chicken into the pot. It was only when she lifted the lid to stir the contents that I saw a chicken bubbling in the water with carrots and onions. Nanny was clever. She did the deed of wringing the hen's neck and plucking its feathers, without me knowing.

One summer's day, when I was thirteen, she needed to put an order of four white eggs together for a customer. She told me I was good at finding eggs in the ditches and sent me out into the half-acre to search for them. I enjoyed searching for eggs because it gave me something to do. Sometimes, it was like going on a treasure hunt.

Out in the half-acre, I took my time searching for nesting hens or eggs that were already laid. After some time, I found two white eggs in a ditch where a black hen had just flown out of. Holding the warm eggs in each hand, I ran across the half-acre to give Nanny the eggs she had been wishing for.

When I walked into the kitchen, Father Cahill, the parish priest, was sitting by the fire talking to Nanny. He smiled when he saw me and gestured for me to come to him. I walked over and stood in front of him. Then he reached out and pulled me towards him and sat me on his lap. Fearing the eggs might break, I gently kept my fists closed around them. Nanny sat opposite me, filling the priest in on the local gossip. As she spoke, Father Cahill drew me closer to his chest and began rubbing my bare arms. My head was near his face, and I could hear his breath growing heavier. Then he moved his hands down the sides of my arms and rested them over my fisted hands. Giving my fists a tight squeeze, I immediately felt the eggs pop. I panicked and didn't know what I should do. I looked at Father Cahill's hands to see if the broken eggs were leaking through his fingers. My stomach churned when I saw the slimy liquid egg yolk and albumen seeping through the priest's fingers. Father Cahill, sensing something was wrong, lifted his hands off mine. Opening his fingers, the egg liquid fell in long sticky slicks onto his black trousers. Nanny, saw what was happening.

She stood up quickly and angrily exclaimed, "Oh *Fadder*. I'm wicked sorry. Will ya just look *atsh whatsh da* young *wan* has gone and done *ta yer* trousers. She'll be *da deash' a* me *yetsh*."

Father Cahill gave me a little shove to get me off his lap, and then stood up. I stood watching him as the slime and eggshells dripped from my hands and onto the stone floor. Nanny found an old grey rag and handed it to the priest. He wiped his hands with it first, and then his trousers. My face flushed with an uneasy feeling when I saw him stretch out his hands in front of him to prevent any further egg spill on his clothing. Nanny was horrified by the situation and kept apologizing to the priest and blaming me for destroying his priestly garb. Not sure what to do next, I turned and faced the fireplace. Shaking the shells off my hands, I scraped off the excess slime with a piece of broken eggshell.

Father Cahill was visibly embarrassed with a beet red face. While mopping the mess off his pants, Nanny continued to fuss over him. When he was done, he finally came to my defense. "Ah, sure, Nora. Leave her be. It was only an accident. Sure, she's a good girl, and didn't mean to do it. She forgot she had the eggs in her hands. Didn't you now?" he said, looking at me, handing the rag back to my grandmother.

After he left, Nanny told me it was a wicked pity I had to go and break the two fine eggs, and what a holy fright it was that I dirtied Father Cahill's trousers.

After Sunday mass that week, I stood with Nanny while she told her friends what I had done to the priest's trousers. The fact that this accident happened to the parish priest, was shocking news for many but comical for others.

At thirteen, I felt it odd the way Father Cahill grabbed me and plopped me on his lap. My father had already stopped sitting me on his lap years before. Looking back, I believe Father Cahill got excited in a strange way when he rubbed my arms and squeezed my fists. In his defense, he didn't realize I was holding two of Nanny's prized eggs in my hands. That was the last time I saw Father Cahill pay a visit to my grandmother's home.

Although Nanny had a series of different roosters, I never saw baby chicks running around in the summertime.

She once sent me to the village grocery store to inquire about new pullets. At the time, I didn't know what a pullet was, and asked the owner if she had any bullets. Luckily, the owner of the store knew what I meant. Smiling, she told me to let my grandmother know that she had sold the last four they had.

Only later did I learn mature chicks were called pullets.

In 1962, the County Council began installing electricity and plumbing in people's homes in rural Ireland. Prior to the installation of plumbing, Nanny had to walk a half mile to a water pump carrying two empty buckets to fill with water. Then she had to carefully return to her house without spilling them. Once the Waterford County Council installed plumbing at the side of her cottage, she no longer had to make that journey. A water faucet was attached to a vertical black hose and secured to the back of a thick wooden board. Having access to running water only steps away from the front door made Nanny's life a lot easier.

However, she adamantly turned down the installation of indoor plumbing. She told the County Council supervisor she didn't need it inside and preferred to live the way she always had.

Even though she enjoyed the convenience of running water at the side of her house, she never dared to use the electricity the County Council installed inside her home. Instead, she continued utilizing candles and a paraffin globe to light her kitchen and bedrooms on dark evenings. Electricity scared her. She believed if she flicked on a light switch, the 220 volts of power would surely electrocute her. Some of her older neighbors thought the same. Like my grandmother, they thought their hands would stick to the switch and electrocute them, from the tales others told them.

In the early days of my grandmother having the use of electricity, she never allowed me to turn on a light switch in her home, even though I was very familiar with the use of electricity from living at the Good Shepherd Convent. Instead, she took advantage of the long summer's evenings, or used paraffin lamps and candles as the evening grew darker.

As I entered my teen years, I found living with Nanny difficult. This was due in part to the lack of indoor plumbing. Uncle Johnny, Peg, Nanny, and me, all had to find creative and practical ways to bathe and use the toilet. At night, or on heavy rain days, we had to use a chamber pot if we needed to go to the toilet. The chamber pots, known as Pos, looked like large teacups, and were kept underneath our beds. They were identical in size and made of white aluminum with a decorative royal blue trim around the rim and the handle.

Living at the convent, I had grown used to indoor plumbing, but had to revert to using a Po at Nanny's house.

Quite often, I woke up at night bursting to go to the toilet and forced myself to wait until morning. As soon as daybreak arrived, I would get up, go outside, and go to the toilet under a tree, where I wouldn't be seen. I also did this to avoid having to empty the Po the next day.

However, sometimes I had no other choice but to use the Po at night. The following morning, it was my responsibility to empty the contents of the Po. If it was urine I had to dispose of, I would carry the Po to the open front door and stop. Holding the Po to the side of me, I peeked out to make sure that no one was passing the front gate. When the coast was clear, I stepped onto the stoop and quickly tossed the urine into the air, where it landed on a row of fuchsia bushes opposite the front door.

If it was solid waste, the same lookout was observed at the front door. When I saw it was safe, I stepped outside with the Po, and speedily crossed the yard to dump the contents onto a dung heap at the far side of the cottage.

On a few occasions, I followed my sister's lead and hurled the Po of urine out the bedroom window. It splashed onto a bushel of orange Iris flowers, where they flourished and grew lush and healthy throughout the summer.

Nanny did her washing on Mondays, and her ironing on Tuesdays. She used two cast iron presses to do her ironing. Placing both directly on a blazing fire, she kept them there until they turned crimson red. Then she removed one of them and carefully dropped it onto a smooth silver plate. Once the iron was secured with a clip attachment, she proceeded with her ironing. When the iron lost its heat, she replaced it with the second iron and continued with the same process until she got all her ironing done.

Nanny was extremely budget minded and begrudgingly monitored every morsel of food I put in my mouth. "*Dats* enough spuds *fer ya* now. *Yer* using too much sugar in *yer tae.* Don't be *puttin'* all *dat butsher* on *yer* bread. *Dats* enough *milk yer pourin'* in *yer tae.*"

Sometimes, I curbed my hunger pangs by searching for blackberries or gooseberries that grew wild along the ditches on her half-acre piece of land. Other times, I waited until she went to bed, and then helped myself to spoons of sugar from the sugar bowl, or would sneak a slice of stale bread from the cupboard, and slather it with butter and jam.

Nanny harvested four types of potatoes, as well as cabbage, carrots, parsnips, and onions on her land. Kerr's pinks, golden wonders, queens, and tiny new potatoes were her favorite spuds to grow. Each day she went out to a section of the half-acre and chose a particular type of spud to boil for supper. Digging at the potato stalk with a prong, she marveled at how many potatoes one stalk gave her.

She did all her cooking over an open fire, with two black pot-bellied cast iron pots. One pot was larger than the other. Depending on the volume of potatoes or food she was cooking, she hung the pots on the appropriate hook on the hob over the fireplace. She was very particular when boiling potatoes, and constantly poked them for softness with the tines of a fork. Once satisfied, she drained the boiling water and put a tea towel over them until they burst into balls of flour. Minutes later she rolled them onto a platter. The broken skin on the potatoes made them easier to eat. It didn't matter which potato she served, all of them tasted delicious with heavy cream and salted butter.

She usually prepared a fry-up of bacon and sausages once a week. It was one of Uncle Johnny's favorite suppers when he arrived home from the forestry. To begin, she removed a lump of lard from her crock jar and dropped it on the frying pan. She placed the pan on top of a triangular cast iron stand to cook them; when the fry-up was ready, she drained off the liquid fat, and poured it back into the crockpot and let it cool down for the next fry-up.

Because Nanny didn't have any top or bottom teeth, it made chewing her food difficult. Over time, her gums became hardened enough to serve as her teeth. One of her favorite meals was a half-smoked pig's head. She often mentioned how cheap it was, which afforded her the opportunity to eat it on a regular basis. After boiling the head for several hours, she took it out of the pot and placed it sideways on a large ceramic platter. While it sat on the kitchen table cooling down, she had to keep swatting the blue bottle flies to stop them from feasting on it. It bothered me having to look at part of an animal I was commonly used to seeing alive and wallowing around in pig sties.

She knew I never liked eating that type of meat. Yet, every time she served it, she insisted I have some too, and cut off a large fatty chunk of it for me. She grumbled when I picked at the meat or if she saw me turn my head away from the butchered half-head.

The meat was tough and full of gristle. To eat it, she had to saw it into portions with a serrated bread knife. To get to the meaty bits, she pulled and hacked around the eye, ear, and snout to separate the fatty lumps from the meaty bits. When she found an edible piece to eat, she popped it in her mouth and rolled it around from side to side to break it down with her gums. With the hard chewy lumps, she held the meat between her lips, and pulled it in and out of her mouth until it turned into a stringy pulp. It turned my stomach having to watch her. To avoid looking at her, I often turned my head to the side. This irked Nanny to no end, especially when she caught me making faces of repulsion. "Look at *ya*. *Dis is* a grand feed. *Tis* a disgrace *da* way *ya won't aitsh*. Another poor young *wan* would love *ta* be *aitin' dis mate*," was her usual refrain.

After breaking down the lumpy bits of meat, she satisfyingly swallowed them back with gulps of buttermilk. I was always glad when she was done eating her feast. She gave the remaining scraps of the pig's head to Pip, her dog. Pip was obedient and stayed under the table watching and waiting for Nanny to share the leftovers with him. She usually fed him the ear and the snout, and he snapped them up before going back under the kitchen table to devour them.

Although Nanny's cottage was small, her fireplace was huge. The fire was lit every day to cook food and provide heat for the house in the winter months. To the right of the fireplace, was a hand-cranked machine. This device was cemented to the floor and acted like bellows. It had a large wheel with a strong, woven, brown strap wrapped around it. Beneath that wheel was a smaller one that resembled a large spool for holding thread. To start the fire each morning, Nanny filled the fire grate with logs and kindling. Then, twisting a piece of newspaper, she lit it, and shoved it under the kindling. To push air through the floor vent, she slowly cranked the large handle of the wheel clockwise. The action of turning the wheel immediately stoked the lighting process.

I had a genuine fascination with the fire machine, and a few times spun the wheel so fast that the large belt derailed. This caused a plume of ash to spew into the kitchen and settle on all the surfaces. Having made such a mess twice, she told me that I wasn't to touch the machine unless she was present.

On long summer evenings, she let the fire die out after she drank her last cup of tea before her bedtime. A few times, out of boredom, I stepped into the unlit fire-grate and looked up the chimney to look at the stars in the night sky. The wide chimney was large enough for any person bold enough to climb down. Having such a wide chimney was bothersome for Nanny. The summer thunderstorms often caused rain to pour down, quenching the fire.

One afternoon, a deluge of hailstones tumbled down the chimney, carrying with it lumps of soot that flew out onto the grey stone floor. To clean the mess, Nanny had to open the front door and sweep the hailstones before they melted their way into the bedrooms.

Nanny was full of superstitions. In the early evenings, she mostly talked about the Banshee she heard wailing and the ghosts she had seen. On the evenings she talked about these ghostly stories, I was petrified to sleep. She mostly dwelled on the 'three death knocks.' She said she heard them the night before my mother died, and again when her other daughter, my mother's sister, Hannah, died. "Oh, *faithin' dat twasn't* in *me 'magination. Dem* were knocks *alrightsh*, and when I opened *da* door, *dere* was no sign of no one *dere*," she said.

After hearing her stories, I had to hide under the bedcovers with my eyes closed and put my hands over my ears. That way,

I could block out any imaginary sounds. I was always glad when I saw daybreak peeking through the bedroom curtains.

One frequent superstition of Nanny's was when she consumed tea. Throughout the day, she brewed tea in what she called, a 'Chaney Pot.' Sometimes, when she poured the tea, a short black stalk floated on top of the teacup. When this happened, she felt sure a stranger would visit her in the next twenty-four hours.

To check who it was she expected to visit, she first had to see what the black stalk was going to tell her.

Scooping the stalk out of the teacup, she placed it on the back of one hand. Then, forming a fist with the other hand, she tapped it with her fisted hand. "Will it be a man, a woman, or a child?" she asked.

Depending on which name caused the stalk to stick to the back of her fist, she got her answer. For the following twenty-four hours, she waited diligently for the stranger to appear. Ironically, quite often, her superstitions came true. When the suggested person arrived on her doorstep, she told them she knew they were coming, leaving the stranger mystified.

Every fortnight, a lady named Mrs. Nugent arrived at Nanny's house to sell her a half-crown's worth of raffle tickets. Mrs. Nugent was short and chubby, and her selling style was very persuasive. Before she departed, she put her index finger in the holy water font by Nanny's front door and blessed herself. "Well, Nora, I'm off. With the help of God, I'll be coming here again in two weeks with some winnings for you," were always her parting words.

Only once did I ever see Nanny win two half-crowns, and she was ecstatic. Although Mrs. Nugent always had the raffle winners' names printed on a sheet of paper, Nanny's half-crown winnings were never posted. When my grandmother told Mrs. Nugent she couldn't find her name in the newspaper, she told Nanny the printing boys must have forgotten to put her name in the paper. She often bragged to my grandmother about all the winners she had, yet she never gave my grandmother a receipt for the money she gave her.

The day Mrs. Nugent gave Nanny the half-crowns, she waited for her to leave. Then she spat on them before she went to her bedroom and placed one of them under the statue of Our Lady of Prague. "That's to increase the luck," she told me.

Within days, the half-crown was transferred into her money box. The statue of Our Lady of Prague was never without a coin taped under it. Looking under the statue, I mostly saw three-penny bits (thrupenny bits).

Because I had very little interaction with people around my own age, I frequently found time at my grandmother's dull and boring. That was until my sister came home. She lived and worked as a nanny taking care of a local farmer's five children on the outskirts of Carrick town. On Wednesdays and Sundays, she was given the afternoons and evenings off, and spent both nights at our grandmother's. As soon as she was released from her work, she got on her bike and rode it seven miles to Rathgormack.

Although Peggy was four years older, we got on well and had fun joking around together. I couldn't wait for her visits and was bursting to fill her in on some funny incidents I encountered in her absence.

It was obvious that Nanny also looked forward to seeing Peggy. The minute she arrived, she poured her fresh tea and served her a slice of her favorite Swiss roll cake. Because Nanny had raised her, Peggy was far more familiar with her country ways.

One evening after supper when I was fourteen, Nanny told Peg and me she was going outside to feed her hens. Soon after Nanny left, my sister came up with a daring plan. "Just for a laugh, why don't you wear some of Nanny's clothes and go outside and call for her hens. You're well able to take her off," she said.

"No, she'll kill me if she catches me. Besides, her clothes are far too big for me," I said.

"Ah, you'll be alright. It'll be a scream. I'll keep a lookout for you," she said.

Normally, I wouldn't dream of doing this when I was on my own with Nanny. But I was eager to please my sister, and thinking Nanny wouldn't catch me, I decided to go along with her idea. While Peggy kept an eye out for me at the open front door, I snuck back to Nanny's bedroom and found some of her clothes draped across a chair. I removed my summer dress and put on her black jumper, heavy-weight black skirts and her crossover apron. Then I rolled her thick, knit stockings all the way up my thighs and tightened them with the garters I found on her windowsill. Finally, I slipped my feet into her lace-up boots. Her boots and clothes were huge on me, and I looked like a ragamuffin. With the hairpins I found on her windowsill, I coiled my shoulder-length hair into a granny knot. My dark hair didn't look anything like Nanny's. When I came out of the bedroom to show Peggy, she almost hit the floor with laughter when she saw me dressed in our grandmother's image. I mentioned how dark my hair was, and she found a small container of Johnson's talcum powder in the bedroom we shared. Holding the container over my head, she shook it all around my hair. Looking in the small kitchen mirror, both of us laughed at the grey appearance it created. Peggy ran back to the front door again. "Go on now. It's safe. I'll keep watching for Nanny," she said.

I stealthily stepped out into the front yard and began calling for my grandmother's hens. "Here, *chick chick, chick. Here chick, chick, chick.*" Within seconds, her hens came running towards me from the side yard. Peggy watched from the front door with tears of laughter rolling down her face. While the hens surrounded me, a car pulled up to the front gate. It was Willie Hickey, one of Nanny's male friends. He got out of his car and stood at the front gate.

"Well, hello, Nora. *Tis* a grand evening out. I was on *me way home* and when I saw *ya* outside, I thought I'd stop and say hello to *ya,*" he said.

I remained motionless when I saw him, and was mortified that he thought I was my grandmother. I tried to ignore him and put my head down.

Peggy heard him too and yelled for me to come back inside. I made a dash to go back inside, but between Nanny's long skirts and the hens crowding around me looking for something to eat, I couldn't move. I tried shooing them away but they barely budged.

"Nora. Do you hear me?" Willie said.

"Hold up, Willie. I'll be right there." I said, nervously. Next, I watched him open the gate and walk toward me.

At the same moment, Nanny walked around the corner and caught me.

"Ha ha, *dere's* two a *ye* in it." Willie said, laughing out loud. My grandmother, seeing me dressed in her clothing, was at first bewildered. But it didn't take her long to realize it was me, and a dissatisfied look appeared on her face.

"*Whash* are *ya doin'* with *me* clothes on *yer* back. Get *dem* off *ya*. You're a little *skelper* dressing like *yer* poor *oul'* grandmother," she said.

"Do *ya* know *whash* it is, Willie, that *wan* will be *da deash a me* yet? Here was I *wanderin'* where *da hins* went off *ta*."

"*Jaysus* Nora, sure I *taush t'was* yourself was in it. Sure, isn't she the image of *ya*? She had me *dere*, Nora, for a minute. I just stopped to say hello on such a grand evening because I *taush t'was yerself* in it."

"*Begodden Willie,* she doesn't look like *meself.*"

I looked for Peggy and caught sight of her sneaking a peek from behind the front door. She was making weird faces which gave me a fit of the giggles, and I couldn't stop. This made Nanny even more cross with me.

Peggy stepped out from behind the door, knowing I was in trouble.

"Nanny, please don't be cross with Noreen. I'm the one who told her to put your clothes on and call the hens."

"*Tis* a fool *yer makin'* of me, Peggy? What business did she have *pokin'* around in *me* room? *Tis* a good job *dash* I have *da* moneybox *kay* in *me* apron pocket."

"Nanny. We were just *blackguarding*," Peggy said.

"Here was I *goin'* around the half-acre looking everywhere for *da hins.*

"What makes her *tink* she can *fitsh* in *me* clothes? Sure, she's *drownin'* in them," Nanny said.

Willie was listening with a wide grin on his face.

"Still and all Nora, she did a grand job trying to make herself look like *yerself.*"

I knew I was in trouble, and told my grandmother I was sorry.

At first she ignored me. Then she looked at me disapprovingly and, pointing her finger, she told me to go and get out of her clothes. The hens were no longer crowded around me, so I quickly fled inside the house.

"That was some craic," Peggy said, when I came back inside, and continued to laugh at the whole spectacle.

If it hadn't been for Willie making light of the situation, Nanny would have been a lot angrier. I believe her friend softened her up, making her see the funny side of my shenanigans.

A few times, Nanny took a notion to play her harmonica. I was with her the day she bought it while shopping in Carrick town. Feeling embarrassed about purchasing it for herself, I was surprised when I heard her tell the clerk she was buying it for me because, she never told me she was buying me one. That same evening, she took it out of the box and began playing two Irish melodies, "Doonaree" by Elish Bolland, and "Believe Me if All Those Endearing Young Charms" by John McDermott. Up to that time, I never knew she could play the harmonica. I believe she taught herself how to play it.

Before playing, she wet the edges of the harmonica with her spit, and, finding the correct note, she began playing. Sitting opposite her, I saw a slick of her saliva dripping from the bottom of the harmonica and falling down onto her skirt. She continued to let it fall until the end of the tune, then she swept it off her skirt and onto the kitchen floor. Apart from Peggy and Uncle Johnny hearing her play the harmonica, I was usually her only audience. She normally pulled out the harmonica when she was happy and was done with all her work.

Nanny couldn't stand to see me idle and looked for ways to keep me occupied. Her incessant jibing drove me crazy. "Why don't *ya* make *yerself* useful. *Go oush* and see if any of *da* hens laid an egg in *da* ditches. Check the calf isn't *aitin' da* spuds. *Rack* me hair (comb). Wash *me faish. Dere* in need of a good *washin'* and *me* toenails need a *clippin'.*

Of all the little jobs she asked me to do, the one I hated the most was having to wash her feet and clip her toenails. She asked me to do this every two weeks, and she knew by the look on my face that I detested this task. Then she piled the guilt on me. "Sure, any *udder* young *wan* your age would love ta do *dat fer dere* poor *oul'* grandmother's *feesh*, except you."

Once Nanny got herself situated comfortably in her seat, she removed her long stockings and set them aside. After pouring water from a cast-iron kettle, I let it cool down before Nanny dunked her feet in the basin of water. She told me to take the kitchen scissors out of a drawer to have them ready to clip her toenails. These were the only pair of scissors she possessed, and she used them to cut literally everything. Not only were they used to clip her toenails, but she also used them to cut sausage links.

Sitting on the stool opposite her, she gave me instructions on how I should proceed. "First, let *me feesh* soak a *bitsh,* and *den ya* can start *cleanin'* between *me* toes. Give *me* ankles a good *washin'* and, *den* work *yer* way up *me* knees." Each time I washed her feet, I had to hold my breath because of the strange musty odor that wafted from them.

At the end of my session, the water was always black, and a greyish black line of scum had settled around the edges.

After drying her feet, it was time to cut her toenails. I started with her small toenails first because they were the easiest to clip. Her big toenails were hard as a rock, and yellow. To trim them, I had to keep digging the blades of the scissors into the nails to snip them. I was always glad when this chore was finished, but I also knew this made my grandmother happy. Luckily, she never asked me to comb, (or rack) her hair, on the same day that I took care of her feet. I usually had a break and waited for at least another week to ten days to do that.

When the day to comb her hair came, I began by removing several hairpins from her granny bun and let it unravel to her mid-back. A sheen of grease showed on her hair from a lack of a good washing. She was of the opinion that if she got her head wet, she would catch a head cold. Her hair was a mixture of grey and white, and her scalp was dotted with tiny spots of black soot. I hated touching her hair because of the greasy film it left on my hands. I cringed with every pass of the hair comb and couldn't wait for a chance to wash my hands. Once I was finished grooming her, she took over. Tossing her head back, she pulled her hair off her face and swirled it back into a tight bun again.

Yet, it appeared no matter what favors I did for my Nanny, she was never fully happy with me. I believe one reason was the striking resemblance I bore to my father, and not to her daughter, my mother. She had no qualms about comparing me to the McGrath's, her side of the family. They were all fair and blue-eyed like her.

"*Ya know, da* more I look at *ya, da* more I see *da* breed of *da* Roches in *ya. Tis da* brown eyes and brown hair *dat ya* have. *Tis* only a Roche would have *dat* color of eyes and hair. Thomas and Peg are more of a McGrath and Whelan like *meself. De* have *da* same blue eyes like *dere* mother, God bless *dem*."

As I grew older, I saw that many members of the Roche family also had blue eyes, and not just brown eyes, as Nanny stated. Her dislike for any 'Roche,' was blatantly obvious. Her bias against the Roches all stemmed from the simple fact that my father married her daughter.

Not only did I attend Sunday mass with Nanny, but she also took me to Rathgormack church to confess my sins every two weeks. I was fifteen when Peggy arrived home unexpectedly and joined Nanny and me for confessions one late afternoon.

I strolled down to the church with Peggy while Nanny went ahead of us. What we didn't realize was Pip, Nanny's dog, had secretly followed us.

There was no sign of Nanny when we entered the church, so we sat in a pew in the mid-section and waited for our turn to enter the confession box. A few moments passed before we heard a dog barking and whining at the rear of the church. Curious to know whose dog it was, Peggy and I turned around to take a look. Pip immediately spotted us and came bounding down the aisle. Trotting into our pew, he slobbered us with wet kisses, causing Peggy and I to get a fit of the giggles. We attempted to shoo him out of the church, but he refused to budge.

When it was my turn for confession, I stepped inside the box and knelt. Father O' Brien, the parish priest, opened the little door that divided us. While I rattled off my usual sins, I could hear Pip outside the box, sniffing, scratching, and crying because he couldn't see me. The priest was aware of who I was after I told him my sins. He moved his head closer to the screen. In a faint voice he said, "Go on now girl, there's more sins than that you need to be telling me."

Taken aback by his remark, I went silent. I wondered if it was because he thought I had intentionally brought Pip into the church, or was it a sin I unknowingly committed, now that I was a teenager. Before I left the confessional, he gave me three Hail Mary's, two Our Father's and an Act of Contrition, for my penance. When I stepped outside the box, Peggy entered.

Pip was so excited to see me again, he urinated on the church floor! Other parishioners who were waiting to have their confessions heard were equally as tickled about the commotion the dog was making.

Someone alerted Nanny about her dog causing a commotion in the church. While sitting in the pew saying my penance prayers, she angrily reached over and took Pip by the scruff of the neck and hauled him outside. It was only later that it dawned on me that Nanny might have told the priest a tall tale or two about me.

Two weeks earlier, my sister had asked Nanny if she could take me out to the local dance with her because she said, I was coming up to sixteen. Nanny immediately refused. I was disappointed with her decision but accepted and spent the evening indoors with her. Yet, when I returned to the Good Shepherd Convent a couple of weeks later, Mother Philomena called me to her office. She had a letter in her hand several pages long. "What's this I hear about you gallivanting around the countryside," she said.

Initially, I didn't know what she was talking about, until she told me my grandmother had written her a letter to tell her how I wanted to go out dancing at night. I blushed standing in front of Mother Philomena, while she read the letter aloud to me. When she was done, she asked me if what my grandmother had written was true. I told her I never went dancing because Nanny refused to let me go. "Are you calling your grandmother a liar then?" she asked.

It was hard to convince her what I said was true. Before allowing me to leave her office, she stepped forward and hit me on the top of my head with the letter.

Looking back, I can only guess Nanny was afraid to let me go out dancing with Peggy, knowing I would be in the company of men. She had taken on the responsibility of caring for me in the summer months, and certainly would not have wanted me going astray and getting in trouble.

Long after her passing, Nanny's country voice still floats in my memory. As I got older, I developed a keener understanding of her warped and eccentric ways, to a point of pitying her. No one ever said life was easy, and for Nanny, that was an understatement. She was shrouded in secrets and lies, not only in her own life, but also with her loved ones, buried beneath the earth.

That Sunday in July when I was twelve years old, I witnessed one such secret; her husband's unmarked grave. Standing in the old church graveyard in Rathgormack, she accidentally revealed her unspoken pain to me.

Life was tough for Nanny, and without the financial and physical support of my Uncle Johnny, she was helpless. She constantly feared he was going to pack up and leave for England as his other siblings had done. He voiced this threat many late nights after he had been drinking. She knew if he were to leave her, he may possibly never return.

Because of Nanny's hold on Uncle Johnny, he didn't get married until he was well into his forties and only after Nanny passed. My uncle feared having two women sharing such a small house would never have worked.

Besides Uncle Johnny, my grandmother had another son named Michael. I never met Uncle Michael because he left for England before I was born, and never again returned to Ireland. Then I discovered she had yet another son she never spoke of.

It happened one sunny day in August when I was thirteen. I was in the kitchen with Nanny when there was a surprise knock on her front door. When she saw who it was, a look of utter shock appeared on her face. In front of her was a handsome, well-dressed man, wearing a wide smile. He introduced himself to her as Lawrence, with a distinctive English accent.

Nanny invited him in and offered him tea. He was friendly and charming, and made small talk with both of us. I noticed how Nanny blushed and flustered when she was around him. Once he finished his tea, he stood up and shook both our hands and left. Looking out the kitchen window, I saw him get into a car he parked outside the gate. At the time, I didn't know he was my uncle, and only found out some years later.

Lawrence was born out of wedlock when Nanny was in her early teens and was adopted shortly thereafter. Looking back on that day, it was easy to see that they were related because the family resemblance was strikingly evident. Both were fair skinned, had the same facial profiles, and sky-blue eyes. After he left that day, Nanny never let on he was a relative, and never again mentioned his name.

I can only guess, the reason she was so awkward in his presence, was she had lived with the shame of giving birth to him out of wedlock. Her ungodly act had labeled her with disgrace. It was easier for her to assume he didn't exist before he showed up at her front door. She had learned to suppress her emotions early in her youth. To curb her emotional pain, she surged ahead and cast away the hazy cobwebs that disturbed her troubled mind.

At age thirty, she lost her thirty-five-year-old husband, John, leaving her to raise six children alone. As soon as her four eldest children came of age, they packed up one by one and left Ireland behind to settle in England. Her youngest son, Johnny, and daughter, Mary, my mother, were all that remained in Ireland. Her daughter, Alice, was the only one of her children that periodically returned from England to visit her.

In 1956, her twenty-eight-year-old daughter, Hannah, living in England and eight months pregnant with her second child, died suddenly of septicemia. Less than two years later, she lost another daughter, Mary (my mother), at thirty. The loss of her two daughters, in such a short time span, had to be genuinely tragic for my grandmother.

Many years after Nanny passed, I was on holiday in Ireland, and paid a visit to see Uncle Johnny. After catching up on our lives, a conversation about his father came up. I told him years earlier I remembered Nanny mentioning a person named 'Johnny' being interred in the old graveyard in Rathgormack and asked him if it was his father.

At first, it came as a bit of a shock that I had asked him. Neither he nor Nanny ever spoke about his father. An uncomfortable few moments passed between us until he finally opened up.

He began by telling me he was only a baby when his father passed, and went on to tell me as much as he knew about him.

He said his father woke up one morning with mild abdominal cramping. The following day the pain grew progressively worse, but he still managed to go about his work on his small farm. A neighbor friend stopped in to visit that same evening. Assessing his condition, he told his father that he guessed it was his appendix that was causing all his pain. Ignoring his friend's suggestion to go to a doctor, he soldiered on in hopes the pain would subside. He was frightened of doctors because of the authority they held in rural communities.

He came in from work the next afternoon and lay on his bed suffering from intense abdominal pain. His belly was swollen and sore and he had a high fever. As the pain worsened, he took matters into his own hands. In desperation, he took a safety pin and inserted it into the side of his abdomen. He hoped to relieve the pain by releasing the pressure of his swollen abdomen. But within an hour, he slipped into unconsciousness and passed away.

Because neither a doctor nor a priest were present when he died, his death was classified as suicide. A postmortem would have shown he died of peritonitis, caused by a ruptured appendix.

It was imperative for all Irish Catholics to receive Absolution from a priest before death. However, the odds were stacked against my grandfather. He lived on an unpaved road, without plumbing, electricity, a telephone, or transportation. To find a priest or a doctor would have proven fruitless in the last hours of his life. Death was far from his mind, and he didn't understand what had befallen him on that fateful day.

Nanny was powerless against the judgement of the church. Her husband was buried without ceremony, in an unmarked grave, in "unconsecrated" ground. She carried on with her life bearing the shame and pain of her husband's supposed suicide.

It was no small wonder that nearly all her children left Ireland. The heartbreaking grief and shame they were burdened with in such a small community must have been devastating for the entire family.

My grandfather was laid to rest along with uncounted men, women, and children, in a deliberately nameless and almost forgotten place. This carefully selected part of The Old Church graveyard in Rathgormack was mostly reserved for those who supposedly offended doctrines of the Catholic Church. Innocent children who died before having the chance to be baptized. Mothers who died with their babies because they were born out of wedlock. Other souls were interred there for committing suicide, along with paupers and criminals.

In August 2010, I was in Ireland visiting my cousin, Margaret. She told me that a blessing of the graves was being performed at the old church graveyard in Rathgormack the following evening, and asked me to join her. I agreed to go and took my husband with me. It was my first time ever to attend the blessing of the graves and I wasn't quite sure what to expect. Sadly, Uncle Johnny and Aunt Kitty wouldn't be present to join us because both of them had passed a number of years earlier.

The next evening, at the graveyard, the weather was sunny, warm, and clear, and the attendance was huge. As I entered the graveyard, I noticed a small altar table had been set up on the unconsecrated ground where the priest was to say Mass. He stood behind the table facing the headstones on the hill. Many of the people gathered had relatives buried on the hillside amongst the ruins of the old church.

When the mass ended, I stood around chatting with the parish priest and other locals. Many of the attendees knew my family and me, and shared stories of their interred family members. As soon as I saw the priest was alone, I walked over to him. After I introduced myself, I told him that I was convinced that where he stood, saying mass, was the exact spot my grandmother had shown me where her husband was buried decades earlier. He flinched when I said this, and I believe I hit a raw nerve.

The priest was pleasant. He told me he was new to the parish and didn't know much about the village or the old graveyard. I asked him if he had any knowledge of the unconsecrated ground he was standing on and if it had ever been blessed. He frowned and seemed stunned by my bold assertions, and said nothing. I tactfully went on to tell him I believed dozens of men, women, and children were buried there, including my grandfather. "Surely, they deserve some recognition to bring closure for the families," I said.

Lowering his head, he told me he would address the matter as soon as possible. Feeling satisfied by his response, I left him, smiling and thankful.

Two years later, back in Ireland, I entered the graveyard to visit my family's grave. I was overjoyed to see a massive sixteen-foot cross had been erected on the unconsecrated land. Standing in front of it, my eyes filled with tears of gratitude. I was grateful the parish priest had taken to heart what I had shared with him. Although this action was long overdue, for my grandfather, and for families who had relatives interred there, their loved ones are no longer lost and forgotten, and can finally Rest in Peace.

A plaque beneath the cross reads:

**"Please pray for the lost and forgotten souls."**

There are hundreds of unmarked graveyards scattered throughout Ireland. They are especially prevalent in rural areas. This practice of burying people deemed unsuitable for Christian burials, continued until the 1960s before it finally ceased. Families were burdened with shame and scorned in smaller communities. The callous disregard for their loved ones must have been truly heartbreaking. They remained in this unknown land without a blessing or headstone. But time had long since passed and most family members took their heartaches with them to their own graves.

Despite my grandmother's torment by what had been done to her husband, she remained true to her faith all her life. She passed away aged eighty-four years, surrounded by those who knew her well and loved her. In retrospect, it was no strange coincidence that she always wore black clothing, having spent her adult life in constant mourning.

I am forever grateful that my grandmother was present in my life. She was a solid anchor in the summer months of my childhood, and ever present to aid me with my own broken wings. If she were alive today, I would thank her, but also ask her why she was sometimes hard on me. I believe she would say that she was only doing what she thought was best for me.

*Family photo. Nanny back row far left. I am six-months old sitting on my
mother's knee. Peggy is front row far left.*

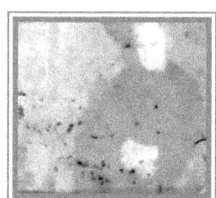

*1968—Nanny.*

*1968, Noreen sitting on a haycock on
Nannie's half acre.*

*Where my grandfather lays buried
in unmarked grave.*

*Ruins of the old church in Rathgormack, Co. Waterford where
mother is buried on hillside.*

## Chapter Twenty-One

# A PLACE TO CALL HOME

Since I was a child, home to me was my grandmother's. Although my father lived only a short distance from her home, it was an understanding I tacitly acknowledged, that since my mother's death, I would never again live in my father's house. Despite having three bedrooms, he only had his own set-up for sleeping. The other two rooms were incomplete and without mattresses.

In my career days, when co-workers asked me where I was going for my annual holidays, I told them I was going home. Yet, friends and acquaintances of my grandmother often referred to the Good Shepherd Convent as my home. "So, when will you be going back home to the nuns?" was one such question.

These people weren't being mean or prying. They just didn't understand the mental punch they were throwing at me. Home for me was Nanny's house.

After my grandmother died in 1975, Uncle Johnny took possession of her house and settled into married life with his new wife, Kitty. The first thing to cross my mind after he got married was, I may no longer have a place to stay when I visited

Ireland. The first Christmas of my uncle's marriage, he sent me a Christmas card stating his home was my home anytime I wanted to come and stay there.

Aunt Kitty was equally as kind as Uncle Johnny. On future visits to their home, both were gracious and gave me a heartwarming welcome. Just as I had done for my grandmother when I became an adult, I always made sure to give them ample advance notice before I arrived and left them money to help defray the cost of my stay.

As much as I enjoyed being in their company, it was getting harder for me to stay with them because of the lack of indoor plumbing. Since leaving Ireland, I had become a creature of twentieth century comforts, and missed the luxury of having a warm bath and shower, as well as the modern use of a flushing toilet.

Soon my trips to Ireland were becoming less frequent as I pursued my life and career. It was 1981, and two years had passed before I returned to Ireland again.

I made my usual arrangement to stay with Uncle Johnny and Aunt Kitty, but this time, only for a few days. Two days before I was due to leave, my cousin, Margaret, cycled out from Carrick to pay me a visit.

Margaret arrived in the early afternoon and Aunt Kitty welcomed her with a fresh-baked Swiss roll and tea. She spent a few hours chatting with us and catching up on life. Before leaving, she decided to use the toilet ahead of riding the seven miles back into Carrick. When she asked where she should go to use the toilet, Uncle Johnny told her to go outside and find a private place under a soft-leafed conifer tree. She politely turned down his suggestion because she didn't like that idea.

She was used to indoor plumbing since her parents had it installed in their home in the early 1960s.

I walked with her to the front gate, and thanked her for cycling out to see me. I usually went to visit Margaret and her parents when I was in Ireland, but because my time was short, I decided to wait until my next trip.

She was about to get on her bike when she asked me if I would prefer to stay in Carrick with her parents. "That way, you can have a nice bath and feel more comfortable," she said.

I was taken off guard by her offer and thought about it a few seconds. Then I told her it might upset Uncle Johnny and Aunt Kitty, but I would talk to them first.

Back inside the house, I waited for the right moment to ask my aunt and uncle about Margaret's suggestion. At first, they seemed sad and went all quiet when I mentioned it. "Will we ever be *seein' ya agin*?" Uncle Johnny asked.

"Yes, of course I will. You know I'll be driving out to see Stevie too. He is only a few miles down the road. If I stay with Margaret's parents, I will also get to spend some time with my brother, Johnjoe," I told them.

Somehow, they both agreed with my decision when they heard that. I thanked them and told them I would never forget their kind hospitality.

I still had a few days of my holiday left. The following morning, I packed my suitcase, said goodbye to my aunt and uncle, and moved in with Aunt Maura and Uncle Jimmy in Carrick.

Uncle Jimmy was one of my father's six brothers. He and Aunt Maura had informally adopted my six-month old brother, Johnjoe, and raised him with their daughter, Margaret.

Aunt Maura had also been a good friend of my grandmother. When Nanny took the Saturday bus into Carrick, Aunt Maura and she often did their shopping together. Walking about the town, they both loved to stop and talk to people they knew.

Returning to her house, Aunt Maura put on a big spread of sandwiches and cake on the table, and the fresh pots of tea were endless. A black kettle sat on her Aga and constantly boiled to make ready for a refreshing cup of tea at any time of the day.

Although Aunt Maura and Uncle Jimmy's home was small, it was very cozy and warm. The Aga dominated the center of the kitchen and blasted out a radiant warmth throughout the entire house. I enjoyed sitting on their cushioned chairs in front of the Aga.

Aunt Maura and Uncle Jimmy sometimes accompanied my grandmother and father when they journeyed to the Good Shepherd Convent to pick me up for the summer. The girls at the convent loved listening to Uncle Jimmy tell them funny stories about his youth. He also performed magic tricks for them with his false teeth. They were fascinated by the way he was able to pull his teeth in and out of his mouth. The younger girls had never seen false teeth before and tried to mimic him by pulling at their own teeth to achieve the same results.

Due to a leg injury he sustained as a young man, Uncle Jimmy had a limp and walked with a cane. Living in his hometown of Carrick, he was often seen sitting on a bench at the fourteenth-century bridge, chatting with pals, and greeting children as they passed. Both he and Aunt Maura were full of wit and good humor. Whenever I walked around the town with my grandmother and Aunt Maura, it was quite apparent how well-liked and respected Aunt Maura and Uncle Jimmy were, especially when people stopped to talk.

After Uncle Jimmy's unfortunate injury, Aunt Maura became the primary breadwinner. She made a living cleaning homes for some local wealthy families and helped the nuns and priests in the parish. She enjoyed her work and the interesting characters she met, and she created an oral portfolio of humorous stories on all of them, each funnier than the last. While working around her house, she dangled a filter-less cigarette from the corner of her mouth. Although it was lit, she never inhaled. Out of habit, she kept it perched on her lip and could laugh without dropping it.

In 1982, Uncle Jimmy died suddenly of a heart attack, at age sixty-nine. Aunt Maura lost her soulmate. She carried on with her life outliving him by nineteen years.

At the ripe age of ninety, Aunt Maura died unexpectedly of heart failure. She was sitting in her daughter's garden, admiring the views of the Slievenamon and the Comeragh Mountains when she collapsed.

I returned from America to attend her funeral. At the viewing, family, friends, and neighbors came to pay their last respects. Some I hadn't seen in decades. I sat close to the coffin as a member of her immediate family, in between Peggy and Thomas. The funeral parlor was crowded with attendees filing past to bid their last farewells. At one point, when I looked up, I recognized a familiar male entering the funeral parlor. He was older and heading toward the chief mourners. It didn't take long for me to realize it was nasty Uncle Morey. Making his way around the coffin, he was wearing a slight smirk. He held his hand out for me to shake it, but I refused. Instead, I stood up without acknowledging him, and I walked to the other side of my aunt's coffin. My family, understanding the predicament I faced, eyed me with approval.

As I moved around to the other side of the coffin, Morey followed me. Despite the sad set of circumstances, I felt a great need to ignore him. He knew that I was deliberately avoiding him and stared at me a few moments. Then he bowed his head at the foot of the coffin, before turning on his heels and leaving the funeral parlor.

Returning to my seat, I sat down and respectfully allowed the remaining mourners to shake my hand. Aunt Maura would have understood if she had witnessed what I had done. Knowing her good sense of humor, she would have laughed, and thought justice had truly been served to such a deplorable man.

That same evening, her remains were taken to the church, where she was to remain overnight. After the priest said some prayers, I headed out of the church with Cousin Margaret. As we drew close to the exit, a female attending the prayer service stepped forward. Offering her condolences to Margaret, she held her hand out while introducing herself. At first, I didn't recognize her and automatically gave her my hand. She shook it briefly, and then quickly turned and left the church. Margaret noted I was confused by the encounter, and leaning into me, she told me it was our cousin, Meg.

Immediately a flood of memories of her and my early childhood came back to me. She was the fourteen-year-old, tattle-tale daughter I lived with after my mother died. Her constant lying and getting me in trouble was part of the reason I ended up in the hospital. It had been years since I had seen her, and believe she too was shocked to see me. She never dreamt I would return to Ireland to attend Aunt Maura's funeral. Was it shame and guilt that caused her to leave the church so swiftly when she discovered it was my hand she had shaken?

The funeral mass was held the next day. When it was over, I followed the family up to the hillside cemetery in Carrick where Aunt Maura was to be interred. I stood next to my brother, Thomas, as the priest recited prayers at the gravesite.

When the ceremony ended, a middle-aged woman walked over to my brother and me. She was smiling and appeared to know both of us. Again, I wasn't sure who this woman was, until she boldly announced herself. "You probably wouldn't remember me, but I reared you two when you were very young."

The minute she said it, I knew who she was. She was Aunt Peg, the one who encouraged her husband, Uncle Morey, to molest me when I was five. I was about to take her hand and shake it but pulled it back instantly. Thomas unknowingly took her hand and shook it. She was perplexed by my rude reaction to refuse her a handshake. Then, I looked directly into her eyes and spoke. "Oh yes, I remember you, and I will never forget you."

Her whole demeanor immediately changed when I said this. Looking back and forth at both of us, she appeared to be dumbstruck. A few seconds passed before she turned and slowly walked away from us. It was out of character for me to be so direct with her. Having Thomas beside me was what gave me the courage to stand up for myself. Once her back was to us, I told Thomas who she was. He was stunned. "Well, in that case, I better find a place to go and wash my hand," he said, giving us both a chuckle. From a distance, I saw her standing in the corner of the graveyard, far away from the other mourners, and eyeing Thomas and me. Then I watched her button her coat, and leave the cemetery.

Almost thirty-five years had passed since I had seen these relatives. Thomas reminded me that if it had not been for Aunt Maura's funeral, we may never have set eyes on them. She never cared for them, but they were brazen enough to show up at her funeral. Standing over Aunt Maura's grave, I quietly thanked her for the opportunity she had given us. Knowing her sense of humor, I imagined her praising me for my boldness, and laughing at how the whole chain of events unfolded.

*1972—Peggy and me.*

**FAMILY PICTURE**

*Back row—Brothers-Thomas and Johnjoe. Aunt Pat, Uncle Johnny.*
*Front row—Noreen, Peggy, Melissa (Peggy's daughter) holding Johnjoe's*
*daughter, Gillian. Aunt Kitty (far right).*

## Chapter Twenty-Two

# TROUBLED WATERS

High winds and giant waves splashed around the old 'Sealink' ferry as it struggled to cross the turbulent waters of the Irish Sea. Three hours had passed since we set sail at seven p.m. from the North Wall Quay, Dublin, Ireland. The ferry would take another six hours before it reached the Liverpool Docks, in England.

It was April 1973, and I was on a night crossing to England with my brother, Thomas. He was joining an Irish friend in the construction trade in the UK. His friend wrote to tell him the company he worked for was in dire need of manual laborers, and Thomas decided to join him.

Weeks before, I received a long-awaited acceptance letter to start nurse's training at a large children's teaching hospital in Surrey, England. On this journey, I was mixed with both nerves and excitement, departing from Ireland to live and work in a country I had never been to before. But the opportunity I had been offered was too tempting to pass up.

Thomas and I looked waif-like and lost. He was eighteen months younger than my nineteen years, and we didn't look like siblings because of our contrasting facial characteristics. Thomas was short and skinny with sky blue eyes and wavy blond hair and looked more like a twelve-year-old than his seventeen years. I stood five feet and three inches tall and was as thin as a rail. My dark brown eyes and long brown hair gave my complexion a pasty white appearance. I was painfully shy and as green as Ireland itself. In the presence of strangers, I had adopted a habit of looking down to avoid any unwanted conversations. But on this journey, I had to bravely cast my insecurities aside, and take charge.

Before sailing away from my homeland, my mind was filled with jumbled thoughts.

"What happens if we get lost in Liverpool?" "Will the English people like us?"

"What if we don't like living there, and want to return to Ireland, how would we get the money to return?"

Growing up in Ireland, I heard many negative stories about the British people and their dislike of Irish settlers in their country. Many older Irish folk I encountered in my youth said the English lacked religion. Some never heard about God. Others hated us for being Irish and Catholic.

On a few occasions, my brother and I second-guessed our decision to leave Ireland. We were unsure of the reception we might get because we only knew of England by name. Apart from our Aunt Pat, we didn't know any other English people.

Aunt Pat certainly was not cut from the same cloth of which they spoke. She was warm and gentle, and oozed love and affection, giving us a sense of solace, and a safe reason to travel to England.

A light drizzle fell, and it was cold, while Thomas and I stood amongst the long queue of passengers waiting to board the ferry. We were wedged somewhere in the middle, shuffling slowly with the voyagers. Looking around me, I saw a mixture of people making the journey. Most were families traveling with their young children. Some of the children had distinguishing British accents. They appeared to be returning to the UK where they had since settled. Several of the men and women were traveling alone. A family ahead of us were dragging a big wheel-less trunk and moved inch by inch to the entrance of the ferry. It was similar in color to the trunk I was hauling, but theirs was larger. Other passengers carried suitcases. A young man standing close to us had his belongings bundled up and tied with twine. Another had a waist belt tightly wrapped around his suitcase to protect his worldly possessions.

Heading out to England by ferry was a treat for most of the passengers. Many were dressed in their Sunday best. Some men wore coats and ties with flat-peaked caps, and some of the women had long, fancy, beaded pins pushed through their felt hats to hold them in place. A handful of travelers were disheveled and shabby looking and didn't have any luggage. I guessed they wore the only clothing they possessed on their backs.

We eventually stepped on board, and I instructed Thomas to dash to a long wooden bench and secure two seats for us. I dragged my trunk to a luggage hold with the help of a gentleman. Once we settled in our seats, a middle-aged woman approached my brother and me. She told us she was from the 'Legion of Mary' and offered us scapulars, rosary beads, and several holy pictures of saints and angels.

"That's to keep *ye* safe on *ye'r* journey," she said. "Are ye two boyfriend and girlfriend?" she asked.

Being shy, I didn't respond immediately. She stood over us waiting for a reply. "No. He's my brother," I said.

"And, what will *ye* be *doin'* when *ye* get to Liverpool?" "We're staying with an aunt and uncle for a bit," I replied. "Oh, I suppose *ye'll* be grand then," she said, dropping her head to one side, showing us a long pitying look.

"Don't be *forgettin' ye'r* prayers to Holy God and the Blessed Virgin, before ye go to sleep now, won't ye?" she said, staring intently at us.

"Yea. We will," I told her.

"Good luck to *ye* now as *ye* head off, and mind *yerselves*."

Then she walked off around the cabin, scanning for other young Irish travelers to offer them the same advice.

By the time everyone was boarded, the cabin was packed with men, women, and children. Sitting quietly beside my brother, I listened in on some of the conversations the passengers were having with each other. Some spoke of returning to England from visits home. Others were heading out for the first time to seek a better life for themselves and their families. Apart from a few scatterings of men, it was mostly women and children who sat in the main cabin. Most of the men gravitated towards the bar once they boarded, and remained there for the duration of the journey.

The noise in the cabin was deafening at the beginning of our journey. People stood chatting to each other and blocked the aisles. Some children shrieked, and babies bawled for attention or out of hunger. Excitable young boys and girls found areas where they could run and play tag while their mothers tried to reign them in. The majority of the young girls had the same short hairstyles. Their hair was parted to the side, and a section of it was gathered and tied up with bright colorful ribbons and hair grips. One woman on the left of me sat alone. She was weeping and fretful, mopping her face with a well-worn handkerchief. Another woman clasped rosary beads in her hands. She was praying, and intermittently tapped her chest, while mouthing a language I didn't understand.

My brother and I had a bird's eye view of the bar. Each time the bar door swung open, plumes of tobacco smoke and the aroma of stale beer wafted into the cabin. It was the same familiar smell of the pub my father frequented at home. Some lucky men found seats at the bar; for others, it was standing room only. Occasionally, a sound of shattering glass was heard when the boat rose over the crest of a wave, causing it to rock from side to side. This made it difficult for the men who were left standing. To maintain their balance, they had to take hold of anything that was bolted down. Some clutched cigarettes or drinks with one hand, while grabbing tight any solid object they could find with the other. However, this uncomfortable situation did not deter the men from proudly belting out ballads of Ireland. Melodies with poetic lyrics flowed through the cabin with rippling emotion.

A few drank as a form of escape, to soothe and blur their worried minds. Alas, for some, it was all in vain when the effects of seasickness crept in. I watched two men hurry out to the deck to purge the contents in their sickly stomachs over the deck's railings. It was dark outside and raining and the men were getting drenched. The fierce April winds picked up the vomit and it scattered carelessly a tither.

The main cabin didn't have any real heating, and every time someone opened the deck door, a freezing chill blew into the cabin and seeped into every gaping crevice. I pulled my red coat tighter around me when a cold shiver gripped me. With each passing hour, the winds grew increasingly stronger, making it unbearable to relax. I closed my eyes to repel an encroaching nausea I sensed churning in my stomach.

A young woman with a toddler bellowed from a bench in front of me. "Jaysus. Who *da* feck vomited on *da* floor *dere*?" she said, pointing to a smelly spill.

"Why *da* feck can't ye clean up after *yerselves* for *Jaysus* sake," she stressed in a Dublin accent.

Her toddler was wrapped snuggly under her wool shawl until she heard her mother speak. Then a little strawberry blonde girl with corkscrew curls peeked out from the top of her mother's shawl. "The stench is *feckin'* rotten, and *meself* and the child can't sleep a wink with it," she continued.

The other passengers gazed at her without emotion, her pleas falling on deaf ears. Frustrated and angry, she pulled her child closer to her bosom, before covering both their heads with the thick shawl.

Thomas and I were close enough to the location of the vomit, and the whiff of it made me wretch. I covered my mouth and nose with the collar of my red coat in an attempt to dispel the odor. *"Swallow, swallow hard. Breath, breathe deeper,"* I told myself to quell the copious amounts of bilious saliva filling my mouth.

I suggested we move to another seat. Thomas stood up and looked around the cabin, but all the seats were taken. I nudged him when I saw a deckhand arrive with a mop and bucket of water. While he efficiently cleaned the mess, the Dublin woman with the child, poked her head out from inside her shawl. "Well, *ya* took *yer bleedin'* time," she said, before tucking her head under the shawl again.

The whooshing and swaying of the ferry continued and I felt nauseous, nervous, and cold. I looked at my brother. He had his eyes closed. His breathing was shallow, and I guessed that he had drifted off to sleep. I snuggled up closer to him to grab some warmth from his body. Tucking my knees to my chest without disturbing him, I gently rested my head on his shoulder. To take my mind off my upset stomach, I lifted the collar of my red coat and pulled it around my neck and face. Taking a deep breath, I closed my eyes and soon fell into a fitful sleep.

Suddenly, the deafening sound of a foghorn roused me from my sleep, and I sat up. Soon the cabin was filled with the moaning, groaning, and the crying of children. It was still pitch-black outside and the queasy feeling I felt hours earlier had now dissipated. In my groggy state, I checked my wristwatch. The time was five-ten a.m. The ferry had just pulled into the Liverpool Docks.

Within minutes, the cabin was full of lively movement. The voyagers gathered up their children and belongings, and stepped in a queue, eager to disembark. I refocused my mind and snapped back into my take-charge mode. Lining up with my brother to disembark, I was ready and prepared for the next step of our journey. We hauled my trunk down the gangplank while a snapping frigid wind brushed my face. When my foot touched the ground of this strange land, I was aware I was at the dawn of a new and daring adventure on a cold and rainy morning in April 1973.

*This is the type of boat I took leaving Ireland.*

# Epilogue

Throughout the 1950s and 1960s, thousands of young women chose to take "Vows of Chastity" and enroll in convents all over Ireland. Although they were rigorously steeped in religious indoctrination, none of them were trained for child-rearing, or knew how to council and nurture children from broken and aberrant homes. Had they been, they would have had a greater comprehension of childhood growth and development. It was perhaps a reflection of the harsh and impoverished Ireland of those times. Quite often their reaction was to reflexively use "the rod" to fix what they perceived as misbehaving.

The nuns never had the experience of rearing children of their own. Adults caring for children are expected to learn patience and understanding of innately curious young children. Children grow or shrivel by learning from the adults who supervise and monitor them.

The so-called "protection program," bestowed on thousands of children by the Irish court system, created a role for the Church. This didn't succeed as the Courts expected it would. The contemporary assumption was that using strict, fear-based, all-encompassing religious indoctrination would result in well-behaved children, backfired in a plethora of ways.

Children's well-being and mental health were never a factor in the courts' decisions. Many were still grieving the loss of a parent, or torn from families where they had known love and affection. Love and affection are the nectars for human survival. Instead, many children who grew into adulthood were severely and emotionally scarred by their rigid upbringing.

Leading up to the Celtic Tiger of the 1990s-2000s, Ireland dramatically changed socially and economically. With the advent of prosperity, a new moral code of conduct evolved, allowing people to be more open-minded, tolerant, and secular.

Television, mobile phones and the internet played a huge role in changing the face of Ireland. People found voices they never had before and entertained brand new ideas. Suddenly these angry voices forced the downfall of the all-powerful grip the Catholic Church had on the Irish nation, operating egregious outrages such as the Magdalene Laundries, ignoring shameful clergy abuse of young children, and kidnapping and selling babies born out of wedlock. Overnight, the Church was almost brought to its knees by these immoral, corrupt practices.

Monetary restitutions were set up for those who had been subjects of draconian mistreatments. But for many abused by this system, it was already too late for recompense. Some died prematurely, some passed naturally, while others took their own lives. Thousands dulled the pain of their past by abusing drugs and alcohol. Then, there were those who refused the payouts, because they had learned to bury their childhoods, so they could safely fit into a society, without reminders of their past. At the time of the payouts, instead of having to revisit my days of living at the Good Shepherd Convent, I chose to turn the money down.

The Good Shepherd Convent facility is now a university. After the nuns departed, it became W.I.T., The Waterford Institute of Technology, from 1995 until 2022. At its inception, I have often wondered why the word, 'Institute' was used to reference the school. That name came awfully close to the word, 'Institution.'

Now, the former dormitories, recreation room, study rooms, refectory etc. are where classes are held at SETU, South East Technological University.

I came back to visit the convent of my youth and found it odd that there is no mention or plaque to commemorate what the edifice once stood for. I wonder if the students walking the cloistered hallways have knowledge of what this place once represented. It is after all a significant part of Waterford's 20th century history.

The looming grey stone walls of what was once the Good Shepherd Convent are now open for all to view. Has the slate been cleverly wiped clean, and the mistreated Irish children of the past been purposely and conveniently forgotten?

For those of us who once treaded and polished the cloisters of the Good Shepherd Convent, our memories have never been erased and will remain with us until the end of our days.

# Addendum

While visiting what was once the Good Shepherd Convent and St. Dominick's in May 2022, I was given a Facebook link to connect with some of the girls from my youth on a private group page. In January 2023, I joined the group and posted a photo I was about to throw out. The photo was in black and white and showed many of the girls I knew. I was around ten years old at the time, and we were performing *The Mikado* operetta at the Theatre Royal in Waterford. Marian was also in this picture.

Although Marian is not on Facebook, her husband is. A few years before, Marian had visited the old convent while on holiday with her husband. The same link had also been shared with them. Her husband took the liberty to join the group page. When he saw my name and the photograph on the page, he immediately contacted me. Within thirty seconds of posting, I was once again in contact with my long-lost friend, Marian.

Fifty plus years had passed since we had last seen or spoken to each other. After all the years we had been apart, this connection was truly phenomenal. As we relived our childhood memories, I broke down. It was like a valve had been released for me that I could finally speak to a person who had walked in the same shoes as I had. Without social media, and Marian's husband's interest in her childhood, we might never have found each other. This has been truly miraculous for both of us.